Free Communities of Color and the Revolutionary Caribbean

The tumult of the Age of Atlantic Revolutions provided new opportunities for free communities of color in the Caribbean, yet the fact that much scholarship places an emphasis on a few remarkable individuals—who pursued their freedom and respectability in a high-profile manner—can mask as much as it reveals. Scholarship on these individuals focuses on themes of mobility and resilience, and can overlook more subversive motives, underrepresent individuals who remained in communities, and elide efforts by some to benefit from racial hierarchies. In these free communities, displays of social, cultural, and symbolic capitals often reinforced systemic continuity and complicated revolutionary-era tensions among the long-free, enslaved, and recently-freed.

This book contains seven fascinating studies, which examine Haiti, Caracas, Cartagena, Charleston, Jamaica, France, the Netherlands Antilles, and the Swedish Caribbean. They explore how free communities of color deployed religion, literature, politics, fashion, the press, history, and the law in the Atlantic to defend their status, and at times define themselves against more marginalized groups in a rapidly changing world.

This book demonstrates that problems of belonging, difference, and hierarchy were central to the operation of Caribbean colonies. Without recalibrating scholarship to focus on this, we risk underappreciating how the varied motivations and ambitions of free people of color shaped the decline of empires and the formation of new states.

The chapters in this book were originally published as a special issue of *Atlantic Studies*.

Robert D. Taber is Assistant Professor of Government and History at Fayetteville State University, USA, where he researches family life in colonial and revolutionary Haiti. He received his Ph.D. from the University of Florida, USA.

Charlton W. Yingling is Assistant Professor of History at the University of Louisville, USA. He studies race and religion in Spanish Santo Domingo during the Age of Revolutions. He received his Ph.D. from the University of South Carolina, USA.

Free Communities of Color and the Revolutionary Caribbean

Overturning, or Turning Back?

Edited by
Robert D. Taber and Charlton W. Yingling

LONDON AND NEW YORK

First published 2018
by Routledge
2 Park Square, Milton Park, Abingdon, Oxon, OX14 4RN, UK

and by Routledge
711 Third Avenue, New York, NY 10017, USA

Routledge is an imprint of the Taylor & Francis Group, an informa business

Chapters 1-7 © 2018 Taylor & Francis
Chapter 8 © 2017 Jessica Vance Roitman

All rights reserved. No part of this book may be reprinted or reproduced or utilised in any form or by any electronic, mechanical, or other means, now known or hereafter invented, including photocopying and recording, or in any information storage or retrieval system, without permission in writing from the publishers.

Trademark notice: Product or corporate names may be trademarks or registered trademarks, and are used only for identification and explanation without intent to infringe.

British Library Cataloguing in Publication Data
A catalogue record for this book is available from the British Library

ISBN 13: 978-0-8153-4761-3

Typeset in MyriadPro
by diacriTech, Chennai

Publisher's Note
The publisher accepts responsibility for any inconsistencies that may have arisen during the conversion of this book from journal articles to book chapters, namely the possible inclusion of journal terminology.

Disclaimer
Every effort has been made to contact copyright holders for their permission to reprint material in this book. The publishers would be grateful to hear from any copyright holder who is not here acknowledged and will undertake to rectify any errors or omissions in future editions of this book.

Contents

Citation Information   vii
Notes on Contributors   ix

1 Networks, tastes, and labor in free communities of color: Transforming the revolutionary Caribbean   1
   Robert D. Taber and Charlton W. Yingling

2 "A true vassal of the King": Pardo literacy and political identity in Venezuela during the age of revolutions   13
   Cristina Soriano

3 Crafting freedom: Race and social mobility among free artisans of color in Cartagena and Charleston   34
   John Garrison Marks

4 Smugglers before the Swedish throne: Political activity of free people of color in early nineteenth-century St Barthélemy   56
   Ale Pålsson

5 Revolutionary narrations: Early Haitian historiography and the challenge of writing counter-history   74
   Erin Zavitz

6 A case of hidden genocide? Disintegration and destruction of people of color in Napoleonic Europe, 1799–1815   92
   Margaret B. Crosby-Arnold

7 West meets east: Mixed-race Jamaicans in India, and the avenues of advancement in imperial Britain   120
   Daniel Livesay

CONTENTS

8 "A mass of *mestiezen, castiezen*, and *mulatten*": Contending with color in the Netherlands Antilles, 1750–1850   137
Jessica Vance Roitman

Index   157

Citation Information

The chapters in this book were originally published in *Atlantic Studies*, volume 14, issue 3 (September 2017). When citing this material, please use the original page numbering for each article, as follows:

Chapter 1
Networks, tastes, and labor in free communities of color: Transforming the revolutionary Caribbean
Robert D. Taber and Charlton W. Yingling
Atlantic Studies, volume 14, issue 3 (September 2017) pp. 263–274

Chapter 2
"A true vassal of the King": Pardo literacy and political identity in Venezuela during the age of revolutions
Cristina Soriano
Atlantic Studies, volume 14, issue 3 (September 2017) pp. 275–295

Chapter 3
Crafting freedom: Race and social mobility among free artisans of color in Cartagena and Charleston
John Garrison Marks
Atlantic Studies, volume 14, issue 3 (September 2017) pp. 296–317

Chapter 4
Smugglers before the Swedish throne: Political activity of free people of color in early nineteenth-century St Barthélemy
Ale Pålsson
Atlantic Studies, volume 14, issue 3 (September 2017) pp. 318–335

Chapter 5
Revolutionary narrations: Early Haitian historiography and the challenge of writing counter-history
Erin Zavitz
Atlantic Studies, volume 14, issue 3 (September 2017) pp. 336–353

CITATION INFORMATION

Chapter 6
A case of hidden genocide? Disintegration and destruction of people of color in Napoleonic Europe, 1799–1815
Margaret B. Crosby-Arnold
Atlantic Studies, volume 14, issue 3 (September 2017) pp. 354–381

Chapter 7
West meets east: Mixed-race Jamaicans in India, and the avenues of advancement in imperial Britain
Daniel Livesay
Atlantic Studies, volume 14, issue 3 (September 2017) pp. 382–398

Chapter 8
"A mass of mestiezen, castiezen, *and* mulatten": Contending with color in the Netherlands Antilles, 1750–1850*
Jessica Vance Roitman
Atlantic Studies, volume 14, issue 3 (September 2017) pp. 399–417

For any permission-related enquiries please visit:
http://www.tandfonline.com/page/help/permissions

Notes on Contributors

Margaret B. Crosby-Arnold is a senior scholar of research in the European Institute and the Department of History, Columbia University, USA. Her work focuses on developing the history of diversity as a new field of historical research.

Daniel Livesay is Assistant Professor of History at Claremont McKenna College, USA. His research focuses on questions of race, slavery, and family in the colonial Atlantic World.

John Garrison Marks is Program Coordinator for Saving Hallowed Ground, a public history and historic preservation non-profit based in Devon, USA. He is currently revising a manuscript that examines racial identity and social mobility for free people of color in the urban Atlantic World.

Ale Pålsson is a Senior Lecturer in History at Stockholm University, Sweden. His interests include Scandinavian colonial history, maritime history, and political language.

Jessica Vance Roitman is a Researcher at the Royal Netherlands Institute of Southeast Asian and Caribbean Studies, Leiden, Netherlands. She works on Caribbean history, particularly the history of the Dutch Leeward Islands, as well as Caribbean Jewish history.

Cristina Soriano is Assistant Professor of History, and Director of the Latin American Studies Program at Villanova University, USA. Her research looks at imperial transformation in Trinidad, and the Spanish Caribbean.

Robert D. Taber is Assistant Professor of Government and History at Fayetteville State University, USA, where he researches family life in colonial and revolutionary Haiti.

Charlton W. Yingling is Assistant Professor of History at the University of Louisville, USA. He studies race and religion in Spanish Santo Domingo during the Age of Revolutions.

Erin Zavitz is Assistant Professor of History at the University of Montana Western, USA. Her research focuses on nineteenth- and twentieth-century Haiti.

Networks, tastes, and labor in free communities of color: Transforming the revolutionary Caribbean

Robert D. Taber and Charlton W. Yingling

ABSTRACT
Scholarship on free people of color in the Caribbean during the Age of Revolutions has focused on themes of mobility and resilience, with emphasis on the few remarkable individuals who pursued their freedom and respectability in imperially visible registers. These themes sometimes mask as much as they reveal. Mobility ignores those individuals who remain in place in families and communities, and resilience elides efforts by some free people of color to secure the benefits of the slave economy for themselves and their descendants. Often figures are assigned subversive motives or subaltern potential they perhaps would not recognize, when in fact their actions sometimes served to legitimate colonial order and strengthen racial divides by distancing themselves from more marginalized groups. Possible displays of respectability complicated revolutionary-era negotiations among the long free, the enslaved, and recently freed. Free people of color frequently defined margins from the enslaved rather than subvert them, including through largely unconsidered realms of taste or conspicuous consumption. This examination raises questions regarding extant conceptions of how Caribbean free people of color acquired and wielded social, cultural, and symbolic capitals. Perhaps more often than operating on socially progressive or latent revolutionary positions they evinced concern for systemic continuity. This essay, which introduces the following research that explores this topic, suggests new avenues of investigating these overlooked complexities in motivations and actions by free people of color, a population of disproportionate importance in the cultural politics of the revolutionary Caribbean. Without this recalibration, we risk underappreciating the legacy of late Caribbean colonialism, minimizing the context of revolutionary change and state formation, and misunderstanding the ambitions and centrality of free communities of color to these processes.

In the 45 years since Jack Greene and David Cohen published *Neither Slave nor Free: The Freedmen of African Descent in the Slave Societies of the New World*, scholarship on free people of color in the Caribbean has focused on themes of social mobility, political resilience, and economic opportunity.[1] These questions became sharper in the latter part of the Age of Atlantic Revolutions (1763–1830), the period between the declaration of abolition in Saint-Domingue (1793) and three key moments: France's recognition of the Haitian state (1825), the publication of David Walker's *Appeal to the Colored Citizens of the World* in the United States (1829), and the dissolution of Gran Colombia and the death of Simón Bolívar (1830). During this period, the contested fact of Haitian independence loomed large in the Atlantic imagination, suggesting novel possibilities for people of color, but also prompting renewed reaction throughout the Atlantic.[2] Families and communities of color navigated these competing forces to provide for the next generation and to protect (not always successfully) often-modest civil rights victories. As the following analyses demonstrate, the monumental and the mundane, including efforts to secure gains through state recognition, reinforcement of color lines and colorisms, and the deployment – at times subversively, sometimes less so – of Eurocentric norms, shaped the tactics deployed by free families and communities of color during this time. These investigations, along with the analytical points in this introduction, suggest commonalities and their important variations among communities of color in the late revolutionary Atlantic, including their boundaries, their desires, and their complicated relationships with retreating Atlantic monarchies and with emerging states.

Discussion of free people of color during the Age of Revolutions has traditionally centered on a few remarkable individuals who pursued freedoms and respectability in imperially visible arenas such as the courtroom, church, press, and battlefield.[3] As a few scholars have noted recently, singular cases of advancement sometimes masked as much as they revealed, in that such upward mobilities were not representative of improvements in group status and sometimes even led to the reinforcement of racial hierarchies. Not only do instances of mobility overshadow the more numerous individuals who remained in their communities, these individuals are often assigned analytical tones of subversive or subaltern potential. Such resilience might also elide the efforts by some free people of color to secure the benefits of colonialist culture or the slave economy for themselves and their descendants.[4]

Between 1793 and 1830, free people of color in the greater Caribbean and across the Atlantic played crucial roles on varying sides of debates over the future of slavery, the slave trade, paths to manumission, and political representation. At the same time, they participated in markets, fashions, religious observances, and circulations of Atlantic print culture.[5] In the aggregate, the studies included here reevaluate the motivations, communities, possibilities, and constraints for free people of color during the late revolutionary period. This volume reconsiders free people of color in the Caribbean during the late Age of Revolutions to highlight themes of politicization in the wider Atlantic, including the Spanish Americas, the Netherlands Antilles, France, Haiti, Jamaica, and the United States, and linkages from these better-known locales to the underappreciated Swedish Caribbean. We contend that examining the mobilities of free people of color in and between their respective communities illuminates the opportunities of revolution, and that exploring the boundaries of revolutionary possibility clarifies the choices made by free people of color to fashion life for themselves, their families, and their neighbors. This examination raises questions regarding extant conceptions of how Caribbean free people of color acquired and wielded social, cultural, and symbolic capitals. This analysis also sheds light on the transition from cosmopolitanism to romanticism in the nineteenth-century Atlantic. We pursue these questions simply to better understand the complexities of this era, not to cast aspersions on those individuals and communities under analysis nor on those who have studied them.

Many scholars have turned their attention to "Atlantic Creoles," Africans and people of African descent who adapted to European colonialist dicta as part of their navigation of structural constraints and their pursuit of personal benefit, subversion of the racial hierarchy, or mediation among cultural groups. Pioneered by Ira Berlin as people of "linguistic dexterity, cultural plasticity, and social agility," the category "Atlantic creole" has been most developed in the scholarship of the eminent historian Jane Landers. Landers argues that their fluid identities and mutability were especially invaluable tools amid the political upheaval of the Age of Revolutions, that Atlantic Creoles were, "extraordinarily mobile, both geographically and socially," and were neither defined or fully constrained by race and slavery.[6] James Sweet praised this approach as having added to our understanding of African-descendants' contributions to ideas and processes of revolution, enlightenment, independence, and society writ large. However, Sweet also criticized this approach as having conflated deeply ingrained African ethnicities of "Atlantic creoles" into an admittedly more nuanced narrative of "Western democratic triumphalism" and "Americanization" in which "Africans are often mechanically inserted in historical processes that are predetermined by the boundaries of European empire and colonialism."[7] While some of the historical figures that appear in this forum might meet the litmus for having been "Atlantic Creoles," we argue that these figures might also fit on a range of free people of color who not only utilized but embraced and embodied European imperial, religious, economic, and cultural norms, all the while subverting those norms by expanding their inclusivity. In doing so for their own benefit, they at times risked legitimizing the colonialist societies in which they lived and latently reinforcing extant exclusionary practices against more marginalized sectors of color, and particularly the enslaved.

In fact, these forms of participation often served to strengthen and legitimize colonial orders. Possibilities for individual liberty and respectability masked the complicated revolutionary-era negotiations between those who had long been free and the enslaved or recently freed. Tactically speaking, some communities of color fashioned new narratives critical of these Eurocentric histories, while others had to navigate exclusionary state policies. Free people of color who were born free, or had long been emancipated, frequently sought to enhance distinctions and margins between slavery and their freedom rather than subvert them, including through the heretofore largely unconsidered realms of taste and conspicuous consumption.[8] They did so through the same imperial channels that some scholars have, at times, cited as evidence of socially subversive positions. Recent advances in scholarship highlight revolutionary potential from these communities without adequately balancing that some communities of color also displayed a distinct concern for systemic continuity and the maintenance of profit, piety, and/or imperial protections of civil rights.

However, other communities faced more constrained opportunities, placing them in counter-point to Eurocentric norms. Many élite free people of color in the Caribbean adapted European hierarchies and sociocultural attitudes even as European societies retrenched from the limited cosmopolitanism of the eighteenth century into the romanticism of the nineteenth century. In prevalent social history traditions influenced by structuralism or Marxian thought, free people of color perhaps appear more subversive and in common cause with their class rights or transgressing racial constraints. The lenses of post-structural, post-colonial, cultural studies, and micro-historical analyses complicate our understandings of personal choice, identity, and rational action.[9]

These complications raise several questions. How did the Age of Revolutions present an opportunity for turning over European domination, while turning back to convenient symbols and ingrained structures of European norms, whether as complicity, subversion, or some aspect of both? How did these groups refract a colonialist *mentalité* through language, education, literacy, dress, craftsmanship, residences, music, civic engagement, and militia service? And finally, did eighteenth-century cosmopolitanisms decline in reaction to the Haitian Revolution?

To pursue answers for these questions, we tip the historiographical pendulum toward analyses of cultural, social, and symbolic capitals. These free people of color under consideration – despite having been blocked from certain career paths due to their race – possessed a skillset, literacy, knowledge, or trade as bureaucrats, authors, artisans, musicians, and soldiers that distinguished them professionally and culturally from more oppressed groups of color. These successes facilitated contacts and the construction of networks among similarly distinguished free people of color through familial ties, churches, civic societies, commerce, and guilds. This mutual acquaintance and community recognition was at many times deliberate to their collective social benefit that implicitly reproduced inequality and exclusion across generations. In such cases, free people of color earned imperial protections often by cultivating connections and earning respect from white élites at the latent exclusion of more marginalized sectors of color – primarily slaves – against whom they contrasted their own trappings of "civility." These individuals often exhibited their distinctions through a performance of European tastes and meanings, and rejection of black or African cultures, through their dress, residences, consumption, music, and language.[10]

The case studies presented here also call into question more specific political ramifications of a retreat from cosmopolitanism in France and the connections between the Napoleonic regime and the rise of Romanticism in the Atlantic. On an individual level, cosmopolitan attitudes in Europe enabled a few ambitious free people of color from the Caribbean to migrate to Europe and experience social mobility. For instance, Joseph Bologne, the Chevalier de Saint-Georges, was born on Guadeloupe to Nanon, an enslaved woman, and became a distinguished classical composer and soldier in Europe. This cosmopolitan space for individuals paved the way for the metropole welcoming colonials at a national level during the revolution. Jean-Baptiste Belley, an ex-slave born in Senegal, was elected from Saint-Domingue's North Province to sit in the National Convention as French citizenship, built on cosmopolitan principles, reached its most universal rendering early in the revolution.[11] The rise and conquests of Napoleon triggered renewed feelings of *patria* in Spain and connections to the *volk* in Germany, and a significant tightening of requirements for French citizenship. The French state retrenched from cosmopolitanism and emancipation, barring free people of color from becoming citizens and bolstering pre-1794 laws policing their movement within the metropole. Meanwhile, racial concerns underpinned the staffing of British imperial projects, suggesting parallels and connections with the reactionary policies imposed on communities of color in the early nineteenth century.

It is possible that, after 1800, the rise of anti-black sentiment in Europe and the stirrings of Romanticism, confining the way Caribbean and African-born people of color could fashion themselves in Europe, were not contemporaneous by coincidence. Hegel may have been inspired by Haiti to argue that the masters depended on the slaves for their sense of self-worth, but as some of the following analyses show, after the experiments of the French Revolution, Napoleonic and post-Napoleonic Europe wanted ex-slaves and their descendants to be far, far away.[12] In sum, all seven studies demonstrate that while for free people of color, revolutionary self-fashioning always had strict limitations, the Americas offered much greater possibility than Romantic Europe, though French and Spanish America offered more than Anglo-America.

Each imperial variation in the Americas wrought key social and cultural differences in the lives and racial systems for free people of color. Of all the variations of Caribbean polities of color, the French Caribbean featured the most powerful and well-off classes of African descent. At its pre-1791 zenith in French Saint-Domingue, the most productive plantation colony in the Americas, people of color comprised almost half of the free population, far greater that the almost 20% in Jamaica. Their roughly one-quarter representation in the free populations of Martinique and Guadeloupe far surpassed the mere 5% in Barbados. With unparalleled legal rights, some well-positioned free people of color could litigate against whites. Intriguingly, this came despite the French metropolitan concern for racial mixing that led to banning interracial unions in the colonies by the 1730s. The exception was Saint-Domingue, where by the 1760s many of the best-off *gens de couleur* were considered "white" by many. Their collective frustration crescendoed as increasing imperial racist constraints unraveled their unrivaled civil rights and social prestige. When Paris demurred at their inclusion under political promises of the Declarations of Rights of Man and the French Revolution, their subsequent protests, most notably by Vincent Ogé in 1790 and the "Rising in the West" in 1791, portended the most radical and momentous civic engagement by free people of color in the Caribbean up to that time. In the Haitian post-revolutionary era, this class suddenly held disproportionate domestic power within a "black" nation of outsized international influence. Their inheritance of pro-European dispositions, including education in France, commercial ties to Europe, consumption and display of ex-metropolitan styles and tastes, and Catholicism, weighed heavily upon Haiti's internal and foreign relations.[13]

In the British colonies that later became the United States a structural binary of blackness and whiteness shaped racial, legal, and social categories. Obvious African ancestry, later classified more severely as the "One Drop Rule" in some US locales, cast free people of color more firmly into blackness than in neighboring societies. In North America, mixed-race individuals never truly comprised a distinct race, legal, and class position as in Latin America, with perhaps the exception of Charleston, a more Caribbean city than other North American ports. However, though their racial strata were precarious, individuals of mixed African and European ancestry were better positioned socially than free blacks who were not only of darker complexion but often had once been slaves themselves. Greater acceptance of cross-race liaisons and extramarital miscegenation enhanced the visibility of mixed-race individuals and their permissibility as a group in the British Caribbean. These outcomes were partly due to demographic dominance of the enslaved (90% in Jamaica, 60% in South Carolina) and sparsity of white women. In these contexts, mixed-race children were less stigmatized and in Jamaica free people of color were granted legislative protections and allowed to legally inherit property.[14]

In the Dutch Caribbean, slaveholders not only manumitted enslaved women with whom they had relationships and their progeny, but also loyal domestic slaves. In Curaçao in particular slaves could also purchase their own freedom. By 1789 Willemstad, Curaçao's capital, was one of the most diverse in the Caribbean, with nearly 23% free people of color and 42% enslaved. By Dutch abolition in 1863, only one-third of the populations were enslaved. Nevertheless, free Curaçaoans were restricted in their consumption, gatherings, and commerce, and by law were taxed more stringently and had to serve in menial public works.[15] As one of case studies here shows, this very flexibility of urban slavery placed free people of color in the Netherlands Antilles in less distinct social and legal category than in neighboring empires.

The Spanish, who introduced African slavery to the Americas, observed more flexible racial gradients and more lenient self-purchasing practices (*coartación*). This process heavily favored urban slaves who could more easily accrue earnings from their artisanal trades and/or small commerce. Furthermore, the absence of a large white population in Cuba and many other Spanish colonies meant that free people of color participated comprehensively as artisans, militiamen, and vendors, especially in cities on the seaboard. Such was the case in Cartagena and Caracas, both featured here. Similar structural influences of slave demographics, miscegenation, and manumission of mixed-race children prevailed. Unlike the enslaved, free populations of color did increase through natural reproduction. By 1800 in all Spanish colonies except Cuba free people of color outnumbered slaves.

However, Spanish categories for free people of color abounded in both formal and informal terminologies. This system of "castes" ranged from *negro libre* (free black, sometimes also *moreno libre*) to *mulato* (child of a white man and black woman), *pardo* (also a person of varied African and European descent), *mulato morisco* (child of a white man and mulata woman), and *zambo* (African and indigenous descent). The usage and meaning of these terms varied across each colonial setting. Overwhelmingly few if any of these free people of color would have self-identified as negro, or black. Furthermore, free people of color with limited detectable African ancestry, and a combination of substantial wealth and public dignity, could petition imperial authorities for legal whiteness through a process called *gracias al sacar*, which could formally provide *limpieza de sangre*, or cleanliness of blood, as hereditary legal property.[16] This diverse group occupied a wide range of social positions.

Within these regional and imperial variations, the particular intersections of gender and autonomy presented unique circumstances for women of color. Women of color could gain freedoms through marital relations, market activities, piety, domestic resourcefulness, and kin networks. Female slaves were more likely to have opportunities for freedom than male slaves – opportunities beyond *marronage*, for example – yet in freedom were more confined than free men of color by norms of class and particularly gender. For example, free women of color dealt with the intersection of their race and attached stereotypes, such as licentiousness. Patriarchy, which also placed limits on economic possibilities for white women, constrained free women of color throughout the Atlantic, though a few acquired significant fortunes.[17]

In the aggregate, free people of color could manipulate the social order to their benefit, often at the expense of the enslaved or racial solidarities highlighted in the Age of Revolutions, but this manipulation had limits. It was predicated upon adopting European ideals, or a colonialist *mentalité*, and was only a successful tactic in certain circumstances.[18]

Self-perception for free people of color under colonialism was diminished by ideas of native inability, racial deficiency, and local marginality, all juxtaposed to metropolitan refinement. This "historical-racial schema" constructed people of color with "a thousand details, anecdotes, and stories." This social arrangement could foster an inferiority complex that propelled their refraction of colonialist culture through emulation or adoption of Eurocentric norms, at times to extremes, and often to the detriment of more "African" populations. By demonstrating European proximity – in speech, dress, and manners – free people of color could partake in the benefits of colonialist conceits, at the expense of reinforcing them. However refined their demonstrations, metropolitans were loath to recognize their whiteness. This colonized person, not fully accepted by the metropolitan society in which they either assimilated their aspirations or aspired to subvert, could become dependent upon white approval and thus alienated from their self.[19] Though at times muted in historiography, these cultural registers formed quotidian material perimeters of social difference. For example, the appearance and feel of their homes and clothing, their tastes in food, the auditory markers of refined pronunciations, and their separation from the smells of unpleasant labor regimes or living conditions, all offered free population of color distinctions from the enslaved, and capital within European milieus.[20]

Finally, although few of the free individuals of color discussed here had access to representative assemblies and high politics, they did, in Michel de Certeau's term, act as "consumers" of their polity's social systems, including plantation slavery and the resulting economic, legal, and cultural structures. In Certeau's schematic, consumers use established language and prescribed forms, but their "trajectories" create "unforeseeable sentences" and "partly unreadable paths" that "trace out the ruses of other interests and desires that are neither determined nor captured by the systems in which they develop."[21] "Trajectories" include two constituent parts: strategy and tactics. In Certeau's use, strategy refers to a subject capable of marshaling enough power to assume a circumscribed place from which to relate to others, i.e., the ability of free people of color to define and manage others as slaves to bolster their own socioeconomic endeavors. Tactics encompass the contingent, shifting efforts to pursue opportunities, and to bend larger trends to the subject's own ends, including legal maneuvers, cunning tricks, and fortunate discoveries of freer spaces.[22] In different locales in the Caribbean and around the Atlantic, free individuals and communities of color had different tactical decisions available to them to dress, behave, and otherwise present themselves in a certain way. Throughout, all were limited by the larger economic context of the Caribbean and broader Atlantic which was built around the general strategy of slave labor.[23]

The seven insightful case studies that follow explore these very themes of capital, self-fashioning, and tactics. Cristina Soriano examines a devoutly Catholic *pardo* musician in Caracas, Venezuela, who was arrested on suspicion of sedition and sent to Spain. Subsequently, the combination of his fervently royalist and insistently pious letters, his craft, and evidence of his character as stated by respected members of his community, contributed to his exoneration and freedom. John Garrison Marks investigates trade networks, consumption, and upward social mobility of free people of color in Cartagena, Colombia, and Charleston, South Carolina. Ale Pålsson analyzes the formation of a community of free Swedes of color. Swedish colonialism on the Caribbean island of St. Barthélemy opened new avenues for subjecthood, legal rights, publishing, and commerce to people of color, including those hailing from other empires. Erin Zavitz explores how Haiti's first generation of authors drew upon contemporary European discourse to justify and legitimize the black nation state. Margaret Crosby-Arnold, without relying on race as a category of analysis, considers Napoleonic oppression against people of color in continental Europe and argues that we should consider it a case of state-sanctioned genocide. Daniel Livesay tracks free people of color in the West Indies who used connections with élite whites to pursue fortune in the East Indies and then sought to shed both sets of colonial connections once they settled in Britain. Finally, in her piece on the Dutch colonies of Curaçao and oft-overlooked St. Maarten, Jessica Roitman studies the legal strivings of the comparatively large free population of color in the Netherlands Antilles amid the flexibility of urban slavery in the century leading to abolition.

This project addresses themes problematic to our understanding of this place and period and pushes beyond common scholarly frames by looking at Atlantic-derived Caribbean ties to bureaucratic emigrants to South Asia, Scandinavian trade and seafaring, Dutch port societies, Napoleonic France, comparisons between emergent American *repúblicas*, and how early Haitian intellectuals linked factually and fictively with an African past. These innovative analyses of free communities of color in the Caribbean and their engagement with the wider world illuminate underexplored ideological and structural continuities that extend beyond the Age of Revolutions. Tying together scholarship on the intersection of social mobility, consumption, and political ideation across empires provides a new perspective on the perpetuation of colonial hierarchies into post-emancipation or post-colonial settings. Examining the nuances of shifting racial categories helps elucidate how free people of color understood and manipulated the relationship between identity and state formation during key moments in the histories of some of the Caribbean's oldest states and most enduring colonies. Without this recalibration, we risk underappreciating the legacy of late Caribbean colonialism, minimizing the context of revolutionary change and state formation, and misunderstanding the ambitions and centrality of free communities of color to these processes.

Notes

1. Cohen and Greene, *Neither Slave nor Free*.
2. Geggus, *Haitian Revolution*; Johnson, *Fear of French Negroes*.
3. Garrigus, *Before Haiti*; Scott and Hébrard, *Freedom Papers*; Lindsay and Sweet, *Biography and the Black Atlantic*; Sensbach, *Rebecca's Revival*; Vinson, *Bearing Arms*; and Twinam, *Purchasing Whiteness*.
4. Sparks, *Two Princes of Calabar*, 9, 44, 85–86, 100; Law and Mann, "West Africa in the Atlantic Community."
5. Johnson, *Fear of French Negroes*, Chapter 4.
6. Landers, *Atlantic Creoles*, 13; Berlin, *Many Thousands Gone*, 24, 64.
7. Sweet, *Domingos Álvares*, 4–5.
8. Candlin and Pybus, *Enterprising Women*; Clark, *Strange History of the American Quadroon*; Rogers, "Les libres de couleur dans les capitales de Saint-Domingue"; and McCleskey, *Road to Black Ned's Forge*.
9. Bhabha, *Location of Culture*, 47, 59–64, 340; Bhabha, "Remembering Fanon," 118–124; Chakrabarty, *Provincializing Europe*, 15–17; and Said, *Orientalism*, 8–15.
10. Bourdieu, *Distinction*; Fanon, *Black Skin, White Masks*; Bourdieu, "The Forms of Capital," 241–258; Taussig, *What Color is the Sacred?*; and Gilroy, *Postcolonial Melancholia*, 52–58.

11. Brubaker, *Citizenship and Nationhood*, 44–48; Reiss, *The Black Count*.
12. Buck-Morss, "Hegel and Haiti." Further study on perceptions and policies regarding racial difference in nineteenth-century Europe, beyond the portrayal of people of color in period literature, will elucidate the construction of whiteness, national belonging, and anti-black sentiment during the Napoleonic and early Romantic period. David Bell touches on the question in *The Cult of the Nation in France*, 104–106. Key recent works include Hoffmann, "Representations of the Haitian Revolution"; Célius, "Neoclassicism and the Haitian Revolution"; Heuer, "The One-Drop Rule in Reverse?"; Miller, *The French Atlantic Triangle*; Vidal, *Français?*; Schüller, "From Liberalism to Racism"; Richardson and Hofkosh, *Romanticism, Race, and Imperial Culture*; Youngquist, *Race, Romanticism, and the Atlantic*; Kirkpatrick, "Constituting the Subject"; Hill, "Categories and Crossings"; and Iarocci, *Properties of Modernity*.
13. Garrigus, "French Caribbean," 186–190; Geggus, *Haitian Revolution*, 48–70; King, *Blue Coat or Powdered Wig*; and Taber, "'The Issue of Their Union'."
14. Lockley, "Race and Slavery," 342–348; Jordan, "American Chiaroscuro," 641–653.
15. Heijer, "Dutch Caribbean," 167; Rupert, *Creolization and Contraband*, 133–136, 146–147, 158–159.
16. Bryant, O'Toole, and Vinson, *Africans to Spanish America*; Andrews, *Afro-Latin America*, 41–45; Childs and Barcia, "Cuba," 94–96; Yingling, "Colonialism Unraveling," 45–64; and Twinam, *Purchasing Whiteness*. Circa 1800 Colombia had roughly 245,000 free people of color out of 787,000 people, only 61,000 of whom were slaves. Venezuela had 444,000 free people of color and 112,000 slaves in a population of 898,000.
17. Scully and Paton, *Gender and Slave Emancipation in the Atlantic World*; Gaspar and Hine, *Beyond Bondage*; Candlin and Pybus, *Enterprising Women*; Beckles, *Natural Rebels*; and Barcia, "Fighting with the Enemy's Weapons."
18. Chartier, *Cultural History*.
19. Du Bois, *Souls of Black Folk*; Fanon, *Black Skin, White Masks*; and Gilroy, *Black Atlantic*.
20. Smith, *How Race Is Made*, 33–34, 78–79, 101–103; Kuti, "Colonial Mentality"; and Taussig, *Mimesis and Alterity*, xiii, 1–32, 236–282.
21. de Certeau, *Practice of Everyday Life*, xviii.
22. Ibid., xix.
23. This discussion of strategy and tactics as applied to Atlantic slave societies is taken from Taber, "'The Issue of Their Union'," 33–34.

Acknowledgements

We would like to thank the editorial board of *Atlantic Studies* for the opportunity to organize this collection, and we are particularly indebted to the support of Manuel Barcia and Dorothea Fischer-Hornung. Thanks to Margaret Crosby-Arnold, Dan Livesay, John Marks, Ale Pålsson, Jessica Roitman, Cristina Soriano, and Erin Zavitz for their contributions of excellent studies, and for their patience with our editorial process. Thanks to Mimi Sheller and Andrew Kettler for their input to our introductory essay, and to the anonymous reviewers who generously gave of their time and expertise.

Disclosure statement

No potential conflict of interest was reported by the authors.

Bibliography

Andrews, George Reid. *Afro-Latin America, 1800–2000*. New York: Oxford University Press, 2004.

Barcia, Manuel. "Fighting with the Enemy's Weapons: The Usage of the Colonial Legal Framework by Nineteenth Cuban Slaves." *Atlantic Studies* 3, no. 2 (2006): 159–181.

Beckles, Hilary McD. *Natural Rebels: A Social History of Enslaved Black Women in Barbados*. New Brunswick, NJ: Rutgers University Press, 1989.

Bell, David A. *The Cult of the Nation in France: Inventing Nationalism, 1680–1800*. Cambridge, MA: Harvard University Press, 2001.

Berlin, Ira. *Many Thousands Gone: The First Two Centuries of Slavery in North America*. Cambridge, MA: Harvard University Press, 1998.

Bhabha, Homi K. *The Location of Culture*. New York: Routledge, 1994.

Bhabha, Homi K. "Remembering Fanon." *New Formations* 1 (Spring 1987): 118–124.

Bourdieu, Pierre. *Distinction: A Social Critique of the Judgement of Taste*. Cambridge, MA: Harvard University Press, 1984.

Bourdieu, Pierre. "The Forms of Capital." In *Handbook of Theory and Research for the Sociology of Education*, edited by John G. Richardson, 241–258. New York: Greenwood Press, 1986.

Brubaker, Rogers. *Citizenship and Nationhood in France and Germany*. Cambridge, MA: Harvard University Press, 1992.

Bryant, Sherwin K., Rachel O'Toole, and Ben Vinson, III, eds. *Africans to Spanish America: Expanding the Diaspora*. Urbana: University of Illinois Press, 2012.

Buck-Morss, Susan. "Hegel and Haiti." *Critical Inquiry* 26, no. 4 (2000): 821–865.

Candlin, Kit, and Cassandra Pybus. *Enterprising Women: Gender, Race, and Power in the Revolutionary Atlantic*. Athens: University of Georgia Press, 2015.

Célius, Carlo. "Neoclassicism and the Haitian Revolution." In *The World of the Haitian Revolution*, edited by David Patrick Geggus and Norman Fiering, 352–391. Bloomington: Indiana University Press, 2009.

de Certeau, Michel. *The Practice of Everyday Life*. Berkeley: University of California Press, 1984.

Chakrabarty, Dipesh. *Provincializing Europe: Postcolonial Thought and Historical Difference*. Princeton, NJ: Princeton University Press, 2001.

Chartier, Roger. *Cultural History: Between Practices and Representations*. Translated by Lydia Cochrane. New York: Cambridge University Press, 1988.

Childs, Matt D., and Manuel Barcia. "Cuba." In *The Oxford Handbook of Slavery in the Americas*, edited by Robert L. Paquette and Mark M. Smith, 90–110. New York: Oxford University Press, 2010.

Clark, Emily. *The Strange History of the American Quadroon: Free Women of Color in the Revolutionary Atlantic World*. Chapel Hill: University of North Carolina Press, 2013.

Cohen, David W., and Jack P. Greene, eds. *Neither Slave nor Free: The Freedmen of African Descent in the Slave Societies of the New World*. Baltimore, MS: Johns Hopkins University Press, 1972.

Du Bois, W. E. Burghardt. *The Souls of Black Folk: Essay and Sketches*. Chicago: A.C. McClurg, 1903.

Fanon, Frantz. *Black Skin, White Masks*. New York: Grove Press, 1952.

Garrigus, John. *Before Haiti: Race and Citizenship in French Saint-Domingue*. New York: Palgrave Macmillan, 2006.

Garrigus, John. "French Caribbean." In *The Oxford Handbook of Slavery in the Americas*, edited by Robert L. Paquette and Mark M. Smith, 173–200. New York: Oxford University Press, 2010.

Gaspar, David Barry, and Darlene Clark Hine, eds. *Beyond Bondage: Free Women of Color in the Americas*. Urbana: University of Illinois Press, 2004.

Geggus, David, ed. *The Haitian Revolution: A Documentary History*. Indianapolis, IN: Hackett, 2014.

Gilroy, Paul. *The Black Atlantic: Modernity and Double Consciousness*. New York: Verso, 1993.

Gilroy, Paul. *Postcolonial Melancholia*. New York: Columbia University Press, 2005.

Heijer, Henk Den. "Dutch Caribbean." In *The Oxford Handbook of Slavery in the Americas*, edited by Robert L. Paquette and Mark M. Smith, 154–172. New York: Oxford University Press, 2010.

Heuer, Jennifer. "The One-Drop Rule in Reverse? Interracial Marriages in Napoleonic and Restoration France." *Law and History Review* 27, no. 3 (2009): 515–548.

Hill, Ruth. "Categories and Crossings: Critical Race Studies and the Spanish World." *Journal of Spanish Cultural Studies* 10, no. 1 (2009): 1–6.

Hoffmann, Léon-François. "Representations of the Haitian Revolution in French Literature." In *The World of the Haitian Revolution*, edited by David Patrick Geggus and Norman Fiering, 339–351. Bloomington: Indiana University Press, 2009.

Iarocci, Michael. *Properties of Modernity: Romantic Spain, Modern Europe, and the Legacies of Empire*. Nashville, TN: Vanderbilt University Press, 2006.

Johnson, Sara. *The Fear of French Negroes: Transcolonial Collaboration in the Revolutionary Americas*. Berkeley: University of California Press, 2012.

Jordan, Winthrop D. "American Chiaroscuro: The Status and Definition of Mulattoes in the British Colonies." In *The Slavery Reader*, edited by Gad Heuman and James Walvin, 641–653. New York: Routledge, 2003.

King, Stewart R. *Blue Coat or Powdered Wig: Free People of Color in Pre-revolutionary Saint-Domingue*. Athens: University of Georgia Press, 2001.

Kirkpatrick, Susan. "Constituting the Subject: Race, Gender, and Nation in the Early Nineteenth Century." In *Culture and the State in Spain (1550–1850)*, 225–251. New York: Garland, 1999.

Kuti, Fela. "Colonial Mentality." In *Sorrow Tears and Blood*, edited by Fela Kuti and Afrika. Kalakuta, vinyl album, 1977.

Landers, Jane. *Atlantic Creoles in the Age of Revolutions*. Cambridge, MA: Harvard University Press, 2011.

Law, Robin, and Kristin Mann. "West Africa in the Atlantic Community: The Case of the Slave Coast." *William and Mary Quarterly* 56, no. 2 (1999): 307–334.

Lindsay, Lisa A., and John Wood Sweet, eds. *Biography and the Black Atlantic*. Philadelphia: University of Pennsylvania Press, 2014.

Lockley, Timothy. "Race and Slavery." In *The Oxford Handbook of Slavery in the Americas*, edited by Robert L. Paquette and Mark M. Smith, 336–356. New York: Oxford University Press, 2010.

McCleskey, Turk. *The Road to Black Ned's Forge: A Story of Race, Sex, and Trade on the Colonial American Frontier*. Charlottesville: University of Virginia Press, 2014.

Miller, Christopher L. *The French Atlantic Triangle: Literature and Culture of the Slave Trade*. Durham, NC: Duke University Press, 2008.

Randy J. *Sparks, the Two Princes of Calabar: An Eighteenth-Century Atlantic Odyssey*. Cambridge, MA: Harvard University Press, 2004.

Reiss, Tom. *The Black Count: Glory, Revolution, Betrayal, and the Real Count of Monte Cristo*. New York: Crown, 2012.

Richardson, Alan, and Sonia Hofkosh, eds. *Romanticism, Race, and Imperial Culture*. Bloomington: Indiana University Press, 1996.

Rogers, Dominique. "Les libres de couleur dans les capitales de Saint-Domingue: Fortune, mentalités et intégration à la fin de l'Ancien Régime (1776–1789)." PhD diss., Bordeaux III, 1999.

Rupert, Linda M. *Creolization and Contraband: Curaçao in the Early Modern Atlantic World*. Athens: University of Georgia Press, 2012.

Said, Edward. *Orientalism*. New York: Pantheon, 1978.

Schüller, Karin. "From Liberalism to Racism: German Historians, Journalists, and the Haitian Revolution from the Late Eighteenth to the Early Twentieth Centuries." In *The Impact of the Haitian Revolution in the Atlantic World*, edited by David P. Geggus, 23–43. Columbia: University of South Carolina Press, 2001.

Scott, Rebecca, and Jean M. Hébrard. *Freedom Papers: An Atlantic Odyssey in the Age of Emancipation*. Cambridge, MA: Harvard University Press, 2012.

Scully, Pamela, and Diana Paton, eds. *Gender and Slave Emancipation in the Atlantic World*. Durham, NC: Duke University Press, 2005.

Sensbach, Jon F. *Rebecca's Revival: Creating Black Christianity in the Atlantic World*. Cambridge, MA: Harvard University Press, 2005.

Smith, Mark M. *How Race Is Made: Slavery, Segregation, and the Senses*. Chapel Hill: University of North Carolina Press, 2006.

Sweet, James. *Domingos Álvares, African Healing, and the Intellectual History of the Atlantic World*. Chapel Hill: University of North Carolina Press, 2011.

Taber, Robert D. "'The Issue of Their Union': Family, Law, and Politics in Western Saint-Domingue, 1777–1789." PhD diss., University of Florida, 2015.

Taussig, Michael. *Mimesis and Alterity: A Particular History of the Senses*. New York: Routledge, 1993.

Taussig, Michael. *What Color Is the Sacred?* Chicago: University of Chicago Press, 2009.

Twinam, Ann. *Purchasing Whiteness: Pardos, Mulattos, and the Quest for Social Mobility in the Spanish Indies*. Stanford: Stanford University Press, 2015.

Vidal, Cécile, ed. *Français? La nation en débat entre colonies et métropole, XVIe-XIXe siècle*. Paris: Editions de l'Ecole des hautes études en sciences sociales, 2014.

Vinson, Ben, III. *Bearing Arms for His Majesty: The Free-Colored Militia in Colonial Mexico*. Stanford, CA: Stanford University Press, 2001.

Yingling, Charlton W. "Colonialism Unraveling: Race, Religion, and National Belonging in Santo Domingo During the Age of Revolutions." PhD diss., University of South Carolina, 2016.

Youngquist, Paul, ed. *Race, Romanticism, and the Atlantic*. Farnham, Surrey: Ashgate, 2013.

"A true vassal of the King": Pardo literacy and political identity in Venezuela during the age of revolutions

Cristina Soriano

ABSTRACT
Eighteenth-century Venezuela was a highly stratified society in which race, education, occupation, honor, family ties, and economic resources all played important roles in defining the place that each member occupied. In this complex social map, not all social groups had equal access to education; literacy was a marker of status and power. Traditionally, literate and formally educated people belonged to the white elite, while the majority of the supposedly "non-literate" population belonged to lower social groups of color, who relied largely on oral media for the transmission of knowledge. By the end of the eighteenth century, this picture began to change: the number of people who owned books increased, an incipient informal market of books began to operate, and original networks for the circulation of books and manuscripts among different social groups proliferated. Increasingly mixed-race groups, known as pardos, learned to read and write through informal means to an education. However, members of the colonial white elite interpreted pardos' access to literacy and education as a way of challenging the proper social order and authority. This article analyzes the case of Juan Bautista Olivares, a literate pardo musician who in 1795 was sent to court in Cádiz, accused by the Venezuelan governor of subversion; Olivares, however, successfully defended himself, declaring his loyalty to the Spanish Monarchy and proving his pious behavior. Pardos, like Juan Bautista, creatively navigated social tensions and the effects of the Atlantic Revolutions by shaping their political identity as royalists, questioning the local government and reasserting their loyalty to the Spanish Monarchy.

When Juan Bautista Olivares disembarked in the port of Cádiz for the first time one warm morning in June 1795, his hands were tied and guards were escorting him to the Royal Prison of Cádiz. Juan Bautista, a *pardo* musician residing in the city of Caracas, capital of the General-Captaincy of Venezuela, never would have predicted that his first visit to Spain would be as a prisoner.[1] The General-Captain of Venezuela, Pedro Carbonell, had sent him to the Council of Indies, accusing him of being a "subversive and arrogant pardo, capable of encouraging the people of his own class to shake off the yoke of obedience and vassalage."[2] Carbonell alleged that Juan Bautista Olivares had read prohibited papers and spread seditious ideas of liberty and equality among fellow people of color and, therefore, that he clearly undermined the public order in Venezuela. Olivares, however, was unaware of these accusations. He considered himself an obedient and loyal vassal of the King, and according to him, his only problem with colonial authorities pertained to his desire to take the holy orders of the priesthood.

Between 1791 and 1794, Olivares presented himself to different ecclesiastical authorities in Caracas seeking permission to be ordained, but he encountered only obstacles and pretexts due to the color of his skin. According to Olivares, these authorities did everything in their power to dissuade him, but they never provided any formal justification for blocking Olivares' ordination.[3] One day, in May 1795, Olivares was unanticipatedly sent to prison in Caracas, and, days later, forced to board the ship *Jesús, María and José* that set sail from the Venezuelan port of La Guaira to Cádiz. No one in Caracas took note of his declaration, nor informed Olivares of the accusations against him. According to the General-Captain, "under the current fragile circumstances," an extraordinary Junta had decided that it was necessary to put Olivares in prison and send him to Cádiz without following "the formality of the legal procedure, proper inquiries, and acknowledgments" because Olivares was "a very dangerous character."[4] Olivares suspected that he had turned into an uncomfortable individual for local authorities, but he never imagined that he would be accused of political subversion because no one had ever charged with such allegations.[5]

The case of Olivares illustrates the complexity of late colonial Venezuela where increasing socio-racial tensions between whites and people of color overlapped with the political forces emerging from the Atlantic revolutions. Eighteenth-century Venezuela was a society founded on social privileges that produced constant tensions within distinct socio-racial groups, especially between white creoles and pardos. Combined, pardos and free blacks represented more than 45% of Venezuelan population and local whites felt threatened by the increasing numbers of free people of color and their aspirations for social mobility.[6]

During the final decade of the century, the circulation of texts and rumors from the Atlantic Revolutions increased white fear of racial confrontations, exacerbated local pressures and disrupted this "tense calmness." Ideas of liberty and equality from the French Revolution reached the coastal towns of Venezuela, and the turmoil of Saint-Domingue and Guadeloupe certainly increased local political anxiety. Colonial authorities and white elites began to pay more attention to the actions of pardos, free blacks, and slaves, and to reconsider their relations with these subordinated groups of color, heightening their suspicions and undermining a sense of confidence that seemed to have existed before the rebellious events of 1791. Before then, white masters in Venezuela rarely questioned their slaves' loyalty, provided them with arms, and even left their haciendas under the supervision of free blacks and pardos.[7]

In this particularly vulnerable context, literate and educated pardos became a source of concern for white elites who believed that educated free people of color were specifically prone to the "revolutionary contagion." In response, the elites further restricted their access to education, religious institutions, and public ceremonies, not only because their presence in those social spaces would dishonor whites, but also because they were convinced that pardos would use their literacy skills to read "evil, infamous, and seditious" pieces, and would use this knowledge to challenge authorities and alter the public order.[8] Pardos and free blacks, on the other hand, used multiple strategies – such as creating alternative means of education, participating in pardo militias and creating religious brotherhoods – to challenge a social system that they perceived as unclear and unfair, but also flexible and manageable enough to allow their intervention.[9]

The myriad revolts and social movements developing in the Caribbean islands in the late eighteenth century mobilized a great number of people of diverse social status, races, and political tendencies across the Americas. This mobilization of people altered, in turn, the social dynamics, the political perceptions, and even the economies of each region.[10] Scholars of this period have often focused on how exceptional individuals of color navigated the turbulent political waters of the Atlantic and made use of an increasingly popular revolutionary language to resist social control, and pursue their freedom and dignity.[11] In the case of Venezuela, an abundant number of studies focus on how local pardos, free blacks and slaves organized and joined local rebellions and conspiracies, and used the revolutionary language to confront both the colonial government and the white elites.[12] Nevertheless, as seen in this article, the pardo political spectrum was more complex and included people like Olivares who resisted colonial social injustice not by making use of revolutionary language, but by exploiting local religious networks, reproducing Spanish reformist cultural practices, and reaffirming his position as a loyal vassal of the King.

In this context, this piece engages with recent scholarship that studies popular royalism in Latin America during the Age of Revolutions. Historians David Sartorius and Marcela Echeverri have invited us to closely analyze the complex and varied reasons that drove people from popular groups and across the color spectrum to remain loyal to the Spanish Crown and to resist those who fought for Independence.[13] Echeverri, in particular, dismantles previous historiographical assumptions that royalists were struggling to restore a traditional, static, and conservative order. She convincingly shows how royalist Indians and slaves in the Northern Andes engaged with ideas of freedom and citizenship, using their political identities to advance profound changes in the system. In so doing, Echeverri proves that the monarchical political culture was dynamic and vulnerable to transformation and that popular groups used royalism as a strategy for mobility.[14]

As this article presents, not many pardos in Caracas had the opportunities that Juan Bautista Olivares did. Juan Bautista perceived himself as an exceptional individual of color who, despite local socio-racial restrictions and limitations, got access to an informal education in music, theology, and law, and directed a religious chorus. Spanish reformist discourses that promoted education and literacy for popular groups such as artisans and peasants had certainly opened new possibilities for distinguished people of color in Venezuela. Juan Bautista still believed his situation could be improved if religious authorities would make the exceptional step of allowing him to take the Holy Orders. However, this seemed an impossibility due to his skin color and lack of a formal education. Juan Bautista was caught between two ideological forces: Spanish reformism and republicanism. In his struggle with Caracas' authorities, Juan Bautista Olivares emphasized his profound Catholic faith and redefined his political identity to express his loyalty to the Monarchy. While solidifying his class' social and political position, Juan Bautista sought new opportunities for himself and for other pardos in Venezuela.

Juan Bautista used his royalism not only to promote changes in the colonial ecclesiastical order but also to defend himself from Caracas government's serious accusations. Reconstructing stories like Juan Bautista's allow us to perceive the nuances on the relationships between free people of color, the colonial government, and the Spanish Crown during colonial times, and gives us a better understanding of the character and weight of popular royalism or, on the contrary, republicanism during the wars of independence in South America.[15]

Social hierarchies and Pardo literacy in late colonial Venezuela

Venezuelan colonial communities, like elsewhere in Spanish America, featured complex and dynamic overlapping of socio-racial, estate, and class structures.[16] Categories of color and status were abstract social constructions that had very specific uses in legal and administrative contexts. Through these categories the colonial state attempted to strategically mold the identities and self-representations of subjects, which were regularly used to legitimize occupational and social exclusion.[17]

Racial or "caste" categories were defined by the people in terms of *calidad* or quality, and were one of the most important criteria of classification in Spanish colonial societies. Some historians have characterized calidad as a racial status defined by legal color, while others have argued that this was a valorizing category used to denote ethnic status, purity of blood, and legal locations.[18] People in Venezuela understood socio-racial or "caste" categories in terms of calidad, a comprehensive category that primordially reflected skin color but that also spoke to one's reputation as a whole. It encompassed education, occupation, integrity, honor, as well as purity of blood.[19] Categories of quality were often confusing and unstable, and changed according to the context in which they were used and/or contested. Nonetheless, it is possible to identify broader classifiers that were commonly used to differentiate (and control) groups and to set rules and restrictions in a society that, in theory, was very attached to ideas of order, harmony, and subordination.

In historical records, people recognized three basic socio-racial groups understood in terms of quality: whites (Spaniards, creoles and *blancos de orilla*), Africans or people of African descent, and Indians.[20] During the colonial period, a large and heterogeneous group – a product of ongoing relations among the three basic groups – became increasingly visible. These people of intermediate quality were known as pardos and, in theory, included all people perceived as mixed-race: *mulatos, zambos, tercerones, cuarterones, quinterones*, etc. The category of pardos was, and still is, difficult to define because it not only referred to the color of the skin, but also represents other features such as education, occupation, literacy, and social practices.[21] For example, pardos and mulattos were both understood to be products of relations between whites and blacks, but sometimes, the term pardo was used to refer to educated mix-race people of slightly fairer skin, while the term mulatto denoted darker and less educated mixed-race individuals.

By the end of the eighteenth century, the population of Venezuela numbered approximately 800,000. Almost 50% – close to 390,000 people – lived in the Province of Caracas. Free people of African descent comprised more than 46% of the population of the Province of Caracas, while enslaved blacks represented 16%, whites represented almost 25%, and 12% were classified as Indians. That means that people of African descent (free and enslaved) constituted over 60% of the population.[22]

The relationships among and within these different socio-racial groups became increasingly strained due to changing political, bureaucratic, and economical circumstances of late colonialism. In theory, in Spanish America exclusively peninsular Spaniards held political positions, yet Ann Twinam argues that until the mid-eighteenth century in Venezuela

"Caraqueños [meaning the white creole elite] experienced Spanish Administration – 'light;'"[23] and enjoyed measured political autonomy and authority. Increasing Bourbon administrative control and restrictions in the political realm created, nonetheless, new tensions between Spanish administrators and the creole elite who continued challenging colonial authorities. By the end of the eighteenth century, white creoles and some elite pardo families (often called *pardos beneméritos*, that is, "worthy" or "meritorious" pardos due to their successes) openly challenged colonial institutions such as the royal audiencia, and even disobeyed Royal Orders that went against their economic interests.[24]

The demographic growth and economic improvement of pardos also exacerbated tensions with whites in areas beyond local politics. White Spaniards and creoles had educational privileges and played important roles in the clergy, government, and military academies. The elites regarded pardos as unsuitable for these positions. Their African blood and their link with their enslaved ancestors, the brown color of their skin, and their supposedly bastard origins coalesced into a stereotyped image of inferiority, which led to various forms of social, spatial, and legal exclusion.[25] White elites depicted pardos as illegitimate children, with no traceable genealogy. For example, a document written by members of the Caracas city council stated: "Pardos, mulattos, and zambos have the defect of illegitimacy, because it is rather rare to find a pardo, mulatto, or zambo with legitimate parents."[26]

In this context, literacy and the possession of books represented markers of social status and power. Most of the literate and formally educated people belonged to the white elite, while the majority of the supposedly non-literate population were part of the lower social groups that barely had the means to buy *pliegos sueltos* (broadsides) and who relied largely on oral media for the transmission of knowledge. By the end of the eighteenth century, however, this picture had begun to change. The number of people who owned books had increased significantly due to the stabilization of the local book market and a greater purchase capacity of the population at large, and the size and diversity of private libraries had grown significantly as a response to the influence of Spanish reformism and enlightened ideas in the region.[27] In a colonial society with no printing press, books and printed texts were expensive, but the lack of money did not prevent Venezuelans of modest means from acquiring printed materials. Social networks, *remates* (public auctions), an expanding circuit of book lending, and a widespread practice of transcription of texts represented some of the strategies that made printed material accessible to a larger population that included people of African descent.[28]

Juan Bautista certainly struggled to get an education, but he proved that Caracas offered several alternatives to pardos who, like him, believed in the power of literacy and instruction to improve their status. "When I couldn't find more instructors to teach me Latin syntax – reflected Juan Bautista – I asked permission to enroll in public classes, but the said permission was denied because I am pardo."[29] Subsequently, Juan Bautista confessed that he decided to educate himself by borrowing books from friends and educated acquaintances, and by "consulting with some of the most instructed and pious individuals."[30] He studied mathematics, grammar, Latin, and philosophy. According to him, he was so "successful" in his studies, that he quickly pursued more advanced studies of theology, sacred scriptures and Law. Soon, he said: "The same individuals who used to look at me with contempt found themselves in situations in which they paid respects to me."[31] In words of the General-Captain, Juan Bautista possessed a "copious library"[32] and most of "pardos of the city venerate him as a *sabio* (wise man)."[33]

It is critical to consider why Juan Bautista was so determined about his education. It seems that his desire to instruct himself was not made in a vacuum. His decisions, in fact, responded to the influences of Spanish educational reformism, a movement that promoted literacy and education for the lower social groups as a way to eradicate perceived ignorance, vice, and idleness among the population at large. Spanish reformists believed that an educated society would lead the empire to the path of civility and progress. Several editions of books by reformists such as Pedro Rodríguez de Campomanes, Melchor de Jovellanos, Fray Benito Jerónimo Feijoo, and Bernardo Ward, among others, arrived in Venezuela during the final decades of the eighteenth century and became quite popular.[34] All of these authors extensively discussed the need to reform the Spanish monarchical system, its administrative and legal structures in order to achieve agricultural and commercial development, while also seeking to produce changes in the public sphere largely through education, labor, and social progress. They built a strong critique against the "lazy and unproductive" nobility, championed public education as an antidote to ignorance, and argued in favor of creating schools to teach peasants, artisans, and urban laborers to draw, read, and write. They suggested that doing so would give birth to an educated society that could use *ciencias útiles* (useful sciences) for the progress of Spain and its territories.[35]

Although, none of these Spanish authors particularly addressed the need to educate the indigenous population or the people of color in the Spanish Indies, in Venezuela's social reality, their proposal meant that pardos and free blacks, the majority of the rural peasants and urban artisans, should become literate and partake of this well-needed social and cultural change. In fact, some Venezuelan teachers enthusiastically adopted the Spanish reformist model that promoted formal education for the common people, advocated for improving the quality of public schools – traditionally attended by whites – and for creating the first *Escuela de pardos* (school for pardos) in the cities of the province.[36]

Their accounts suggest that although some wealthy pardo families could afford to hire private tutors, the vast majority of the pardo population learned to read and write at the shops of barbers and shoemakers, or thanks to the assistance of improvised teachers such as carpenters and musicians. Therefore, it was clear that there was a middling group of people of color who collaborated in developing an alternative system of education to provide their kids with basic skills on reading, writing, and counting.[37] Juan Bautista did not reveal who taught him to read and write, but given that his father, a mulatto silversmith, was literate and that his older brother, Juan Manuel Olivares, was a student of music, there is a good chance that he learned with the assistance of members of his family. Later, both Juan Manuel and Juan Bautista had the good fortune of continuing studying music and religious studies under the guidance of two white priests, Father José de Osío and Father Pedro Palacios Sojo, who were close friends of the Olivares' family.[38]

The Olivares family was known for having musical instruments in their home, such as violins and a harpsichord (or French clavecin) that was fabricated by Father Osío himself. Father Osío offered music lessons to the Olivares brothers and taught Juan Manuel how to fabricate and play musical instruments as well. Later, the Olivares actively collaborated with Father Sojo on the development of the School of Music of Chacao, where they taught young men how to play the violin, the chamber organ, and the harpsichord. Juan Manuel also composed several pieces of liturgical music that musicians performed at religious ceremonies in the city.[39]

The Olivares brothers were known for organizing concerts of classic and religious music in the private houses, haciendas, and churches of Caracas. They became active participants in Spanish cultural and religious practices, and this allowed them to stand on a higher social status in regards to other pardos. Juan Bautista not only played musical instruments, from 1780 to 1792 he also directed a chorus and played in mass celebrations and religious events in different churches of Caracas.[40] The Olivares family looked like the typical pardo family of artisans in Caracas. These families afforded their kids with a modest and informal education that allowed them to become distinguished artisans, such as musicians (like the brothers Juan José and José Luis Landaeta, and Lino Gallardo), painters (like Juan Lovera, Blas Miguel Landaeta and Francisco José de Lerma y Villegas), and silversmiths.[41] If the Olivares brothers were part of an expanding network of educated pardos who dedicated themselves to artisanal activities, what made Juan Bautista an exceptional character? What turned him into a *persona non-grata* for colonial Authorities?

The "exceptionality" of Juan Bautista and white fears of revolutionary contagion

In 1789, Juan Manuel Olivares married Sebastiana Velázquez, a free mulata who was the daughter of a black slave and sister of the recognized black musician José Francisco Velázquez. His younger brother, Juan Bautista, considered a different destiny for himself. His close relationship with the fathers and brothers of the Temple of San Felipe de Neri made him think about the possibility of becoming a priest.[42] Although, Juan Bautista never revealed who specifically contributed to his religious education, his account and other testimonies of the Captain-General show that he cultivated a close relationship with members of the church of San Felipe de Neri, a place "he attended frequently to meet with musicians and priests."[43] These same priests were probably the ones who held discussions with him, "rigorously examined [my] knowledge and vocation," and even advised him on his inclination to become a priest.[44] No one seemed to be concerned about Juan Bautista's exceptional path until he asked permission to take the Holy orders, and it was only then that he seemed to have transgressed social boundaries.

Juan Bautista knew that his desire to be ordained confronted two important obstacles in Caracas: he was pardo and he lacked the formal education (neither from the university nor monastery) necessary for priesthood. He expressed that he talked about his case with different "doctos and santos" (wise and pious men) and asked them for guidance. Some of them told him that he was condemned and there was nothing he could do, but "others [expressed] that this was a vocation for God, and that [he] should do the pertinent diligence and present [his] case to the Bishop."[45] Olivares, then, decided to present himself to the Bishop of Caracas, Don Mariano Martí, and "after examination," the Bishop told him that "his vocation was perfect,"[46] and "there was no obstacle for [his] ordinance other than the folly of the patricians, that he did not know where they got that idea from."[47] But soon the Bishop passed away, and Olivares' destiny remained in the hands of those who fervently opposed his ambitions.

In 1791, Olivares submitted a petition to the diocesan authorities to enter an ecclesiastical order, but the church official attorney ignored his petition for three years, and "kept his file hidden in a drawer." Later, in 1794 the attorney-general of the diocese opposed Olivares' petition again alleging that the pardo was a descendent of "blacks and mulattos" and that someone with impure blood could not have access to "positions exclusive to people who are clean of all bad race."[48] Olivares continued writing challenging letters to different ecclesiastical authorities until the Captain-General unexpectedly imprisoned him.

According to colonial officials, the problems with Juan Bautista Olivares started when rumors circulated that two subversive documents – the "Extract of the Manifest that the National Convention made for all the Nations" and a "Sermon from the Constitutional Bishop of Paris, Mr. Embert" – were found in the hands of a group of pardos in Caracas.[49] Allegedly the pardo musician Juan Bautista Olivares had been reading these papers to them. Additionally, ecclesiastical authorities accused Olivares of writing and circulating letters containing "arrogant and seditious phrases" against the ecclesiastical authorities. Suddenly, Juan Bautista – a literate, educated, and pious pardo – precipitated the greatest political concern.

Colonial and ecclesiastical authorities had strong reasons to be worried about Juan Bautista's seditious public readings. For them, reading and writing during revolutionary times could open dangerous paths of political awareness to groups of color and compromise traditional socio-racial hierarchies, undermining also the authority of the church and of the colonial institutions.[50] Therefore, authorities developed a strong censorship campaign in which local priests read aloud titles of prohibited books and papers at Sunday Masses, and also posted indexes on the doors of the Church and walls of the squares. Agents of the Inquisition visited private houses to collect or censor prohibited books, or to rip out particularly offensive pages.[51] During Sunday sermons, priests reprimanded readers of seditious tracts and described the hellish punishments they would suffer for reading such "evil texts."[52]

The lack of printing shops, the absence of formal booksellers, and the significance of smuggling activities along Venezuela's long coast made efforts at controlling and censoring readings much more difficult.[53] From 1789 to 1795, samizdat materials – copied by hand – along with pamphlets printed in Europe, Trinidad, and Saint-Domingue, flooded cities and port towns of Venezuela, and networks for borrowing and copying books and newspapers flourished. In May 1796, Captain-General Carbonell confessed that his "greatest fear was the spread of papeles sueltos, and the political instruction that simple people [gentes sencillas] might receive from them, especially the slaves who in this Province [Caracas] alone number more than 100,000."[54]

Colonial officials and Church representatives feared that the ongoing tensions between socio-racial groups, the revolutionary events in France and the Caribbean, and the increasing circulation of revolutionary texts would "infest the most humble vassals with a revolutionary contagion" that would lead them to anti-religion, disobedience, and chaos.[55] José Ignacio Moreno, a white creole priest, knew all too well that the literate elite was not the only social group partaking in political conversations, and that local free blacks and slaves were having debates about the effects of the revolutions. According to Moreno, slave rebellions and the planning of republican conspiracies offered clear evidence that "the poison of liberty had invaded the hearts of the innocent and less intelligent people."[56]

There is evidence that these popular groups did in fact have access to prohibited papers and gazettes. On occasion members of the pardo militia presented copies of prohibited papers they collected among the population of color to colonial authorities. By doing so, they demonstrated their loyalty to the Crown and the local government; however, they never revealed how they had come by these documents. They never mentioned the names of the people who provided them with the documents nor the places they collected them.[57]

At the beginning of 1795, the Captain-General of Venezuela and members of the Junta in Caracas were convinced that the literate pardo Juan Bautista Olivares had intended to undermine their authority by "spreading the seed of equality among mulattos."[58] They finally decided to put an end to the problem by abruptly sending Olivares to prison in Cádiz without even questioning him, presenting proof of accusations, or following regular legal procedure.[59] They justified this irregularity by saying that the fragility of the current circumstances, and that the risk of allowing Juan Bautista to defend himself would bring more attention from the public to an issue that required "the most profound stealth."[60]

Ignorant of the accusations and of his own destiny, Juan Bautista left the Port of La Guaira in May 1795. "I couldn't – he confessed – find any crime in my heart." His pain grew even more when he overheard a conversation between the Capitan of the ship and the General-Captain in which the latter, refusing to pay for Juan Bautista passage, said: "if there is no food for him, then don't feed him. Tie him to the mast or throw him to the sea."[61] It is clear that the General-Captain had flagrantly broken the requirements of the law. He was so blinded by the Olivares case that he risked the fulfillment of the 1774 royal decree that compelled colonial authorities to "allow those sentenced to give evidence and present a legitimate self-defense."[62] Carbonell's disregard for the law was risky and could have had devastating effects for him because in these cases the King could "proceed against those who became transgressors of his sovereign intentions."[63]

Olivares' exceptional petition to be ordained as a priest was transfixed between two ideological forces: Spanish reformism and French republicanism. While his desire for a more socially inclusive church could have been framed within the Spanish reformist spirit, colonial authorities in Venezuela insisted on interpreting the audacity of the pardo as having been directly influenced by French revolutionary ideals. Juan Bautista's fate was placed in the hands of the Council of Indies.

"A true vassal of the King": Juan Bautista's case

By the end of July 1795, the Council of the Indies in Madrid revised the charges that the General-Captain and the Junta in Caracas made against Olivares. Carbonell accused Olivares of disturbing the tranquility of the Province by reading seditious texts to others and by writing letters and petitions in which he not only referred to revolutionary ideas but where he also expressed a haughty and defiant character. After analyzing Carbonell's letters, the Council decided it was absolutely necessary to follow the regular legal procedure. They demanded Carbonell to immediately send any documentation that he might have about Olivares. They also appointed members of the Court in Cádiz to conduct Juan Bautista's trial.[64]

First, the judges inquired about Olivares' written correspondence. They asked him if he had written a letter to a mulatto in which he had stated that "the powerful of this world triumph over the humble" and concluded that "they [the powerful] will be favored while the dark times last." Olivares answered that he did write the letter to a mulatto named Lauro (the musician of the Parish of Altagracia, Juan Gabriel Landaeta), in which he complained about a stingy priest who, while calling him "thief," did not pay him for his work as a musician. He admitted that he had written the quoted sentences, but insisted that his intentions had not been evil, as he had taken the sentences directly from Father Nieremberg's book *Diferencias entre lo Temporal y lo Eterno*. By "dark times," he added, "I meant the time of mortal life, nothing else."[65]

Olivares implied that his notion of light and darkness was, by no means, related with the revolutionary perception of "Light" as the Republican system and Darkness as the monarchical system. Contrary to what his accusers in Caracas believed, his references to light and darkness were profoundly Catholic: light represented the immortal life and the grace of the company of God, and darkness, the mortal time of humanity on earth. Moreover, the original source of Olivares' sentences – Nieremberg's book – was one of the most popular religious books read in Spanish America. In fact, almost 45% of late eighteenth-century private libraries in Caracas contained a copy of Nieremberg's book.[66] Olivares quoted a well-known and widely accepted religious reference, and proved that his statements were neither anti-religious nor anti-monarchical, but profoundly Catholic and pious.[67] The judges asked him whether he had read and explained to another mulatto named Victor Arteaga a sermon attributed to the Archbishop of Paris. Olivares answered:

> On one occasion, a friend of mine, named Pedro de Silva, brought to my house another mulatto known by the name Acuña, with the purpose of reading a manuscript sermon that was said to be written by the Archbishop of Paris [...] I read the sermon and Acuña immediately took it [the paper] with him, although I asked Acuña to lend me the paper so that I could copy it, I have not seen him again. I learned afterwards from a Priest of the San José de Chacao Parish, that the sermon was forbidden, and I desisted of the idea.[68]

Clearly, Olivares tried to disclaim responsibility for having read "seditious" papers to others. Although his account allows us to imagine a complex scenario in which he and other pardos met to read potentially seditious papers, he tried to clarify that this was not his idea, nor his intention. Olivares confessed that he was unaware that the paper they read was prohibited. In fact, he declared that he diligently followed the warning of the priest. When the judges asked him if he knew that the text of the Archbishop of Paris was infused with maxims of freedom and equality, he answered: "Although it is true that I wanted to copy it, it was only to feed my curiosity; I have always detested these maxims."[69] His confession revealed that his curiosity could have led him to commit sedition, but he rapidly reaffirmed that he despised the republican values. After all Juan Bautista was just one of the many Caracas readers who were caught reading seditious materials. Between 1791 and 1795, the General-Captain sent several notifications to the Council of Indies informing about cases in which colonial authorities uncovered individuals reading, translating, copying, and spreading revolutionary texts.[70] The most evident differences between Juan Bautista and these other white readers is that he was a pardo petitioning to be ordained as a priest.

The Judges then asked Olivares if he had read, copied, and circulated other documents on the French Revolution or republicanism. He answered that he had not read any other papers regarding this issue, except for "La *Gaceta de Madrid* and the testament of the King of France."[71] Many Spanish-American readers learned about the French Revolution through the pages of the *Gaceta* since it was a popular newspaper that was widely read in different corners of Spanish America. Olivares, then, proved that his source of information about the revolutions was pretty much the same source that anyone had both in Spain and in Venezuela, part of the common knowledge shared by the literate population of the Hispanic Atlantic.[72]

At the end, the judges touched an important issue: they asked Olivares if it was true that he had petitioned to be ordained as a priest. He answered affirmatively. Then the judges asked him if it was true that his letters of petition addressed to the clergy authorities were written with haughtiness and pride. Olivares responded that after facing several obstacles he had written a letter asking the said authorities to provide him with clear and sound reasons why he was not being allowed to take the holy orders. Olivares argued that this rejection on the part of the local authorities was arbitrary and contradicted not only "the positive Law, but it went against the Divine Law, against the Sacred Scriptures, the Holy Fathers, against the designs of God, against the Church and against the King."[73]

Although Olivares knew he had not received the education for ordination, he believed there were not legal reasons to deny him this possibility. According to him, even the Bishop Martí recognized there were not real obstacles for his ordination. Assiduously, Olivares added that he never entertained the idea of undermining the public peace, on the contrary, his strongest desire was to fulfill God's designs and to incite others of his class to be faithful and to offer their services to the Church and to the King. In this way, Olivares advocated for a more racially inclusive Church. Vocation of faith, in his opinion, was not related to quality or status, it responded instead to a "call from God."

During his time in prison, Olivares wrote a revealing letter in which he explained the hardships he had to confront in Caracas.[74] The letter provided the Council with a clear description of "misfortunes" and discrimination regularly experienced by pardos in the province, where they were not allow to pursue an education or to attend the seminary, and therefore could not be priests. Olivares sought to prove that the Captain-General and the Real Audiencia had sent him to Cádiz not because he was a "subversive person" but because, as a loyal and faithful vassal of the King, he was anxious to join the clerical order and he engaged in a struggle with the church authorities of Caracas who aggressively opposed his petition. In fact, in one of Olivares' letters to Caracas' ecclesiastical authorities he argued there were mestizos priests in other bishoprics of Spanish America, such as the one in Charcas or Cusco.[75] He therefore could not understand why in Venezuela he could not follow this pious vocation. Olivares argued that his quality was not a strong reason to deny him the possibility to take the holy orders:

> after reading more than sixty authors, and consulting almost thirty theologians and jurists, supported by a decree the Holy Congregation of the Concilio, I alleged [to church authorities] that priesthood cannot be denied to the son of a white and a black.[76]

The other obstacle to be ordained would be his lack of education, but Olivares was convinced that his was in perfect condition to take the most rigorous exams and proof his solid preparation.

Olivares' petition was made during a particularly tense period of confrontation between white elites and pardos – especially the lighter-skinned, educated, and wealthy elite – who had devised legal strategies to gain access to positions that the elites denied from them. Among these was a Royal Edict – known as the *Real Cédula de Gracias al Sacar* – which could bestow on the wealthiest pardos a "dispensation of color" (*dispensa de calidad*), granting them honorary white status.[77] As Twinam shows, Venezuela was the most notable geographical cluster of petitioners of the Gracias al Sacar in the Spanish Indies, both because the region had a particularly large and growing pardo population and because white elites ferociously opposed any of their attempts to improve their social power. Many of these petitions for whitening were made by men who wanted to extend whiteness to their wives or their offspring, so that, for example, their sons could marry whites, enroll in the University, or take the sacred orders and become priests.[78]

Venezuela was also the place were these petitions encountered the most aggressive opposition from white creole elites who argued that these edicts violated the Crown's policy against social mobility and compromised the tranquility and order of the Province. In a letter presented by the local *Cabildo* to the King of Spain at the end of 1796, white creoles insisted that the honor of whites could not be extended to pardos, because honor and tradition depended on "proper order and subordination." Members of the City Council pleaded for

> [...] guarding the honor of their ancestors and the thoughts of their elders, saving them from the outrage of having to mix with pardos favored by a Royal Decree that promises elevation for them, that announces equality, disorder, and corruption.[79]

Regarding the issue of pardos' access to priesthood, the Caracas elite emphasized through several letters sent to the Council of Indies, that pardos lacked both the education and the honor to become priests. First they could not "receive sufficient education to take the holy orders"[80] because imperial ordinances barred them from the university and from monastery schools, secondly they could not hold "holy" or "distinguished" positions because, as Twinam mentions, how would whites show respect to ordained mulattos "who currently were not offered seats in our houses not our arms on the streets?"[81]

Juan Bautista clearly became a particularly uncomfortable character for local whites, church authorities, and colonial officials not because he wanted to become white, but because he was pleading for a more racially inclusive Church administration. His case clearly contradicted elites' allegations: although he did not have the formal education necessary for priesthood, he had prepared himself, he took informal examinations, and even the previous bishop, Don Mariano Martí, believed he could perfectly be ordained. Olivares was so confident of his instruction and preparation that he even challenged local ecclesiastical authorities to examine him and confront him in a formal theological dispute. For local whites, Olivares had transgressed too many limits and authorities needed to put him back in his place. These are probably the reasons that prompted the Captain-General to put him in prison so abruptly and with complete disregard of the formal judicial procedure on suspicions of subversion and disruption of the public order. The sudden and poorly supported accusations of sedition also proved that Caracas' church authorities were not willing to engage in a formal debate with Juan Bautista, either because this would give him a sort of honorability or attention that a pardo did not deserve, or because they were not sure they could prove him wrong.

After a close examination to Olivares' testimony and revealing letter, in October 1795 the King and the Council of Indies determined that the accusations that the Captain-General made against Olivares were dubious and have decided that Juan Bautista "should be liberated and allowed to go back to Caracas."[82] The Council's sentence do not offer detailed explanations for their decision, it is rather simple and austere. The decision, however, confirmed that the King nor the Council of Indies believed that Olivares was actually a subversive. It implied that the General-Captain directed a paranoid aggression, even violating the regular judicial procedure, against someone who was not only a fervent Catholic but also loyal vassal of the Crown. The Council's decision declared Olivares' innocence but did not say anything about his petition to be ordained. In December 1795, after six months in the prison of Cádiz, Juan Bautista was set free. He was granted permission to return to Caracas on the condition that he would behave with the utmost prudence. Madrid's decision enraged the Captain-General who complained that Olivares's return would encourage "pardos to challenge the proper order in a province covered by a pestilent poison." He concluded: "They [pardos] always try to present themselves as the equals of whites by any imaginable means."[83]

Olivares' case put in evidence the internal tensions that developed within the Spanish empire and the nature of the circumstances that disconnected the American Province with the metropolis during the Age of Revolutions. Juan Bautista's literacy and education was consistent with the Spanish reformist spirit but his desire to join the clergy embroiled him in a complex and dangerous situation. The case certainly confirms the idea that Venezuelan colonial officials and elites did everything in their power to oppose and protest against pardos,[84] especially against those who, like Juan Bautista, believed they could reach a respectable position in colonial society. Caracas' officials used Spanish "Francophobia" and the menace of revolutionary contagion to obstruct Olivares' aspirations, but their violation of judicial procedure and the poor presentation of the proofs made the Monarchy question their actions and favor the rights of Olivares, who defined himself as a loyal vassal of the King.

When Olivares returned to Caracas in 1796 he could never take the holy orders but he resumed his work as a musician, directing a religious chorus in the cathedral of the city. He had defended himself in front of the Council of Indies. During the turbulence of the Atlantic Revolutions, Olivares confirmed his political identity as a loyal subject of the Crown. His Catholic faith and loyalism made him deserve the "royal piety of Your Majesty"[85] which saved him of spending the "darkest times oppressed in an abyss of calamities."[86]

Notes

1. Pardo was the name used by Venezuelans to refer to people of mixed-race (combining whites, blacks, and Indians); this group demographically represented around 45% of the population of the Province of Caracas, Venezuela. "Manuscrito de Juan Bautista Olivares, Cárcel de Cádiz, 16 de Julio de 1796." Archivo General de Indias (hereafter AGI): Caracas, 346.
2. "Del Gobernador al Duque de Alcudia, 16 de febrero de 1795." Archivo General de la Nación-Caracas (hereafter AGN): Gobernación y Capitanía General, LIV, 126–127. See also AGI: Caracas, 346.
3. "Manuscrito de Juan Bautista Olivares, Cárcel de Cádiz, 16 de Julio de 1796." AGI: Caracas, 346.
4. "Representación del Consejo de Indias sobre el caso de Juan Bautista Olivares, 30 de Julio de 1795." AGI: Caracas 346, no. 56.

5. "Manuscrito de Juan Bautista Olivares, Cárcel de Cádiz, 16 de Julio de 1796." AGI: Caracas, 346. See also Pérez Vila, "Juan Bautista Olivares" in *Diccionario de Historia de Venezuela*, 399–400.
6. Focused primarily on studying rebellions and political movements, Venezuelan traditional historiography has characterized this period as particularly conflictive. Authors like Federico Brito Figueroa and Laureano Vallenilla Lanz argued that late colonial Venezuela is characterized by permanent tension between locals and colonial rule. By way of contrast, a more recent historiography that focuses on every-day life and economic growth describes this time as the "golden years" of colonial Venezuela. A period in which the province expanded economically and reached an unprecedented political maturity, what Michael McKinley characterized as a "harmonious and stable society." These narratives suggest that conflicts were processes of adaptation to the new administrative transformations triggered by the Bourbon reforms, and not responses to unequal access to power. This debate has been recently addressed by historian Ann Twinam who argues that this historiographical discrepancy results from the use of different sources and scopes, but that there was certainly a combination of factors in Venezuela (substantial presence of free blacks and pardos, significant social mobility, and intense repression from the elites) that created a tense atmosphere in which social groups engaged in constant confrontation and power struggle. See Brito Figueroa, *Las insurrecciones de los esclavos negros* and *El Problema de la tierra y esclavos*; Vallenilla Lanz, *Cesarimso democrático*; McKinley, *Caracas antes de la independencia*, chapter 1; Twinam, *Purchasing Whiteness*, 206.
7. I have found several cases of free blacks and slaves serving as overseers of Haciendas and plantations during the eighteenth century. One example was a captured slave named Juan Alexandro who had escaped from José Antonio Bolívar's hacienda. Bolívar "had proposed him to be the mayordomo of the hacienda," and although he did not want to do this job, he was forced into it. "Procedimientos contra esclavos fugitivos en los montes de Capaya y sus declaraciones." AGN: Diversos, LXVI, 469–569, 481v. See also the communication from the General-Captain prohibiting the use of slaves of free blacks as mayordomos, "Comunicación del Capitán General a todos los dueños de haciendas de los Valles de Río Chico, Panaquire y Tapipa, Caracas, 19 de marzo de 1801." AGN: Gobernación y Capitanía General, Vol. XCVI, 156.
8. See letters from both the Cabildo and Faculty of the Caracas' University regarding the negative consequences of allowing pardos to attend the university, the seminary, or to be part of a monastery. "Representación del Cabildo de Caracas solicitando la revocación de la Real Cédula de 10 de febrero de 1795, 28 de noviembre de 1796." AGI: Caracas, 180; "Informe de la Universidad de Caracas sobre prejuicios que pueden segurise de permitir que los hijos de Diego Mexías y otros reciban en los estudios generales de ella, 6 de octubre de 1803," in Cortés, *El régimen de las Gracias al Sacar*, vol 2, 190–192.
9. On religious brotherhoods as strategies for social mobility, see Soto, "Purchasing the Status," 72–97. For a rich discussion on ways people of African descent in late eighteenth-century Venezuela used the colonial legal system to defend their honor, see Laurent-Perrault, "Black Honor: Intellectual Marronage in Venezuela."
10. For views on the impact of mobilization of people in the Atlantic World during the Haitian Revolution. See Gaspar and Geggus, *A Turbulent Time*; Geggus, *The Impact of the Haitian Revolution in the Atlantic*; Geggus and Fiering, *The World of the Haitian Revolution*; Scott, "The Common Wind"; Gómez, *Le Syndrome de Saint-Domingue*; and Nesbitt, *Universal Emancipation*.
11. Scott, "The Common Wind"; Landers, *Atlantic*; and Scott and Hébrard, *Freedom Papers*.
12. Such as the rebellion of Coro in 1795; Brito Figueroa, *Las insurrecciones de los esclavos negros en la sociedad colonial*; Gil, Dovale, and Bello, *La insurrección de los negros de la sierra coriana*; Córdova Bello, *La independencia de Haití y su influencia en Hispanoamérica*; Grases, *La conspiración de Gual y España y el ideario de la independencia*; and Soriano, *Tides of Revolution*.
13. Sartorius, *Ever Faithful*; Echeverri, *Indian and Slave Royalists in the Age of Revolutions*.
14. Echeverri, *Indian and Slave Royalists in the Age of Revolutions*.
15. Scholars have provided ample evidence that during the Venezuelan war of independence, many elite pardos but also poor people of color and slaves sided with the Spanish Crown and not with the republican forces. However, there has been little attention to popular

royalism during colonial times. For popular royalism, see Zahler, *Ambitious Rebels*; Miller, "Status and Loyalty of Regular Army Officers in late Colonial Venezuela"; and Uslar Pietri, *Historia de la rebelión popular de 1814*.
16. Salcedo Bastardo, *Historia fundamental de Venezuela*, chapter 2; Soriano, *Venezuela 1810–1830: aspectos desatendidos*, 33–57; Pellicer, *La vivencia del honor en la provincia de Venezuela*, 40–46; and Rappaport, *The Disappearing Mestizo*.
17. On how colonial documents reproduce and legitimize social categories, Stoler, "Developing Historical Negatives," 155–188, and Stoler, *Along the Archival Grain*. See also the recent work by Rappaport, *The Disappearing Mestizo*.
18. Gutiérrez, "Sex and Family;" McCaa, "Calidad, Clase and Marriage in Colonial Mexico," 477–501; Martínez, "The Black Blood of New Spain"; O'Toole, *Bound Lives*; and Twinam, *Purchasing Whiteness*, 50–55. For an analysis of the complexity of honorability, race and status in Colonial Spanish America, see Twinam, *Public Lives, Private Secrets*.
19. Purity of blood (*Limpieza de sangre*) refers to a concept used to differentiate truly Christian communities from outsiders. This idea crystalized in late fifteenth-century Spain when a series of edicts were used by Spaniards to discriminate against those who were believed not to have a clean blood, such as Jews, Moors, heretics, and people of African ancestry. On purity of blood, see Martínez, "The Black Blood of New Spain" and Twinam, *Purchasing Whiteness*, 49–51.
20. *Blancos de orilla* were white Spaniards from the Canary Islands who, because of their origin, artisanal occupation and education, occupied lower a stratum than both Spaniards and local creole whites. Soriano, *Venezuela 1810–1830*, 33–57.
21. Fréderique Langue argues that in Venezuela the word "pardo" was regularly used for all "non-whites," understood in both anatomical and cultural terms. But historians Pellicer and Rodríguez believe that this definition merely echoes the views of local whites, who tended to lump pardos with other mixed races. Pardos, on their other part, had a different perception of their status: they believed themselves superior to other mixed-race groups because only those who had some portion of European blood could be considered pardos. Langue, "La pardocratie ou l'itineraire d'une 'classe dangereuse,'" 57–72; Pellicer, *La vivencia del honor*, 40–46; and Rodríguez, "Los pardos libres en la Colonia y la Independencia," 30–40.
22. Data from Lucena Salmoral, "La sociedad de la provincia de Caracas," 8–11; Arcila Farías, *El régimen de la encomienda en Venezuela*, 70.
23. Twinam, *Purchasing Whiteness*, 212.
24. Soriano, *Venezuela 1810–1830*, 56–57; McKinley, *Caracas antes de la independencia*.
25. See Cortés, *El régimen de las gracias al sacar en Venezuela*; Pellicer, *La vivencia del honor*, 40–90; Leal Curiel, "La querella por una alfombra."
26. "Informe que el Ayuntamiento de Caracas hace al Rey de España referente a la Real Cédula de 10 de febrero de 1795. Caracas, 28/11/1796," in Cortés, *El régimen de las gracias al sacar en Venezuela*, vol. 2, 93–94.
27. Leal, *Libros y bibliotecas en Venezuela*; Soriano, "El correr de los libros en la cotidianidad caraqueña," 229–49; and "Bibliotecas, Lectores y Saber en Caracas," 247–253.
28. Soriano, "Bibliotecas, Lectores y Saber en Caracas," 247–253.
29. "Manuscrito de Juan Bautista Olivares, escrito en la cárcel de Cádiz," AGI: Caracas, 346.
30. Ibid.
31. Ibid.
32. "Representación del Capitán General de Caracas sobre las gravísimas causas que lo han obligado a remitir a la peninsula a Juan Bautista Olivares, 16 de febrero de 1795." AGI: Estado 65, no. 24.
33. "Representación del Consejo de Indias sobre el caso de Juan Bautista Olivares, 30 de Julio de 1795." AGI: Caracas 346, no. 56.
34. See book lists in "Registros de Navíos," AGI: Contratación 1693 (1770–1773), 1694 (1774–1776), 1695 (1777–1778); and AGI: Indiferente General 2173, 2177, and 2178. On the intellectual impact of Spanish reformism in Spanish territories, see Martínez Shaw, "El despotismo ilustrado en España"; Aguilar Piñal, "La Ilustración española."

35. See Rodríguez de Campomanes, *Discurso sobre el fomento de la industria* and *Discurso sobre la educación popular de los artesanos y su fomento*; Jovellanos, *Memorias de la real sociedad económica de Madrid*; Feijoo, *Theatro crítico universal* and *Cartas eruditas, y curiosas*; and Ward, *Proyecto económico*. All of these titles are frequently found in both Caracas' post-mortem inventories and ship inventories from 1760 to 1790.
36. See reports by schoolteachers José María Bañuelos and Simón Rodríguez written in 1786 and 1792, respectively. Rodríguez, "Reflexiones sobre los defectos" in *Rodríguez, Escritos*, 5–27. See also "Expediente sobre la Aprobación de una escuela de Primeras letras para la enseñanza de los pardos de la Ciudad de Caracas, año 1805" and Leal, *Documentos para la historia de la educación en Venezuela*, 349–362.
37. Leal, *Documentos para la historia de la educación en Venezuela*; Rodríguez, "Reflexiones sobre los defectos," 5–27..
38. Pérez Vila, "Juan Bautista Olivares," 399–400; Duarte, *Los Olivares en la cultura de Venezuela*.
39. Pieces such as *Stabat Máter* a cuatro voces, *Lamentación primera del Viernes Santo* para solo de tenor, a *Salve Regina* a tres voces, and a *Salmo primero para las Vísperas de Nuestra Señora de La Merced* were written by Juan Manuel Olivares. Duarte, *Los Olivares en la cultura de Venezuela*.
40. Pérez Vila, "Juan Bautista Olivares," 399–400; Duarte, *Los Olivares en la cultura de Venezuela*.
41. Sosa, *Los Pardos*, 45–48; Duarte, *Los Olivares en la cultura de Venezuela*.
42. Duarte, *Los Olivares en la cultura de Venezuela*.
43. "Representación del Capitán General de Caracas sobre las gravísimas causas que lo han obligado a remitir a la peninsula a Juan Bautista Olivares, 16 de febrero de 1795." AGI: Estado 65, no. 24.
44. "Manuscrito de Juan Bautista Olivares, Cárcel de Cádiz, 16 de Julio de 1796." AGI: Caracas, 346.
45. Ibid.
46. "Respuesta del Fiscal sobre caso de Juan Bautista Olivares, Junio 1795." AGI: Caracas, 15.
47. Ibid., by "patricians," Olivares referred to the white elite and the groups of power in Caracas.
48. "Documento relativo a la petición que hace Juan Bautista Olivares ante el Provisor y Vicario General para que le conceda licencia para vestir los hábitos clericales, Caracas, febrero 1795." AGN: Gobernación y Capitanía General, LIV.
49. "Representación del Capitán General de Caracas sobre las gravísimas causas que lo han obligado a remitir a la peninsula a Juan Bautista Olivares, 16 de febrero de 1795." AGI: Estado 65, no. 24.
50. "Representación del Cabildo de Caracas solicitando la revocación de la Real Cédula de 10 de febrero de 1795, 28 de noviembre de 1796." AGI: Caracas, 180; "Informe de la Universidad de Caracas sobre prejuicios que pueden segurise de permitir que los hijos de Diego Mexías y otros reciban en los estudios generales de ella, 6 de octubre de 1803," in Cortés, *El régimen de las Gracias al Sacar*, vol 2, 190–192.
51. See the 26 book prohibition edicts published between 1762 and 1809, "Edictos de Prohibición de Libros." Archivo Arquideocesano de Caracas: Santo Oficio, carpetas I and II; Soriano, *Tides of Revolution*, chapters 1 and 2.
52. "Carta Pastoral del Arzobispo de Caracas, Narciso Coll y Pratt, junio 1812," in Suria, *Iglesia y Estado*, 118–140.
53. For a discussion on Censors' bureaucratic operations in Latin America, see Nesvig, *Ideology and Inquisition* and Guibovich, *Lecturas prohibidas*.
54. "Representaciones que remite el Gobernador de Caracas sobre noticias sediciosas, y sublevaciones. 22 de junio de 1799." AGI: Estado, 67, No. 67.
55. Ibid.
56. "Observaciones de un Ciudadano sobre la conspiración descubierta en Caracas el día 13 de Julio del presente año y de los medios a qué podrá ocurrir el Gobierno para asegurar en lo sucesivo a sus habitantes de iguales insultos by José Ignacio Moreno." AGI: Caracas, 434, folio 798.
57. For example, Josef Luis Aleado, a veteran of the pardo militia, submitted copies of prohibited pamphlets such as "Extract of the Manifest that the National Convention made for all the Nations," and "extracts from a French Gazette." "Informe que da cuenta de lo ocurrido con

aquella Audiencia sobre darle el voto consultivo en un expediente grave relativo á la Introducción de un papel sedicioso de la Asamblea de Paris que se aprehendio." AGI: Estado, 58, no. 5.
58. "Documento relativo a la petición que hace Juan Bautista Olivares ante el Provisor y Vicario General para que le conceda licencia para vestir los hábitos clericales, Caracas, febrero 1795." AGN: Gobernación y Capitanía General, LIV, 127.
59. "Del Gobernador al Duque de Alcudia, 16 de febrero de 1795." AGN: Gobernación y Capitanía General, LIV, 126–127; also AGI: Caracas, 346.
60. "Representación del Capitán General de Caracas sobre las gravísimas causas que lo han obligado a remitir a la peninsula a Juan Bautista Olivares, 16 de febrero de 1795." AGI: Estado 65, no. 24.
61. "Manuscrito de Juan Bautista Olivares, Cárcel de Cádiz, 16 de Julio de 1796." AGI: Caracas, 346.
62. "Disposición general de las Leyes y demas reales resoluciones sobre los artículos diecisiete y diecinueve de la Real Pragmática de diez y siete de Abril de 1774." AGI: Estado 58, no. 22.
63. Ibid. This is not the only case of violation of legal procedure in late colonial Venezuela. In the rebellion of Coro in May 1795, the violation of the law was even more critical: colonial authorities executed dozens of blacks without testimonies or trials. See Soriano, *Tides of Revolution*, chapter 4.
64. "Auto en Cádiz sobre la Acusación del Capitán General de Venezuela a Juan Bautista Olivares, 31 de Julio de 1795." AGI: Caracas, 346, and "Respuesta del Fiscal sobre caso de Juan Bautista Olivares, junio de 1795." AGI: Caracas, 15.
65. See "Declaración de Juan Bautista Olivares, acusado de promover la intranquilidad pública, haciendo circular ideas sediciosas de libertad e igualdad, trasladado a Cádiz, donde se le siguió declaración indagatoria." AGI: Caracas, 346.
66. I have studied more than 90 inventories of private libraries in the Province of Caracas from 1770 to 1810, AGN: Testamentarías, 1770–1810. See also Soriano, "Bibliotecas, Lectores y Saber en Caracas," 243–252.
67. See Nieremeberg, *Diferencias entre lo temporal y lo eterno*.
68. "Declaración de Juan Bautista Olivares."AGI: Caracas, 346.
69. Ibid.
70. "Expediente formado con las disposiciones referentes a evitar la introduccion en esta Provincia de papeles procedentes de la Francia, que contengan señales alucivas a la libertad." AGN: Diversos, LXVI, 290–293, "Expediente de la Intendencia relativo a asuntos de Francia." AGN: Diversos, LXVI, 290–295.
71. "Declaración de Juan Bautista Olivares." AGI: Caracas, 346.
72. From 1790 to 1793, this periodical published details of the King's mounting difficulties and the potential eruption of a new political order. After the execution of the Louis XVI in January 1793, and despite the abrupt interruption of communication between France and the rest of Europe, the Gaceta dedicated a significant number of pages to the French Revolution. *Gaceta de Madrid*, no. 67, 20 August 1793, 827–828. Ada Ferrer notes that the Captain General of Cuba, the Marquis of Someruelos, expressed his mortification in regards to the public circulation and spread of the *Gaceta* in different corners of the island of Cuba: "Everyone buys them, and they circulated widely amongst the blacks," he expressed revealing his concern. Ferrer, "Noticias de Haití en Cuba," 687–699.
73. "Declaración de Juan Bautista Olivares." AGI: Caracas, 346.
74. "Manuscrito de Juan Bautista Olivares, escrito en la cárcel de Cádiz." AGI: Caracas, 346.
75. "Petición del Olivares para vestir hábitos clericales, Noviembre de 1791." AGI: Caracas, 346.
76. "Manuscrito de Juan Bautista Olivares, escrito en la cárcel de Cádiz." AGI: Caracas, 346.
77. For a comprehensive study and a documentary compilation of this Royal Decree, see Cortés, *El régimen de las gracias al sacar*; Twinam, *Purchasing Whiteness*, chapter 7.
78. Thirteen out of a total of 40 petitions of the Spanish Indies were issued in Venezuela. The most comprehensive analysis of pardos in Venezuela and their quest to upgrade their social conditions is found in Twinam, *Purchasing Whiteness*, chapters 4–7.

79. See "Informe que el Ayuntamiento de Caracas hace al Rey de España referente a la Real Cédula de 10 de febrero de 1795. Caracas, 28 de noviembre de 1796," in Cortés, *El régimen de las gracias al sacar*, vol. 2, 93–94.
80. Twinam, *Purchasing Whiteness*, 215.
81. Ibid., 216.
82. "Representación de Consejo de Indias, 6 de octubre de 1795." AGI: Caracas, 15.
83. "El Gobernador al Príncipe de la Paz, Agosto, 1796." AGN: Gobernación y Capitanía General, LIX, 234.
84. Twinam, *Purchasing Whiteness*, 232–234.
85. "Representación del Consejo de Indias, Octubre de 1795." AGI: Caracas, 246, No. 4.
86. "Manuscrito de Juan Bautista Olivares, escrito en la cárcel de Cádiz." AGI: Caracas, 346.

Acknowledgements

I thank the Albert R. Lepage Endowment of the History Department, Villanova University, which supported archival research in Seville and Caracas, in 2013 and 2015. I am grateful to the editors of this special issue, Charlton Yingling and Robert Taber, for the enthusiasm on this project and thoughtful comments to this piece. I appreciate the contributions and thoughtful criticism of Manuel Barcia and the two anonymous readers.

Disclosure statement

No potential conflict of interest was reported by the author.

ORCID

Cristina Soriano http://orcid.org/0000-0002-6879-4236

References

Aguilar Piñal, Francisco. "La ilustración española, entre el reformismo y el liberalismo." In *La literatura española de la Ilustración: homenaje a Carlos III*, 39–51. Madrid: Universidad Complutense de Madrid, 1989.
Arcila Farías, Eduardo. *El régimen de la encomienda en Venezuela*. Caracas: Instituto de Investigaciones, Facultad de Economía, Universidad Central de Venezuela, 1996.
Brito Figueroa, Federico. *El problema de la tierra y esclavos en la historia de Venezuela*. Aragua: Asamblea Legislativa del Edo, 1973.
Brito Figueroa, Federico. *Las insurrecciones de los esclavos negros en la sociedad colonial venezolana*. Caracas: Cantaclaro, 1961.
Córdova Bello, Eleazar. *La independencia de Haití y su influencia en Hispanoamérica*. Caracas: Instituto Panamericano de Geografía e Historia, 1967.
Duarte, Carlos. *Los Olivares en la cultura de Venezuela*. Caracas: Separata del Boletín Histórico, Fundación John Boulton, 1967.
Echeverri, Marcela. *Indian and Slave Royalists in the Age of Revolutions. Reform, Revolution, and Royalism in the Northern Andes, 1780–1825*. Cambridge: Cambridge University Press, 2016.

Feijoó, Fray Benito Jerónimo. *Theatro crítico universal, o discursos varios, en todo género de materias, para desengaño de errores communes, dedicado al General de la Congregación de San Benito de España*. Madrid: Lorenzo Francisco Mujados, 1726–39.

Ferrer, Ada. "Noticias de Haití en Cuba." *Revista de Indias* LXIII, no. 229 (2003): 675–694.

Gaspar, David B., and David Patrick Geggus, eds. *A Turbulent Time: The French Revolution and the Greater Caribbean, 1789–1815*. Bloomington: Indiana University Press, 1997.

Geggus, David P. *The Impact of the Haitian Revolution in the Atlantic World*. Columbia: University of South Carolina Press, 2001.

Geggus, David P., and Norman Fiering, eds. *The World of the Haitian Revolution*. Bloomington: Indiana University Press, 2009.

Gil Rivas, Pedro, Luis Dovale, and Luzmila Bello. *La insurrección de los negros de la sierra coriana; 10 de mayo de 1795*. Caracas: Universidad Central de Venezuela, 1996.

Gómez, Alejandro. "Le Syndrome de Saint-Domingue. Perceptions et représentations de la Révolution haïtienne dans le Monde Atlantique, 1790–1886." PhD diss., Ecoles de Hautes Etudes en Sciences Sociales, 2010.

Grases, Pedro. *La conspiración de Gual y España y el ideario de la independencia*. Caracas: Academia Nacional de la Historia, 1997.

Guivobich, Pedro. *Lecturas prohibidas. La Censura Inquisitorial en el Perú tardío colonial*. Lima: Fondo Editorial Pontificia Universidad Católica del Perú, 2013.

Gutiérrez, Ramón. "Sex and Family: Social Change in Colonial New Mexico, 1690–1846." PhD diss., University of Wisconsin, 1980.

Jovellanos, Gaspar Melchor de. *Memorias de la real sociedad económica de Madrid*. Madrid: Antonio Sancha, 1795.

Landers, Jane. *Atlantic Creoles in the Age of Revolutions*. Cambridge, MA: Harvard University Press, 2010.

Langue, Frédérique. "La pardocratie ou l'itineraire d'une 'classe dangereuse' dans le Vénezuela des XVIIIe et XIXe siècles." *Caravelle* 67 (1997): 57–72. doi:10.3406/carav.1996.2708

Laurent-Perrault, Evelyne. "Black Honor. Intellectual Marronage in Venezuela." PhD diss., New York University, 2015.

Leal, Ildefonso. *Documentos para la historia de la educación en Venezuela*. Caracas: Academia Nacional de la Historia, 1968.

Leal, Ildefonso. *Libros y bibliotecas en Venezuela colonial (1633–1767)*. Caracas: Academia Nacional de la Historia, 1978.

Leal Curiel, Carole. "La querella por una alfombra, o la cuestión del buen orden de la república. Valencia, Venezuela, finales del siglo XVIII." *Revista Historia y Memoria* no. 9 (julio-diciembre, 2014): 163–187.

Lucena Salmoral, Manuel. "La sociedad de la provincia de Caracas a comienzos del siglo XIX." *Anuario de Estudios Americanos* XXXVII (1980): 157–189.

Martínez, María Elena. "The Black Blood of New Spain: Limpieza de Sangre, Racial Violence, and Gendered Power in Early Colonial Mexico." *William and Mary Quarterly*, 3rd series, 61, no. 3 (2004): 479–520.

Martínez Shaw, Carlos. "El despotismo ilustrado en España y en las Indias." In *El imperio sublevado: monarquía y naciones en España e Hispanoamérica*, edited by Víctor Mínguez and Manuel Chust, 123–178. Madrid: Consejo Superior de Investigaciones Científicas, 2004.

McCaa, Robert. "Calidad, Clase and Marriage in Colonial Mexico: The Case of Parral, 1788–1790." *Hispanic American Historical Review* 64, no. 3 (1984): 477–501. doi:10.2307/2514936

McKinley, Peter M. *Caracas antes de la independencia*. Caracas: Monteávila, 1993.

Miller, Gary. "Status and Royalty of Regular Army Officers in Late Colonial Venezuela." *The Hispanic American Historical Review* 66, no. 4 (1986): 667–696.

Nesbitt, Nick. *Universal Emancipation. The Haitian Revolution and the Radical Enlightenment*. Charlottesville: University of Virginia Press, 2008.

Nesvig, Martin A. *Ideology and Inquisition: The World of the Censors in Early Mexico*. New Haven, CT: Yale University Press, 2009.

Nieremeberg, Juan Eusebio. *Diferencias entre lo temporal y lo eterno, crisol de desengaños en la memoria de la eternidad, postrimerías humanas y misterios divinos*. Madrid: Manuel Martin, 1762.

O'Toole, Rachel. *Bound Lives, Africans, Indians, and the Making of Race in Colonial Perú*. Pittsburgh, PA: University of Pittsburgh Press, 2012.

Pellicer, Luis. *La vivencia del honor en la provincia de Venezuela, 1774–1809, estudios de casos*. Caracas: Fundación Polar, 1996.

Pérez Vila, Manuel. "Juan Bautista Olivares." In *Diccionario de Historia de Venezuela*, Vol. 3, 399–400. Caracas: Fundación Polar, 2010.

Rappaport, Joanne. *The Disappearing Mestizo, Configuring Difference in the Colonial New Kingdom of Granada*. Durham, NC: Duke University Press, 2014.

Rodríguez, Manuel Alfredo. "Los pardos libres en la Colonia y la Independencia." Discurso de Incorporación como Individuo número de la Academia Nacional de la Historia, 23 de Julio de 1992. In: *Discursos de Incorporación 1992–1998*, vol. VIII. Caracas: ANH, 2002.

Rodríguez, Simón. "Reflexiones sobre los defectos que vician la escuela de primeras letras de Caracas y medio de lograr su reforma por un nuevo establecimiento 19 de mayo de 1794." In *Simón Rodríguez, Escritos*, edited by Pedro Grases, 5–27. Caracas: Imprenta Nacional, 1954.

Rodríguez de Campomanes, Pedro. *Discurso sobre el fomento de la industria*. Madrid: Antonio Sancha, 1774.

Rodríguez de Campomanes, Pedro. *Discurso sobre la educación popular de los artesanos y su fomento*. Madrid: Antonio Sancha, 1775.

Rodulfo Cortés, Santos. *El régimen de las gracias al sacar en Venezuela durante el período Hispánico*, 2 vols. Caracas: Academia Nacional de la Historia, 1978.

Salcedo Bastardo, Jose. *Historia fundamental de Venezuela*. Caracas: Fundación Gran Mariscal de Ayacucho, 1977.

Sartorious, David. *Ever Faithful. Race, Loyalty, and the Ends of Empire in Spanish Cuba*. Durham, NC: Duke University Press, 2013.

Scott, Julius, III. "The Common Wind: Currents of Afro-American Communication in the Era of the Haitian Revolution." Ph.D. diss., Duke University, 1986.

Scott, Rebecca J., and Jean M. Hébrard. *Freedom Papers, an Atlantic Odyssey in the Age of Emancipation*. Cambridge, MA: Harvard University Press, 2012.

Soriano, Cristina. "Bibliotecas, lectores y saber en Caracas durante el siglo XVIII." In *El libro en circulación en la América Colonial: producción, circuitos de distribución y conformación de bibliotecas en los siglos XVI-XVIII*, edited by Idalia García and Pedro Rueda, 239–258. México: Edit. Quivira, 2014.

Soriano, Cristina. "El correr de los libros en la cotidianidad caraqueña. Mercado y redes de circulación de libros en Caracas durante el siglo XVIII." In *Mezclado y sospechoso: movilidad e identidades, España y América (siglos XVI-XVIII)*, edited by Gregoire Salinero, 229–249. Madrid: Casa de Velázquez, 2005.

Soriano, Cristina. *Tides of Revolution. Information and Politics in Late Colonial Venezuela*. Albuequerque: University of New Mexico Press, forthcoming.

Soriano, Graciela. *Venezuela 1810–1830: aspectos desatendidos de dos décadas*. Caracas: Lagoven, 1988.

Sosa Cárdenas, Diana. *Los Pardos, Caracas en las postrimerías de la Colonia*. Caracas: Universidad Católica Andrés Bello, 2010.

Soto, Andreína. "Purchasing the Status: Religious Confraternities in Late-Colonial Venezuela." *Concept, an Interdisciplinary Journal for Graduate Students* 39 (April 2016): 72–97.

Stoler, Ann Laura. *Along the Archival Grain. Epistemic Anxieties and Colonial Common Sense*. Princeton, NJ: Princeton University Press, 2009.

Stoler, Ann Laura. "Developing Historical Negatives: Race and the (Modernist) Visions of a Colonial State." In *From the Margins: Historical Anthropology and Its Futures*, edited by Brian Keith Axel, 156–188. Durham, NC: Duke University Press, 2002.

Suria, Jaime. *Iglesia y Estado*. Caracas: Ediciones del Cuatricentenario de Caracas, Editorial Sucre, 1967.

Twinam, Ann. *Public Lives, Private Secrets: Gender, Honor, Sexuality and Illegitimacy in Colonial Spanish America*. Stanford, CA: Stanford University Press, 1999.

Twinam, Ann. *Purchasing Whiteness. Pardos, Mulattos, and the Quest for Social Mobility in the Spanish Indies*. Stanford, CA: Stanford University Press, 2015.

Uslar Pietri, Juan. *Historia de la Rebelión Popular de 1814*. Caracas: Monteávila Edit., 2014.

Vallenilla Lanz, Laureano. *Cesarismo democrático: Estudios sobre las bases sociológicas de la Constitutición efectiva de Venezuela*. Caracas: Tipografía Garrido, 1961.

Ward, Bernardo. *Proyecto económico en que se proponen varias providencias dirigidas a promover los intereses de España*. Madrid: Joaquín Ibarra, 1779.

Zahler, Reuben. *Ambitious Rebels. Remaking Honor, Law, and Liberalism in Venezuela, 1780–1850*. Tucson: The University of Arizona Press, 2013.

Crafting freedom: Race and social mobility among free artisans of color in Cartagena and Charleston

John Garrison Marks

ABSTRACT
Throughout the urban Atlantic World, skilled work proved central to the ability of free people of color to achieve economic and social mobility during the late eighteenth and early nineteenth centuries. Through their labor in a wide variety of artisan occupations, free people of color gained the opportunity to publicly demonstrate their skills, industriousness, and public worth. As such, free people of color used their role as artisans to gain distinct economic advantages, to cultivate relationships with prominent whites and fellow artisans of color, and to obtain a measure of social distinction. Through their labor, artisans of African descent improved their reputations and increased their bargaining power with white authorities, gaining the opportunity to claim distinctions and privileges that improved their daily lives – ones often closed to other African-descended people. Yet this effort to achieve social and economic advancement often hindered a broader racial identification, as artisans of color attempted to draw class, color, and status distinctions between themselves and the city's popular classes of African descent. While free artisans of color sometimes succeeded in improving their place within the social order of Atlantic World societies, that success often required them to accommodate the broader logic of American racial hierarchies.

In late eighteenth-century Cartagena, a *pardo* artisan named Pedro Romero worked as a blacksmith. He maintained a workshop in the prominent, mixed-race neighborhood of Santa Catalina within the walls of the colonial Caribbean city, and he later operated a foundry just outside them. Romero's status as an artisan allowed him to claim significant social privileges and rights, ones not typically open to people of African descent in colonial Spanish America. Some 1500 miles to the north across the Caribbean Sea, in the city of Charleston, South Carolina, a free man of color named Jehu Jones derived many similar advantages – if from different sources – from his work as a tailor and hotelier. Through his work, Jones not only gained the opportunity to purchase his freedom, he cultivated social links with a number of prominent whites and established a reputation for himself as one of the city's most respectable free men of color. Through their work, both Romero and Jones gained a measure of social prestige, and while they may have been uncommonly successful, their reliance on skilled labor to support claims to various rights and privileges represents a common thread in the lived experience of race and freedom that linked African-descended people throughout the urban Atlantic World.

Throughout the urban Atlantic, people of African descent found work as artisans. As barbers and carpenters, stonemasons and tailors, free and enslaved people of color labored in skilled trades in the urban centers of the Americas and Caribbean, and their status as artisans often became central to their social lives and identities. Skilled labor allowed a segment of the free colored population to distinguish themselves from the black popular classes, including not only the enslaved people laboring on the plantations and *haciendas* in the hinterlands of urban centers, but also free and enslaved people of color engaging in unskilled or marginally skilled work in cities themselves. By publicly demonstrating their skills, industriousness, and public worth, free people of color gained distinct economic advantages, cultivated relationships with prominent whites and fellow artisans of color, and gained a measure of social distinction. Through their labor, artisans of African descent improved their reputations and increased their bargaining power with white authorities, gaining the opportunity to claim distinctions that improved their daily lives. While the nature of these distinctions could vary widely, examining the experiences of artisans of color in the urban Atlantic begins to reveal the centrality of skilled work to the efforts of African-descended people to achieve social mobility in the Atlantic World.[1]

This article focuses on the social and cultural worlds of free artisans of color in two urban Atlantic communities: Cartagena, along the Caribbean coast of the Kingdom of New Granada (modern day Colombia), and Charleston, located along the southern Atlantic coast in the South Carolina Lowcountry. In many respects these cities were very different places during the eighteenth and nineteenth centuries, particularly in regard to the role of slavery in the local economy and in the lives and interests of white authorities. Cartagena, which remained under colonial rule until 1811, was a society with slaves and mainly served as a commercial entrepôt, while Charleston was a slave society and one of the US South's primary ports for importing enslaved people and exporting the agricultural staples they produced. Thus, while during the eighteenth and nineteenth centuries enslaved people constituted the vast majority of the population of Charleston District along with a small community of free people of color, in Cartagena the opposite was true: free people of color comprised the largest demographic group in the city, along with a relatively small (and declining) enslaved population. These differences in the role of slavery directly affected the challenges and opportunities free people of color faced during the late eighteenth and early nineteenth centuries. Yet these cities held a great deal in common as well, particularly their status as two of the most important ports for their respective continents, providing crucial links to the broader Caribbean and Atlantic Worlds. While white Charlestonians were far more directly involved in all aspects of slavery than their counterparts in Cartagena, white authorities in both cities governed as a minority and struggled to maintain control – physical, ideological, and political – over majorities of African descent. And in both Cartagena and Charleston, people of African descent, particularly free people of color, played an important role in the local labor force, providing goods and services crucial to the well-being of communities, nations, and empires.

Thus, in both cities – indeed, throughout the urban Atlantic World – free people of color recognized the advantages they could gain through skilled work, and they used their work as artisans to gain distinctions and privileges that could improve their lives and those of their families. Through their work, free artisans of African descent throughout the urban Atlantic World gained the opportunity to cultivate client and patronage networks among the city's elite, to maintain social ties to other artisans matching their racial, economic, and social profiles, and ultimately to bend Spanish and Anglo institutions and cultural values to their specific needs. Artisans of African descent in the Atlantic World used the elevated social status and economic advantages of skilled work to claim privileges and rights that improved their individual circumstances, even while the sources of such advantages cold vary widely between Latin America and the USA. While free artisans of African descent in Cartagena used their position as artisans to demand rights and privileges from the Spanish crown, for example, their counterparts in Charleston more often used their status as artisans to demonstrate shared cultural values with whites and at times a shared commitment to the racial order through their ownership of enslaved people. While social prestige and stability in Charleston hinged on the cultivation of private social links and reputations, artisans in Cartagena relied on public, corporately ordered institutions like the voluntary militia to support their claims to social privileges. Yet despite these differences, as artisans of African descent engaged white authorities throughout the Atlantic World and worked to distinguish themselves from the black popular classes, free artisans of color challenged their place within Atlantic social hierarchies, even as they accommodated themselves to broader systems of white authority.

This article contributes to the growing body of literature examining the role of labor in the lives of African-descended people in the Atlantic World. By employing an explicitly comparative approach, this article re-frames the way we consider the lived experience of racial difference in the various cultural contexts of the Americas, with a particular focus on the place of labor. Historians have devoted significant attention in recent years to examining the daily lives of African-descended people, exploring in particular how labor informed black identities, social lives, and political participation. Scholars like Zephyr Frank, Lyman Johnson, Matthew Restall, Michele Reid-Vazquez, Sergio Paulo Solano, Ann Twinam, Ben Vinson III, and a host of others have explored how labor impacted the efforts of Afro-Latin American populations to improve their individual circumstances. In the US context, historians like Philip D. Morgan and T. Stephen Whitman have observed the early racialization of urban work, while others have more recently examined the working worlds of African Americans in US urban centers.[2] By examining the daily lives and lived experiences of free artisans of color, this article begins to offer new ways of considering how the racial dynamics of Atlantic World societies affected the daily lives, challenges, and opportunities of African-descended people. By investigating how skilled work offered a path to social mobility to people of African descent in both Latin America and the USA, this article reconsiders the relationship between race and labor in the urban Atlantic World. This article also focuses on divisions within populations of African descent. While existing scholarship has explored the ways people of African descent used skilled work to improve their individual circumstances, this article examines more fully the efforts of artisans of color to gain social distance from other African-descended people. By examining how artisans of African descent distanced themselves from the black popular classes in two American communities, this article sheds light on how racial hierarchies and categories of racial difference could affect populations of African descent in profoundly different ways both within and across American communities, and begins to reveal the ways some free people of color accommodated and accepted the racial order of Atlantic World societies.

Cartagena

In Cartagena, free people of color dominated artisan trades during the eighteenth and nineteenth century. This is in part attributable to the general disdain for manual labor exhibited by Spaniards and white *criollos*, as whites' unwillingness to engage in skilled manual trades created significant opportunities for people of African descent. As tailors, carpenters, barbers, silversmiths, and in a host of other skilled occupations, free people of color – mostly *pardos* and mulattoes but a small number of *negros* as well – gained a degree of both economic and social independence.[3] This degree of self-sufficiency allowed artisans to distinguish themselves from free and enslaved people of African descent working in more subordinate positions throughout the city – particularly those engaged in unskilled labor or domestic service. Likewise, the personal nature of work like tailoring and barbering provided free artisans of color the opportunities to interact with wealthy whites and Spaniards in the city and perhaps to begin crafting reputations for themselves as respectable members of their local community. Likewise, some free artisans of color gained further prestige by maintaining independent workshops in prominent neighborhoods inside the walled city, a distinction not just from the black and colored popular classes but from less wealthy African-descended artisans as well. Finally, and perhaps most importantly, skilled work provided many male artisans of color the opportunity to join the voluntary *pardo* militia, further distinguishing them from the popular classes of African descent in the city and providing them additional leverage to gain privileges capable of improving their social standing and individual circumstances.

The rejection of manual labor by whites in Cartagena allowed people of African descent to carve out an important niche for their labor during the late eighteenth and early nineteenth century. While free people of color constituted the largest population group in the city, they constituted an even greater majority of the city's artisans, most of whom were classified as *pardos*.[4] Of the 391 free people of color in Cartagena for whom occupational information was recorded in the 1777 census, the last major census of the colonial period, fully 241 worked as artisans of some kind, with tailors, shoemakers, carpenters, and masons constituting the most popular skilled occupations.[5] The relatively small number of individuals for whom census administrators recorded occupational data – just over 1100 for the entire city – suggests they only recorded such information for individuals of higher economic status; that free people of color were so frequently recorded as artisans thus suggests a strong link between skilled labor and economic opportunity in Cartagena.

The census of artisans in Cartagena conducted in 1780 further confirms the extent to which free people of color dominated skilled trades in the city. Of the 230 artisans enumerated in the neighborhood of Santo Toribio in 1780, only 22 (9.5%) were whites (listed explicitly as *blancos*, rather than simply left blank as in other census returns), along with 182 *pardos* (79.1%), 24 *negros* (10.4%), and two *zambos* (less than 1%).[6] Whites also did not constitute a significant portion of any individual trade in the neighborhood, with only barber and scribe providing work to more than three *blancos*.[7] Tailor, shoemaker, carpenter, barber, and stonemason represented the five most popular trades in Santo Toribio, accounting for 136 (59.1%) of the 230 artisans recorded there. Of those 136 artisans, 109 (80.1%) were classified as *pardos*, 19 (13.9%) as *negros*, and just 8 (5.9%) as *blancos*, with whites having no representation at all among carpenters and shoemakers (see Table 1). Though they constituted just over 50% of the total population of the city, free people of color comprised *nearly 90*% of all the artisans inside the walled city, and 94% of the artisans in the city's five most popular artisan occupations. And though causation may be impossible to determine (and it seems likely that it may have in fact been circular) people of mixed racial ancestry or lighter complexion were far more likely than Africans and *negros* to be engaged in skilled work, and thus more likely to have achieved an elevated economic status.

Nearly identical patterns emerge in the city's other neighborhoods, particularly in Santa Catalina and Las Mercedes, also inside the walled city.[8] Unfortunately, the 1780 artisan census only extended to neighborhoods inside the walled city and did not include the lower class, largely *negro* and *pardo* neighborhood of Getsemaní. Using the 1777 general census, however, it is clear that while a number of artisans lived in that neighborhood as well (reflecting the general trend of African-descended people dominating artisan trades), many of Getsemaní's artisans were engaged in occupations like carpentry and shoemaking, jobs that elsewhere in the city tended to include more *negros* and fewer *pardos*.[9] Though they represented the largest demographic group in the city, free people of color were still drastically over-represented in artisan occupations relative to their proportion of the population. The rejection of even skilled manual labor by Cartagena's whites opened up a significant sphere of economic opportunity for enterprising free people of color.[10]

Much of that opportunity stemmed from the ability of artisans of color in Cartagena to own residences and maintain independence workshops within the walled city, increasing their social and economic ties to prominent whites. The situation of blacksmith Pedro Romero reveals the kinds of opportunities available to artisans of African descent in the city. In 1780, the 24-year-old Romero worked as a blacksmith in the neighborhood of Santa Catalina, operating out of an *asesoría*, an independent workshop attached to a larger residence, likely with its own entrance and exit. Romero's neighbors, in addition to many military, religious, and other royal officials, included at least four white blacksmiths and armorers who operated on his block, men with whom Romero likely had significant contact, if not collaboration.[11] Furthermore, because of the intensive nature of work like blacksmithing, it seems likely as well that Romero employed apprentices, perhaps of African descent, and may have employed or owned enslaved people as well. Operating a successful independent business in a prominent neighborhood like Santa

Table 1. Racial classification of five most popular artisan occupations in Santo Toribio, Cartagena (1780). "Relación que manifiesta los Artesanos que existen en el Barrio de Santo Thorivio el presente año de 1780." AGN: CO/MI, vol. 31. Compiled by the author.

Occupation	Blanco	Negro	Pardo	Total
Barber	5 (26%)	0 (0%)	14 (74%)	19
Carpenter	0 (0%)	9 (29%)	22 (71%)	31
Shoemaker	0 (0%)	9 (27%)	24 (73%)	33
Stonemason	1 (7%)	1 (7%)	12 (98%)	14
Tailor	2 (5%)	0 (0%)	37 (95%)	39
Total	*8 (6%)*	*19 (14%)*	*109 (80%)*	*136*

Catalina afforded him access to the institutional life of the city and likely allowed him to forge social ties with prominent whites. For artisans of African descent, living inside the walled city and maintaining workshops there would have been an important distinction, facilitating interaction with prominent neighbors and engagement with the social and cultural life of the city's elites. The ability to maintain independent residences or workshops in prominent neighborhoods offered free artisans of color in Cartagena the ability to accentuate their class status and social distinction through physical separation. Living in racially mixed neighborhoods that were separated from the black lower classes of Getsemaní, free artisans of color gained geographic proximity to wealthy whites and colonial officials as well as greater access to both religious and civil institutions in the city. Free artisans of color used the economic advantages of skilled labor to achieve a physical distance between themselves and the black lower classes that mirrored the social distance they attempted to achieve.

Many free people of color inside the walled city occupied the lower floors of large residences, while prominent Spaniard and creole-born whites occupied the upper floors. This kind of vertical segregation meant they were largely excluded from the social world of elites, resigned to occupying dank basement apartments seemingly a world away from the prominent residents living above them.[12] Others, however, likely derived some distinction or tangible benefits from the maintenance of well-located workshops, particularly for artisans of color engaged in trades that served wealthy clientele. This was perhaps particularly true for artisans of color who lived within the walled city not in the "*casa en lo bajo*" of a prominent house, but, like Pedro Romero, plied trades that demanded the maintenance of independent "*asesorias*." Pardo brothers Manuel Blanquezel, José Concepción Blanquezel, and Mateo Blanquezel, all tailors, kept one such workshop, attached to a large house directly on the Plaza de Santo Toribio. The 1777 census reveals that the head of this household was *Don* Juan Marzan, who lived there with his wife *Doña* Feliciana Hurtado de Mendoza and their seven children, each of whom received the same honorific title. In addition to this family, 8 other households comprised of a total of 33 people occupied this house. Included within that 33 are Joseph and Pedro de Vega, a silversmith and tailor, sons of *quarterón* Joseph Antonio; Mauricio Yturre, a pardo shoemaker and son of a retired militia sergeant; and Joseph Montaño and Pasqual Hurtado, both tailors. Similarly, 18-year-old pardo shoemaker and *miliciano* Francisco Hurtado lived and worked in an *asesoria* attached to the house of white military officer *Don* Nicolas Garcia, who lived in Casa Alta N. 15 with his wife and six children (all of whom received honorific titles), along with four enslaved women who likely served the family as domestics. *Negro* carpenter Manuel Ynitola maintained an *asesoria* near or attached to the house of Spanish merchant *Don* Bartholome Javier Marquecho, who lived there with his wife, three children, and five enslaved people.[13]

While some artisans of African descent in Cartagena would have remained in first floor and basement residences and workshops of little distinction, the many who maintained more independent houses and workshops would have gained prestige and economic benefit from their prominent location. The ability of artisans of color to count wealthy whites among their clientele would have allowed them to not only cultivate social ties with prominent community members, but to craft reputations for themselves as respectable. Even as whites may have wanted to keep artisans of African descent close – both for convenience and social control – the proximity of free artisans of color to white elites and fellow artisans, coupled with the service-oriented nature of their trades likely allowed them to craft reputations for themselves as industrious and respectable members of their communities, neighborhoods, and cities.[14] In 1810, for example, prominent merchant and public official José Ignacio de Pombo described Pedro Romero by stating,

> We have in the master Pedro Romero and his son Stephen two intelligent artists in this profession [blacksmithing], or better yet, two intelligent men that the force of their genius […] has elevated to a degree of perfection and delicacy that is truly admirable.[15]

Through his work as a blacksmith, Romero distinguished himself in Cartagena. Romero and his family capitalized on their social prominence, as several of Romero's daughters married well-to-do whites. Romero also sent a petition to the Spanish crown requesting permission for his son to pursue university studies, a privilege normally exclusive to whites, "excusing his condition of mulatto."[16] Further, as Sergio Paulo Solano has demonstrated, Romero gained additional distinction within the class of artisans of color through his ability to win military contracts with the Spanish crown – perhaps facilitated by his close contact with prominent Spanish officials.[17] For Romero, his success as a skilled worker not only allowed him to gain a measure of social distinction in the city, but to use his reputation for industry and respectability among Cartagena's prominent whites to gain very tangible benefits.

Finally, as a successful artisan, Romero was also able to join the city's voluntary *pardo* militia – one of the most prominent benefits of skilled work for artisans of African descent. Nearly all militiamen of African descent were artisans during the late colonial era, and African-descended militiamen made up a huge portion of the city's voluntary militia. Romero, through both his individual social connections and institutional affiliations – both of which were open to him primarily through his work as an artisan – improved his individual circumstances and gained social distinction that he successfully parlayed into very real benefits. Of the 230 artisans recorded in Santo Toribio in 1780, just 56 did not serve in the military in some capacity, 17 of whom received exemptions. Of the remaining 31 non-military artisans, 13 (33%) were whites. Just five white artisans (2%) served in the militia or military in some capacity. Among artisans of African descent, meanwhile, 200 were militiamen or *matriculados*, fully 87% of artisans. That whites constituted such a large portion of artisans who did not present for military service, and that nearly all artisans of African descent did, speaks to the social prestige and tangible benefits militia service could offer. For *pardo* and *negro* artisans, their status as militiamen improved their social standing within the local community and it increased their bargaining power with the Spanish crown.[18]

This strong overlap between artisan work and militia service among free people of color reveals as well the way the boundaries of respectability were strongly gendered in late colonial Cartagena, as the artisan censuses rarely listed occupational information for women, some of whom were surely engaged in artisan or craft work as seamstresses, dressmakers, and petty merchants, as well as in culinary occupations and a wide variety of other work. It seems likely that this disregard for the skilled work of free women of color stems directly from the relationship between artisan work and military service – the crown was likely concerned only with those whose labor could contribute to the city's defense. This seeming disregard for women's work among Cartagena's colonial administrators suggests that while African-descended people could use their labor to claim rights and privileges capable of boosting their social prestige, women's exclusion from important occupational and institutional realms made this eminently more possible for free men of color than for women.

One of the most pressing concerns of militiamen of African descent was the acquisition of the *fuero militar* a significant social distinction in colonial Spanish America. The *fuero militar* placed those serving in the military under the jurisdiction of special military tribunals, rather than of the civilian court system, and limited the power of civilian authorities in a number of ways. Because of the security needs of such a crucial port city, free militiamen of color in Cartagena could likely expect to receive more equitable treatment from a military tribunal than from civilian courts. The privilege and distinction of the *fuero militar* was one free people of color throughout Spanish America fought hard to obtain and keep. While artisans of African descent broadly crafted reputations for respectability among their clients and neighbors, the voluntary militia afforded them the opportunity to use their labor to demand and claim more concrete benefits from the Spanish crown. Because they played such crucial roles in the city's defense, artisans of color in Cartagena demanded and won the privilege of the fuero not only for themselves but for their families as well. The success of militiamen of African descent in securing the military fuero likely proved significant in the desire of artisans to volunteer for militia service.[19]

In addition to the military fuero, militiamen of African descent also used military service to gain visual distinction from the black popular classes, claiming for themselves and their families the right to wear uniforms and symbols afforded to white. In 1794, when the colonial government in Madrid suspended the right of pardo officers to wear the same insignia as white veteran officers, they provided an exception for pardo officers in Cartagena, an exemption that speaks to the outsize importance of militiamen of African descent there and the potential value of militia service for free people of color.[20] Throughout Caribbean New Granada, militiamen of African descent demanded the ability to wear hats similar to those of white militia members and to mourn the death of King Carlos III using similar insignia. They demanded as well that their wives be granted the right to wear certain garments, like velvet skirts with precious stones, items they believed were befitting the social station of militia members.[21] In Cartagena and throughout Caribbean New Granada, artisans of African descent demanded the right to the distinction of military uniforms, a visual signifier that would have immediately marked them as reputable and respectable individuals.

Militia service enhanced the bargaining power of artisans of African descent in Cartagena, allowing them to claim from the crown a variety of rights and privileges not typically afforded to people of African descent. Access to special military tribunals and the visual distinction of military uniform lent social prestige to artisans of African descent, distinguishing them from less wealthy artisans as well as from the city's free and enslaved black popular classes. The over-representation of free people of color among both the artisan class and the ranks of militiamen reveals how skilled work could directly aid the entry of African-descended people into a respectable, corporately ordered body, and thus reveals how one's status as an artisan provided access to privileges that free artisans of color increasingly viewed as rights.

Artisan labor allowed some free people of color to cultivate social contacts and client-patron relationships with prominent whites, provided the opportunity to maintain independent workshops in prominent neighborhoods, and for some aided their entry into the city's voluntary militia. Thus, not only did artisan work facilitate the development of respectable reputations among free people of color, the central importance of both their labor and their militia service increased their bargaining power with crown, allowing them to claim a variety of rights and privileges. These rights, however, demanded free artisans of color to defend, quite literally, white interests as their efforts to distance themselves from the black popular classes reinforced both white authority and established racial hierarchies.

Charleston

Remarkably similar racial-occupational patterns emerged in the US southern port city of Charleston, South Carolina. Although free people of color comprised a far smaller proportion of the population in Charleston than they did in Cartagena – never rising above about 5% of the total population of Charleston District, compared to an enslaved population that remained around 70% for most of the eighteenth and nineteenth centuries – free people of color there found opportunities in many of the same occupations.[22] These parallels in racial-occupational patterns reveal the way skilled labor represented a link in the experience of freedom for African-descended people throughout the Atlantic World and across national, imperial, and cultural boundaries. Like in Cartagena, free people of color in Charleston used their engagement with skilled work to achieve social mobility, to cultivate reputations as respectable, and to claim a variety of privileges not typically open to people of African descent in the US South. Yet the challenges and opportunities open to artisans of color differed in important ways as well. While *pardo* and *negro* artisans in Cartagena used their affiliation with the voluntary militia to support claims to rights and privileges, such public institutions were never open to free people of color in Charleston. Rather, free people of color in Charleston – especially members of the city's mixed-race artisan class – founded private organizations and attempted to demonstrate on a more personal level a commitment to shared values with whites, including not just a reputation for industriousness and sobriety but sometimes a commitment to slave ownership as well. Free artisans of color challenged their place within the racial order, attempting to gain exceptions to attitudes and policies that proscribed the opportunities available to them. Yet, by distinguishing themselves from enslaved people and the free black poor, artisans of color also reinforced, and at times strengthened, existing racial hierarchies.

As a growing port city, enslaved and free blacks plied a wide variety of skilled trades to help drive the city's growth and provided services to the city's permanent and transient populations. As bricklayers and barbers, carpenters and cooks, tailors and tradesmen of a variety of other kinds, people of African descent, particularly free people of color, found ample opportunity for skilled, artisan labor throughout the eighteenth and nineteenth centuries, from the colonial era through the Civil War.[23] While data on the extent to which free blacks engaged any particular occupation is more difficult to discern for Charleston than for Cartagena – much of the data for Charleston has necessarily been drawn from a later era than for Cartagena – an analysis of censuses, city directories, and legislative petitions reveals not only the centrality of skilled labor to the free black experience in Charleston, but also that free artisans of color engaged many of the same occupations as in Cartagena.[24] Unlike in Cartagena, however, free artisans of color in Charleston had to compete with whites and with enslaved people in many skilled trades.

The 1831 city directory of Charleston recorded just a small number of the city's most prominent free people of color, but nearly all of these individuals found employment in artisan occupations of some kind.[25] Barred by both custom and law from higher professional occupations, artisan professions were often the highest positions to which people of African descent could aspire. For free men of color recorded in the 1831 directory, barber (13), tailor (12), and carpenter (9) were by far the most popular occupations, revealing significant overlap with Cartagena. The census of the City of Charleston conducted in 1848 likewise reveals barber, carpenter, shoemaker, and tailor were the four most common artisan occupations for free people of color. Of all the free people of color listed with occupations in the 1848 census, fully 35% are employed in just these four occupations.[26] Like in Cartagena, the most popular trades among free black Charlestonians included occupations that would have allowed free people of color to develop and cultivate a client base and social contacts among prominent whites, as well as to craft reputations for themselves as skilled, hard-working members of the Charleston community.

Further, the 1848 city census reveals not just that free people of color engaged frequently in artisan work, but the extent to which they are over-represented in these occupations relative to their proportion of the population. Although in 1848 free people of color made up just 5.6% of the total population of the city of Charleston, they comprised 77.8% of its barbers, 10.6% of its carpenters, 48.2% of its shoemakers, and 30.3% of its tailors (see Table 2).[27]

Their extreme over-representation relative to their proportion of the population illustrates the desirability of these occupations for free Charlestonians of color, the success of free people of color entering into these trades, and the centrality of skilled work to the lives of free people of color in Charleston.[28]

As the table above illustrates, free artisans of color in Charleston competed in these occupations with both enslaved people and whites in a way that free colored artisans in Cartagena did not, in large part because free people of color constituted such a small portion of Charleston's population. For example, while 48 free people of color worked as tailors, making it the most popular occupation among that class, 74 whites and 36 enslaved people worked as tailors as well. Likewise, while many free people of color worked as carpenters (the second most popular occupation), they were far outnumbered in that profession by both whites (117) and slaves (110). In barbering, by contrast, free people of color seem to have had the arena to themselves.[29] While the servile nature of barbering turned whites away from the trade, it likewise made it an area of significant opportunity for free people of color – a trend applicable to a much larger portion of artisan occupations in Cartagena.

Table 2. Most popular artisan occupations for free men of color in Charleston, with racial classifications (1848). *Census of the City of Charleston, South Carolina, for the year 1848, exhibiting the condition and prospects of the city*. Charleston, SC: J. B. Nixon, 1849. Compiled by the Author.

Occupation	Whites	Free Blacks	Slaves	Total
Barber	0 (0%)	14 (77.8%)	4 (22.2%)	18
Carpenter	117 (46.1%)	27 (10.6%)	110 (43.3%)	254
Shoemaker	13 (44.8%)	14 (48.2%)	2 (6.8%)	29
Tailor	68 (46.6%)	42 (28.8%)	36 (24.7%)	146
Totals	198 (44.3%)	97 (21.7%)	152 (34.0%)	447 (100%)

Such significant competition existed between black and white artisans in Charleston that white workers regularly complained to South Carolina's legislature, requesting restrictions on the activities of black workers. In 1783, a group of over 30 white bricklayers and carpenters in Charleston complained about the "jobbing Negro Tradesmen," who "deprived [whites] of the means of gaining a livelihood by their industry."[30] In the early 1820s, over 100 "Sundry Mechanics of Charleston" complained that "the competition of negro and colored workmen, whether bond or free," undercut the value of their work, made their occupations less than prosperous, and disinclined a younger generation towards artisan trades. They bemoaned the fact that: "almost all the trades, but especially those of carpenters, bricklayers, plasterers, wheelwrights, house painters, shoemakers, &c., are beginning to be engrossed by black & colored workers."[31] As late as 1858 white tradesmen in Charleston continued to petition the legislature complaining of the "baneful evil" of black artisan work. They urged the legislature to "take into consideration the [...] free negroes," and requested "that a tax be imposed upon them [...] that shall at least place us in such a position that we may be able to compete with them, if they are to be on an equality with us."[32]

In an entirely different spirit, a group of 129 white Charlestonians petitioned South Carolina's legislature two years later in 1860, testifying to the ubiquity and necessity of free black artisan labor. As free blacks faced increasing pressure to remove from South Carolina, these prominent whites testified that many free blacks were "good citizens" who exhibit "patterns of industry, sobriety, and irreproachable conduct." More importantly, they noted, "their labour is indispensable to us in this neighborhood." According to the petitioners, the people of Charleston could not "build or repair a house [...] without the aid of the coloured carpenter or bricklayer."[33]

These petitions help illustrate the centrality of artisan work to free people of color in late eighteenth- and nineteenth-century Charleston. Free people of color constituted a sizeable portion of the individuals plying many of the skilled trades in the city, to the extent that white workers worried about their ability to compete. Yet, by proving themselves "indispensable" to their "neighborhood," free artisans of color crafted reputations as industrious and respectable members of their local community.

The case of Free Charlestonian of color Jehu Jones helps reveal how artisans of color could capitalize on these relationships and reputations for respectability among prominent whites. Jones, of mixed racial ancestry, was born a slave in the late 1760s to a white tailor named Christopher Rodgers, from whom he likely learned the trade. Like many skilled slaves in the urban US South, Jones used his skills as a tailor to achieve a degree of functional autonomy as well as the ability to earn and save money for himself. Jones purchased his freedom in 1798. In the years that followed, Jones continued to work as a tailor and began to acquire property throughout the city. In 1809, he purchased a lot on Broad Street and six years later acquired the adjacent property as well, establishing what would ultimately become "Jones' Long Room" and later the Jones Hotel, located in one of the busiest areas of Charleston. This hotel would eventually become regarded, at least according to one observer, as "unquestionably the best in the city."[34] Though Jones' role as a caterer and hotel proprietor replaced his tailoring, he must have trained his son in the trade, as Jehu Jr. is listed as a tailor in the city's 1831 directory. For Jehu Jones, artisan labor not only provided for his freedom, but also allowed him to amass a personal estate that could provide for him and his family.[35]

Jones Sr. used his occupation in service-oriented occupations to establish and cultivate relationships with prominent whites and to solidify his reputation as respectable. By crafting such a reputation among whites in Charleston, Jones was well positioned to request privileges normally denied to free people of color. In 1823, for example, Jones marshaled the support of a number of prominent white Charlestonians to gain an exemption to the state's restrictions on the movement of free blacks across state lines, passed in the wake of the Denmark Vesey insurrection scare the year before. A man named John L. Wilson petitioned the legislature on behalf of Jones, who wished to visit his wife and daughter who had earlier relocated to New York. Wilson reported that Jones was "a man of good moral character, attached to the laws and government of this state." In another petition four years later, over 90 prominent Charlestonians certified that Jones and his wife Abigail possessed a "genial and good character" and were both "honest, industrious, and decent people, and have always sustained that reputation." Jones was sure, should the legislature require it, that "satisfactory testimonials" could be provided from "many respectable citizens of this place." Many of these supporters were likely people Jones came to know through his work. That he was able to garner the support of over a hundred prominent whites reveals how artisan labor allowed free people of color to establish crucial social connections with local whites, and how the development of reputations as respectable and industrious through their work as artisans could allow free people of color to request privileges from the state not normally afforded to free people of color.[36]

Because free artisans of color in Charleston lacked the kinds of public-institutional opportunities so crucial to artisans of African descent in Cartagena, however, they developed ways to privately or personally demonstrate their distinction from the city's enslaved populations as well as its free black poor. One of the most prominent ways artisans of color in Charleston crafted reputations for respectability was through membership in a variety of voluntary organizations that grouped men of similar racial, economic, and social profiles. Organizations like the Brown Fellowship Society, Friendly Union Society, and Friendly Moralist Society – founded in the late eighteenth and early nineteenth centuries – restricted membership both on complexional and racial considerations as well as reputational ones, marking members as people of means and respectability. Membership in these organizations was restricted almost exclusively to Charleston's light-skinned or mulatto artisan class, and they offered a way not only to reinforce social links between individuals who shared similar backgrounds and professions, but as a means of demonstrating to the broader Charleston community their commitment to values like industry, sobriety, and charity. These voluntary organizations helped reinforce the link between artisan work and respectability among free people of color in the city.[37]

Prominent artisans would have had the opportunity to distinguish themselves by maintaining workshops in prominent neighborhoods as well. For much of the eighteenth and nineteenth centuries, walking for more than a few blocks almost anywhere in the city's center would have brought an individual into contact with a number of prominent free artisans of color. For whites, this would have meant that the sight of relatively affluent, skilled free people of color would have been a daily occurrence in the city. For free people of color, particularly artisans, they would have had the opportunity to further cultivate social ties with individuals matching their occupational and racial profiles. To return to Jehu Jones, we can imagine the contact he would have had with other prominent free artisans of color in his day-to-day life. Just three doors down from Jones's hotel on Broad

Street, Edward Lee maintained a barbershop. If Jones headed west from the door of his boarding house and walked a single square block, he would have encountered the shops of many prominent artisans of color: Jane Monies worked on Meeting Street as a manuta maker, Thomas Ingliss as a hairdresser, and John McBeth as a carpenter; Eliza Lee worked as a pastry cook on Tradd Street; John Brown's a cabinet making shop and William Irving's barber shop were located on King Street; on Broad Street was the tailor's shop of Gilbert Wall; and Camilla Johnson also worked nearby as a pastry cook.[38]

Artisans of color established themselves as part of the fabric of their neighborhood, maintaining businesses and residences in the heart of Charleston. The ability to live and work in the center of Charleston was distinction that likely allowed free artisans of color to cultivate social ties with neighbors, both black and white, and generate a client base that likely included prominent, wealthy members of the community. As we saw with the case of Jehu Jones, such a social network could be called upon during times of need. Later in the antebellum era, artisans of color continued to distinguish themselves by living in prominent areas of the city, particularly as less wealthy blacks moved north to the more affordable Charleston Neck.[39] Yet even as skilled work provided many artisans of color the opportunity to cultivate social contacts with prominent whites and maintain workshops and residences in the city, success and stability for artisans in Charleston often depended on the ability not just to demonstrate one's respectability, but to demonstrate a commitment to the existing racial order as well. Some artisans of color, including many of the most prominent, did so through the ownership of enslaved people.

Through slave ownership, free artisans of color could more firmly distinguish themselves from enslaved people and the free black poor, and the buying, selling, and owning of slaves allowed free people of color to share social spaces with prominent whites.[40] When Jehu Jones's wife and two grandchildren moved from Charleston to New York City in 1823, for example, they brought with them "a girl named Martha, a slave."[41] Among the prominent artisans of color living within a square block of Jones, at least four owned enslaved people. As social pressure on free people of color increased in Charleston during the antebellum era, slave owning among free people of color seemed to grow in importance. While hundreds of free people of color in the city owned enslaved people during the eighteenth and nineteenth centuries, the prevalence of slave ownership among free people of color in the city increased later in the antebellum era – and artisans represented the vast majority of slave owners among free people of color.[42] While some free people of color in the South owned family members or friends they were unable to manumit, it seems at least as likely that artisans of color owned enslaved people for their own benefit. Through slave ownership, free artisans of color would have distinguished themselves among local whites and demonstrated a shared commitment to the institution of slavery. By allowing them to enter into the slave owning class, skilled work proved central to the ability of some free people of color to improve their standing among local whites and avoid the worst effects of a racial climate increasingly hostile to black freedom.

Artisan labor proved crucial to free people of color in eighteenth- and nineteenth-century Charleston. Through skilled work, they cultivated social links with prominent members of the community, built economic foundations on which their families could stand, and crafted reputations for themselves as respectable and indispensable residents of the city. These benefits of skilled work allowed some free people of color to occasionally claim specific privileges from the state, and it allowed many others to survive and sometimes thrive in a city whose white authorities regularly expressed disdain for and distrust of free people of color. While whites generally viewed the free colored population in the city as a threat to the stability of slavery and as a group uncommonly predisposed to lives of vice and crime, free artisans of color used their engagement with wealthy white clients, their membership in prominent voluntary organizations, and sometime slave ownership to demonstrate that they were respectable members of the local community and individuals committed to the same cultural values as the city's white elite. By demonstrating a willingness to abide the existing racial order in Charleston, free artisans of color gained support in their efforts to claim privileges from the state and to achieve a degree of social and economic mobility.

Conclusion

For a segment of the free colored population in the urban Atlantic World, skilled work functioned as the key to economic stability and social mobility. Through their work as tailors, barbers, carpenters, and in numerous other roles, free artisans of color positioned themselves as key contributors to their local communities, providing them not just social distinction but the opportunity to claim a variety of rights and privileges unavailable to most other people of African descent. The service-oriented nature of skilled work allowed free artisans of color to develop social ties and relationships with prominent whites and to develop local reputations as hard-working, honest, and trustworthy individuals. For some artisans of African descent, the nature of their work and the success they encountered allowed them to maintain independent workshops and residences in prominent, mixed-race neighborhoods, providing further distinction from enslaved people and the free black poor and offering greater, if still limited, access to channels of institutional authority and the social world of white elites. Skilled work provided distinction and prestige to some free artisans of color, and they attempted to emphasize and capitalize on that distinction in a variety of ways.

For free artisans of color in Cartagena, one of the primary methods by which they distanced themselves from the city's popular classes was through membership in the city's militia – an opportunity available almost exclusively to artisans. As self-sufficient artisans and militiamen, free people of color claimed a variety of rights and privileges that improved their daily lives and those of their family. They demanded access to the *fuero militar*, placing them and their families under the jurisdiction of military tribunals likely to treat them more fairly than civilian courts. They likewise gained the opportunity to don military uniforms, a visual distinction that would have marked them as distinguished in the local community. They fought for the right of their wives and families to gain similar visual distinctions as well. For artisans in certain trades, like Pedro Romero's metalwork, military contracts, not just military service, could further improve the bargaining power of free people of color and increase their chances of claiming additional rights, privileges, and distinctions. By dominating the skilled trades so essential to the functioning of an urban commercial center and playing such a crucial role in the city's defenses, artisans of African descent in Cartagena uniquely positioned themselves to improve their economic fortunes and social standing while distancing themselves from the black popular classes.

In Charleston, artisans of color likewise sought to draw distinctions between themselves and enslaved people and the city's free black poor – though they did so in different ways. Without access to the kinds of public institutions so crucial to the lives of African-descended artisans in Cartagena, Charleston's artisans of color used private institutions and personal relationships to gain distinction. Artisans of color founded and joined voluntary organizations dedicated to moral improvement and mutual aid, often explicitly excluding poorer and darker skinned members of the city's free community of color. These organizations emphasized values like thrift, sobriety, and hard-work, and their members built reputations for themselves that ingratiated them with the city's white elite. Artisans of African descent also purchased and owned enslaved people, not only allowing them to occasionally share social spaces with whites but, more importantly, demonstrating a commitment to upholding Charleston's existing racial order. This expression of shared cultural values and the relationships with prominent white Charlestonians it facilitated shielded artisans of color from various restrictions as the racial climate in South Carolina became increasingly hostile to black freedom over the course of the nineteenth century. At times, free people of color called this support into action directly, as whites supported the claims of artisans to various privileges and exceptions in petitions to the legislature. While artisans of color in Charleston used skilled work to distance themselves from the enslaved and free black poor, the benefits of artisan labor there often came from very different sources than in Cartagena.

Indeed, if a comparison of the lived experiences of free people of color reveals how skilled work offered a path to social mobility throughout the urban Atlantic World, it reveals just as clearly the differences in opportunities available to African-descended people and the ways strategies for improving one's individual circumstances could vary in different cultural contexts. While free people of color in Cartagena could use their affiliation with a key colonial institution to claim rights from the crown, by-passing local officials and at times gaining privileges over their objections, the opportunities available to free artisans of color in Charleston were more circumscribed – more local, more private, and more personal. Though free artisans of color in Charleston occasionally petitioned the state, such requests were in large part dependent on the support of prominent local whites, individuals perpetually concerned with the impact and influence of free people of color on the institution of slavery. While artisans of African descent throughout the Atlantic World used artisan work as a means of improving their social standing and gaining privileges otherwise denied to African-descended people, the sources of prestige and distinction differed in crucial ways.

Finally, social mobility for artisans of color often depended, in various ways, on an acceptance of established racial hierarchies. Even as they challenged their own place within the racial order of American societies, their efforts to place themselves above the free and enslaved popular classes frequently involved at least a tacit acceptance of the racial hierarchies and structures of white authority that undergirded them. In both Cartagena and Charleston, free people of color did not mount challenges to white rule despite the demographic majority people of African descent represented. In Cartagena, they actively defended the city during the colonial era and did not mount a broader challenge to white rule during Cartagena's and New Granada's wars of independence. In Charleston, free artisans of color not only distanced themselves from less skilled, less wealthy, and darker skinned free blacks, they actively participated in the institution of slavery, buying, selling, and owning enslaved people. Likewise, they declined to use their engagement with whites to push for broader racial reforms, unlike their counterparts in northern US cities. Thus, while investigating the social worlds and daily lives of free artisans of African descent illuminates the way skilled work supported the claims of free people of color to rights and privileges and provided an avenue to social mobility throughout the urban Atlantic World, it likewise offers a way to begin exploring divisions among African-descended people in a variety of urban contexts. While free artisans of color often succeeded in challenging their place within the racial order of Atlantic World societies, that success often required them to accommodate the broader logic of the racial order itself.

Notes

1. This article is drawn from Chapter 3 of: Marks, "Race and Freedom in the African Americas.".
2. For work on labor and the worlds of free people of color in Latin America, see for example: Johnson, *Workshop of Revolution*; McGraw, *The Work of Recognition*; Restall, *The Black Middle*; Reid-Vazquez, *Year of the Lash*; Solano D. and Flórez Bolívar, "'Artilleros pardos y morenos artistas'," 11–37; and Twinam, *Purchasing Whiteness*; Vinson, *Bearing Arms for His Majesty*. For work on the USA, see Morgan, "Black Life in Eighteenth-century Charleston"; and Whitman, *The Price of Freedom*; Rockman, *Scraping by*; Johnson and Roark, *Black Masters*. Additional scholarship has focused on the role of black labor in creating the built environments of Atlantic World cities. See for example, Dantas, *Black Townsmen*; and Hart, *Building Charleston*.
3. I have consulted all the available census returns for both the 1777 general census of the population of Cartagena, and the 1780 census of artisans in the city. By compiling the information from these manuscript census returns into a database, I have been able to generate a rather detailed racial-occupational portrait for the city. For the 1777 census, returns are available for four of the city's five neighborhoods: Santo Toribio, La Merced, San Sebastian, and Getsemaní: "Padrón del barrio de Sto. Thoribio, año de 1777." Archivo de la Nación Colombia (hereafter AGN): Sección Colonia (hereafter CO), Fondo Miscelánea (hereafter MI), vol. 41, ffs. 1004–1079 (hereafter "Padrón del barrio de Sto. Thoribio"); "Padrón que comprehende el barrio de Nra. Sa. de la Merced, y su vecindario, formado en el año de 1777, por su comisario Dn. Francisco Pero Vidal, Capitan de Milicias de Blancos." AGN: CO, Fondo Censos Remidibles (hereafter CR), Various Departamentos (hereafter VD), vol. 8, ffs. 132v–64v.
   "Padrón que comprehende el barrio de Nra. Sa. de la Merced"; "Barrio de San Sebastián, Año de 1777." AGN: CO/MI, vol. 44, ffs. 945–958 (hereafter "Barrio de San Sebastián"); "Padrón general ejecutado por Dn. Mariano José de Valverde, regidor interino de M.Y.C.J. y Regimiento de esta ciudad de Cartagena de Indias en el ella comisario del Barrio de la Santísima Trinidad de Getsemaní en el presente año de 1777." AGN/CO/CR/VD, vol. 8, ffs. 75–133 (hereafter "Padrón general […] del Barrio de la Santísima Trinidad de Getsemaní.") The 1780 artisan census includes the neighborhoods of Santo Toribio, La Merced, and Santa Catalina: "Relación que manifiesta los Artesanos que existen en el Barrio de Santo Thorivio el presente año de 1780." AGN: CO/MI, vol. 31, ffs. 148r–55v (hereafter "Relación que manifiesta los Artesanos que existen en el Barrio de Santo Thorivio"); "Lista de los Artesanos que comprehende el Barrio de Nra Sra de las Mercedes, en sus Manzanas, Calles, y Casas." AGN: CO/CR/VD, vol. 6, ffs. 259r–60v (hereafter "Lista de los Artesanos que comprehende el Barrio de Nra Sra de las Mercedes"); "Lista de los artesanos que comprehende el padrón general del barrio de Santa Cathalina año de 1780." AGN: CO/CR/VD, vol. 6, f. 618v (hereafter "Lista de los artesanos […] del barrio de Santa Cathalina.")
4. In 1777, free people of color constituted slightly less than half of Cartagena's 13,690 inhabitants, with slaves comprising just below 20%, making people of African descent a majority in the city. Nearly 30% of the city's residents were classified as whites, a relatively large

proportion compared with the province more broadly (where whites constituted only 11% of the total population) owing in large part to the presence of a number of merchants, military officials, and crown administrators. Indians made up just over a half percent of the city's population. Meisel Roca and Aguilera Díaz, "Cartagena de Indias en 1777," 233. In contrast with Charleston and many Caribbean cities, the peak of slavery and slave trading in Cartagena lay in the mid-seventeenth century, not the eighteenth or nineteenth. The Atlantic slave trade to Cartagena had largely ended before the city of Charleston was even founded.
5. Ibid., 264–268.
6. *Pardo* was a racial classification used to identify individuals of mixed racial ancestry. In practice, it seems to have been used as a relatively imprecise category including not just mulattoes, but for various other admixtures of African and European ancestry. It was likely used for any individual of lighter complexion or not solely of African ancestry. *Zambo* refers to individuals of mixed African and indigenous ancestry.
7. Given the popularity of barbering as an occupation among people of African descent throughout the urban Americas, it is at least somewhat surprising that even this many whites engaged in the trade. For more on barbering among African-descended people, see: de Carvalho Soares, "African Barbeiros," 207–230; and Bristol, *Knights of the Razor.*
8. "Lista de los Artesanos que comprehende el Barrio de Nra Sra de las Mercedes," ffs. 259r–60v; and "Lista de los artesanos que comprehende el padrón general del barrio de Santa Cathalina año de 1780," f. 618v.
9. "Padrón general [...] del Barrio de la Santísima Trinidad de Getsemaní," ffs. 75–133.
10. "Relación que manifiesta los Artesanos que existen en el Barrio de Santo Thorivio," ffs. 148–155.
11. "Lista de los artesanos que comprehende el padrón general del barrio de Santa Cathalina," f. 618v.
12. Such an arrangement fits neatly with Charles Walker's assessment of mid-eighteenth-century Lima, Peru, in which he argues that the use of architecture and space served as a "key social and cultural marker," particularly the desire of upper class whites to achieve a spatial arrangement that matched their social status, one "high above the masses." Walker, "The Upper Classes," 58.
13. "Relación que manifiesta los Artesanos que existen en el Barrio de Santo Thorivio"; and "Padrón del barrio de Sto. Thoribio, año de 1777."
14. See also Cope's *The Limits of Racial Domination* for a fuller exploration of the relationship between race, class, and labor in Mexico.
15. de Pombo, "El informe," 130.
16. Helg, *Liberty and Equality*, 122. While Romero attempted to gain educational opportunities for his son despite his mulatto background, it would seem many more African-descended people in Spanish America attempted to purchase whiteness through *gracias al sacar* petitions to the crown. See: Twinam, *Public Lives, Private Secrets;* and Twinam, *Purchasing Whiteness.*
17. Solano D., "Pedro Romero," 151–170.
18. This general trend in which people of African descent used the militia to achieve social prestige dovetails neatly with the situation elsewhere in Spanish America and the Hispanic Caribbean. See: Vinson, *Bearing Arms for His Majesty*; Belmonte, "El Color de los Fusiles," 37–51; Contreras, "Artesanos mulatos y soldados beneméritos," 51–89; For discussions of the *pardo* militia in Cartagena in particular, see: Helg, *Liberty and Equality*; Lasso, *Myths of Harmony*; Kuethe, "The Status of the Free Pardo,"105–117; Kuethe, "Flexibilidad racial," 177–192; and Solano D. and Flórez Bolívar, "'Artilleros pardos y morenos artistas'," 11–37; Ben Vinson has found a similar overlap between artisan work and military service among free coloreds in colonial Mexico; see: Vinson, *Bearing Arms for His Majesty.*
19. A flurry of legal challenges emerged from Cartagena in regard to the military fuero after the crown reorganized voluntary militias in 1773. Over the subsequent decades, they would claim and defend the right of the military fuero for themselves and their families. See: "Domingo Esquiaqui, su comunicación sobre goce del fuero militar," AGN: CO/Fondo Milicias y Marina

(hereafter MM), vol. 30, ffs. 199–201; "Tomás Morales [...] con derecho al goce de fuero militar," AGN: CO/MM, vol. 46, no. 32, ffs. 492–580.
20. Helg, *Liberty and Equality*, 104.
21. "Honores fúnebres," AGN: CO/MM, vol. 2, 234–235; AGN/CO, Fondo Policía, vol. 2, ffs. 516–539; "Felix Martinez Malo, comandante de milicias de Panamá; su acusación por violación de los reglamentos militares," AGN: CO/MM, vol. 40, ffs. 668–687.
22. In 1800, Charleston District was home to 50,890 people: 35,914 (70.6%) slaves, 13,823 (27.2%) whites, and 1153 (2.3%) free people of color. In 1820, the population was 80,212: 57,221 (71.3%) slaves, 19,376 (24.2%) whites, and 3615 (4.5%) free people of color.
23. Unfortunately, the federal decennial census not record did specific occupational information until 1850. Nevertheless, the 1850 returns, along with data culled from other sources like city directories, allow for the development of a statistical and demographic sketch of Charleston during the first half of the nineteenth century. Leonard Curry observed a similar difficulty in his impressive statistical analysis of urban America, and noted that, through a combination of other sources, he could conclude that patterns of black occupations in 1850 "prevailed throughout the entire period." He argued that in Charleston, along with Boston and Baltimore, "there was no appreciable shift in the patterns of occupational opportunity for free persons of color" between 1800 and 1850. See: Curry, *Free Black in Urban America*, 30–31. Additionally, Philip D. Morgan's work on eighteenth-century Charleston suggests that the general pattern of enslaved and free people of African descent frequently finding work in skilled trades persisted in Charleston for more than a century; see: Morgan, "Black Life in Eighteenth-century Charleston."
24. While this section relies primarily on data from 1850 – some 70 years after the data I utilized for Cartagena – other sources strongly suggest that these trends were present for much of the eighteenth century as well.
25. While the 1830 federal census for Charleston County recorded 3594 free colored persons – 1554 men and 2040 women – the city's 1831 directory listed only about one hundred (and only 82 with occupations). Goldsmith, *Directory and Stranger's Guide*, 120–128.
26. *Census of the City of Charleston*, 29–35.
27. The 1848 census for the City of Charleston marks the first time since at least 1790 that whites outnumbered blacks in the city. That year, the city was home to 14,187 whites, 10,772 slaves, and 1492 free people of color. Between the federal census of 1840 and the city census of 1848, the black population of Charleston declined precipitously, by 24.4%. The editors of the 1848 census attributed the decline to the fact that "slaves and free colored have removed to the Neck, beyond the corporate limits of the city, where the class of houses suited to their condition are numerous, and obtainable at moderate rents." *Census of the City of Charleston*, 2–3.
28. Data culled by historians like Leonard Curry and Ira Berlin suggest that these occupational patterns among free people of color persisted throughout the antebellum era. For example, Curry calculated that in Charleston between 1845 and 1855, just over 50% of free black men engaged artisan trades, compared with just 16% of the free population generally. Berlin calculated that fully three-quarters of free black Charlestonians performed some type of skilled labor in 1850. According to Berlin, Charleston's free blacks "enjoyed a level of occupational skill which surpassed that of most whites." [28] See: Curry, *Free Black in Urban America*, 266. Berlin, *Slaves Without Masters*, 221.
29. *Census of the City of Charleston*, 27–35.
30. "Bricklayers and carpenters of Charleston, petition concerning Negroes who are underpricing them for work, asking the honorable House to stop such practices," 19 July 1783. South Carolina Department of Archives and History (hereafter SCDAH): Series S165015, Roll AD1321, No. 159, 647–651.
31. "Sundry Mechanics of Charleston, Petition to form the Charleston Mechanics Association and for Legislative Relief from Colored Mechanics and Tradesmen." SCDAH: Series S165015, Roll 1287, no. 48, 142–145. This petition is dated 1811 in the SCDAH, but given the reference made to the law passed in 1822 prohibiting enslaved people from hiring out their own time, the petition is likely from 1823 or 1824. Given this timing, it seems possible that these

32. "South Carolina Mechanics Association, petition to indict the hirer and owner of a slave hiring out his own time and that a tax or other remedy be placed on free blacks to insure more equitable competition for jobs," 11 November 1858. SCDAH: Series S165015, Roll 1374, no. 25, 285–288.
33. By 1860, as southern slavery come under increasing scrutiny in national politics, efforts emerged among some South Carolinians to drive free people of color from the state entirely. While these efforts may have gained more widespread support within the state's rural and plantation zones, these white urbanites objected. "Petition opposed to bill professing to drive our free coloured people from the state." SCDAH: Series S165015, Roll ND1304, no. 2801, 895–899.
34. Nell, *The Colored Patriots*, 244.
35. "Manumission of Jehu Jones," SCDAH: Miscellaneous Records (hereafter MR), vol. HHH, 442–443; "Rules and Regulations of the Brown Fellowship Society." (Charleston: J. B. Nixon, 1844), in "Brown Fellowship Society Records, 1794–1990." Avery Research Center for African American History and Culture, College of Charleston: AMN 1005, Box 1; Goldsmith, *Directory and Stranger's Guide*. See also: Johnson, Jr. and Romero, "Jehu Jones," 425–443; Johnson and Roark, *Black Masters*, 252; Powers, *Black Charlestonians*, 43–47, 57; Wikramanayke, *A World in Shadow*, 110–111.
36. "Petition of John L. Wilson, Guardian of Jehu Jones," ca. 1823. SCDAH: Series S165015, No. 1871, 322–324; "Report of the Special Committee for the Petition of John L. Wilson, Guardian of Jehu Jones a colored man," ca. 1823. SCDAH: Series S165005, No. 1302A; and "Petition on behalf of Jehu and Abigail Jones," 6 November 1827. SCDAH: Series S165015, No. 102, 810–815.
37. Bowler and Drago, "Free Black Benevolence in Antebellum Charleston"; "Holloway Family Scrapbook," Avery Research Center: AMN 1065, College of Charleston, Lowcountry Digital Library. http://lcdl.library.cofc.edu; "Rules and Regulations of the Brown Fellowship Society;" and Harris, Jr., "Charleston's Free Afro-American Elite." See also: Berlin, *Slaves Without Masters*, 57–58, 312–313; Fitchett, "The Free Negro in Charleston, South Carolina," 1–2, 163; Johnson and Roark, *Black Masters*, 215; and Wikramanayake, *A World in Shadow*, 78–83.
38. Goldsmith, *Directory and Stranger's Guide*, 120–128.
39. While the 1848 city census noted that many slaves and free blacks had recently "removed to the Neck, beyond the corporate limits of the city, where the class of houses suited to their condition are numerous, and obtainable at moderate rents," analysis of the federal census conducted two years suggests that wealthier, more highly skilled free people of color were able to maintain their presence in the city proper. This ability to continue to maintain workshops and residences in the city thus likely increasingly became a source of social distinction as the antebellum era wore on. See: *Census of the City of Charleston*, 2–3; Seventh Census of the United States (1850), Schedule I, Free Inhabitants; and Schedule II, Slave Schedule; both for Parishes of St. Philip's and St. Michael's, Charleston District, South Carolina.
40. See for example, Johnson, *Soul by Soul*.
41. "Petition on behalf of Jehu and Abigail Jones," 6 November 1827, SCDAH: Series S165015, No. 102, 810–815.
42. While Carter G. Woodson calculated that in 1830, slave ownership among free people of color was roughly equal in the Charleston and Charleston Neck, by 1850 it had grown in importance in the city. Compared with their counterparts in the neck, artisans in the city owned more enslaved people and the enslaved people they owned tended to be younger. Slave owners comprised a larger proportion of the free black population in the city than they did in Charleston Neck, as well. These conclusions are drawn from my own calculations, using the Free Schedule and the Slave Schedule of the 1850 Federal Census, which I used to create a database that could provide me with summary statistics. Unlike the 1830 census, which provides the name of the head of household and the number of people within the household, both free and enslaved, the 1850 separates out free individuals from enslaved ones. The Slave Schedule

(Schedule II), which identifies slave owners and the age, race, and sex of the enslaved people they owned, did not identify the race of the slave owner. This required me to create and manipulate a database to create the statistics I could compare with 1830. First, I created a database of the entire Slave Schedule for 1850 in the parishes of St. Philip's and St. Michael's, being the parishes that included the four wards of the city and Charleston Neck. Then, I used various functions in Microsoft Excel to compare this list to the list of free blacks listed in the 1850 Free Schedule with occupations. I first compared the lists using the CONCATENATE function, taking just the first three letters of the name and surname so as to avoid false negatives (i.e., so that "Edwd Lee" and "Edward Lee" could be identified as the same person). I then went through these matches manually, to eliminate resultant false positives. This allowed me to identify all of the free black slave owners for each of the city wards and for the Neck. While this method surely misses many free black slave owners (particularly free black women slave owners, who are the majority of slave owners in 1830 but are far less likely to be listed with occupations in the 1850 census), I feel these omissions are reasonably likely to be evenly spread across the city's neighborhoods, thus rendering the statistics still valid. See: Seventh Census of the United States (1850), Schedule I, Free Inhabitants; and Schedule II, Slave Schedule; both for Parishes of St. Philip's and St. Michael's, Charleston District, South Carolina.

Acknowledgements

The author would like to thank the editors of this special issue, Robert D. Taber and Charlton Yingling, the editors at *Atlantic Studies*, and the peer reviewers for their help in improving the quality of this article. The author would also like to thank James Sidbury, Alida C. Metcalf, W. Caleb McDaniel, James H. Sweet, and Jenifer L. Bratter for their reading of the longer chapter from which this work is drawn.

Disclosure statement

No potential conflict of interest was reported by the author.

Funding

Finally, thank you to the Rice University Department of History and Rice University's Wagoner Foreign Study Scholarship for supporting the research for this article.

Bibliography

Belmonte Postigo, José Luis. "El Color de los Fusiles. Las milicias de pardos en Santiago de Cuba en los albores de la Revolución Hatiana." In *Las armas de la nación. Independencia y ciudadanía en Hispanoamérica (1750–1850)*, edited by Manuel Chust and Juan Marchena, 37–51. Madrid: Iberoamericana/Vervuert, 2007.

Berlin, Ira. *Slaves Without Masters*: *The Free Negro in the Antebellum South*. New York: Pantheon Books, 1974.

Bowler, Susan M., and Edmund L. Drago. "Free Black Benevolence in Antebellum Charleston: The Proceedings of the Friendly Moralist Society, with Supporting Documents." Charleston, SC: Avery Research Center. n/d.

Bristol, Douglas Walter. *Knights of the Razor: Black Barbers in Slavery and Freedom*. Baltimore, MD: Johns Hopkins University Press, 2009.

Census of the City of Charleston, South Carolina, for the Year 1848, Exhibiting the Condition and Prospects of the City. Charleston, SC: J. B. Nixon, 1849.

Chakrabarti Myers, Amrita. *Forging Freedom: Black Women and the Pursuit of Liberty in Antebellum Charleston*. Chapel Hill: University of North Carolina Press, 2011.

Contreras, Hugo. "Artesanos mulatos y soldados beneméritos. El batallón de infantes de la Patria, en la guerra de independencia de Chile, 1795–1820." *Historia* 44 (2011): 51–89.

Cope, R. Douglas. *The Limits of Racial Domination: Plebian Society in Colonial Mexico City, 1660–1720*. Madison: University of Wisconsin Press, 1994.

Curry, Leonard P. *The Free Black in Urban America, 1800–1850: The Shadow of the Dream*. Chicago: University of Chicago Press, 1981.

Dantas, Mariana L.H. *Black Townsmen: Urban Slavery and Freedom in the Eighteenth Century Americas*. New York: Palgrave-Macmillan, 2008.

de Carvalho Soares, Mariza. "African Barbeiros in Brazilian Slave Ports." In *The Black Urban Atlantic in the Age of the Slave Trade*, edited by Jorge Cañizares-Esguerra, Matt D. Childs, and James Sidbury, 207–230. Philadelphia: University of Pennsylvania Press, 2013.

de la Fuente, Alejandro. "From Slaves to Citizens? Tannenbaum and the Debates on Slavery, Emancipation, and Race Relations in Latin America." *International Labor and Working Class History* 77 (Spring 2010): 154–173.

de la Fuente, Alejandro and Ariela Gross. "Comparative Studies of Law, Slavery and Race in the Americas." *Annual Review of Law and Social Science* 6 (2010): 469–485.

Degler, Carl N. *Neither Black Nor White: Slavery and Race Relations in Brazil and the United States*. Madison: University of Wisconsin Press, 1986.

Fitchett, E. Horace. "The Free Negro in Charleston, South Carolina." PhD diss., University of Chicago, 1950.

Goldsmith, Morris. *Directory and Stranger's Guide for the City of Charleston and Its Vicinity, from the Fifth Census of the United States*. Charleston, SC: Office of the Irishman, 1831.

Harris, Jr., Robert L. "Charleston's Free Afro-American Elite: The Brown Fellowship Society and Humane Brotherhood." *South Carolina Historical Magazine* 82, no. 4 (Oct 1981): 289–310.

Hart, Emma. *Building Charleston: Town and Society in the Eighteenth-century British Atlantic World*. Charlottesville: University of Virginia Press, 2010.

Helg, Aline. *Liberty and Equality in Caribbean Colombia, 1770–1835*. Chapel Hill: University of North Carolina Press, 2004.

Historical Census Data Browser. University of Virginia, Geospatial and Statistical Data Center. Accessed 1 March 2016. http://mapserver.lib.virginia.edu.

Johnson, Lyman L. *Workshop of Revolution: Plebian Buenos Aires and the Atlantic World, 1776–1810*. Durham, NC: Duke University Press, 2011.

Johnson, Walter. *Soul by Soul: Life Inside the Antebellum Slave Market*. Cambridge, MA: Harvard University Press, 1999.

Johnson, Michael P., and James L. Roark. *Black Masters: A Free Family of Color in the Old South*. New York: W. W. Norton Press, 1984.

Johnson, Jr., Karl E., and Joseph A. Romero. "Jehu Jones (1786–1852): The First African American Lutheran Minister." *Lutheran Quarterly* 10, no. 4 (Winter 1996): 425–443.

Klein, Herbert S. *Slavery in the Americas: A Comparative Study of Virginia and Cuba*. Chicago: University of Chicago Press, 1967.

Kuethe, Allan J. "The Status of the Free Pardo in the Disciplined Militia of New Granada." *The Journal of Negro History* 56, no. 2 (April 1971): 105–117.

Kuethe, Allan J. "Flexibilidad racial en las milicias disciplinadas de Cartagena de Indias." *Historia y Cultura* 2 (1994): 177–192.

Lasso, Marixa. *Myths of Harmony: Race and Republicanism During the Age of Revolution, Colombia, 1795–1831*. Pittsburgh, PA: University of Pittsburgh Press, 2007.

Marks, John Garrison. "Race and Freedom in the African Americas: Free People of Color and Social Mobility in Cartagena and Charleston." PhD diss., Rice University, 2016.

McGraw, Jason. *The Work of Recognition: Caribbean Colombia and the Postemancipation Struggle for Citizenship*. Chapel Hill: University of North Carolina Press, 2014.

Meisel Roca, Adolfo, and María Aguilera Díaz. "Cartagena de Indias en 1777: un análisis demográfico." In *150 años de la abolición de la esclavitud en Colombia: desde la marginalidad a la construcción de la nación*, edited by Museo Nacional de Colombia, 224–289. Bogotá: Minsterio de Cultura, 2003.

Morgan, Philip D. "Black Life in Eighteenth-century Charleston." *Perspectives in American History* 1 (1984): 187–232.

Múnera, Alfonso. *El fracaso de la nación: región, clase, y raza en el Caribe colombiano, 1717–1821*. Bogotá: Banco de la República, 1998.

Nell, William C. *The Colored Patriots of the American Revolution: With Sketches of Several Distinguished Colored Persons, to which Is Added a Brief Survey of the Condition and Prospects of Americans*. Boston, MA: Robert F. Wallcut, 1855.

de Pombo, José Ignacio. "El informe de la Junta Suprema de Cartagena de Indias de 1810." In *Ensayos Costeños, de la Colonia a la República, 1770–1890*. Compiled by Alfonso Múnera, 130. Colombia: Colcoturra, 2004.

Powers Jr., Bernard E. *Black Charlestonians: A Social History, 1822–1885*. Fayetteville: University of Arkansas Press, 1994.

Reid-Vazquez, Michele. *The Year of the Lash: Free People of Color in Cuba and the Nineteenth Century Atlantic World*. Athens: University of Georgia Press, 2011.

Restall, Matthew. *The Black Middle: Africans, Mayas, and Spaniards in Colonial Yucatan*. Stanford, CA: Stanford University Press, 2009.

Rockman, Seth. *Scraping by: Wage Labor, Slavery, and Survival in Early Baltimore*. Baltimore, MD: Johns Hopkins University Press, 2009.

Solano D., Sergio Paulo. "Pedro Romero, el artesano: trabajo, raza y diferenciación social en Cartagena de Indias a finales del dominio colonial." *Historia Crítica* 61 (July–Sept 2016): 151–170.

Solano D., Sergio Paulo and Roicer Flórez Bolívar. "'Artilleros pardos y morenos artistas': artesanos, raza, milicias y reconocimiento social en el Nuevo Reino de Granada, 1770–1812." *Historia Critica* 48 (Sept–Dec 2012): 11–37.

Tannenbaum, Frank. *Slave and Citizen*. New York: Alfred A. Knopf, 1947.

Twinam, Ann. *Public Lives, Private Secrets: Gender, Honor, Sexuality, and Illegitimacy in Spanish America*. Stanford, CA: Stanford University Press, 1999.

Twinam, Ann. *Purchasing Whiteness: Pardos, Mulattoes, and the Quest for Social Mobility in the Spanish Indies*. Stanford, CA: Stanford University Press, 2015.

Vinson III, Ben. *Bearing Arms for His Majesty: The Free-colored Militia in Colonial Mexico*. Stanford, CA: Stanford University Press, 2001.

Walker, Charles. "The Upper Classes and Their Upper Stories: Architecture and the Aftermath of the Lima Earthquake of 1746." *Hispanic American Historical Review* 83, no. 1 (Jan 2003): 53–82.

Whitman, T. Stephen. *The Price of Freedom: Slavery and Manumission in Baltimore and Early National Maryland*. Lexington: University Press of Kentucky, 1997.

Wikramanayke, Marina. *A World in Shadow: The Free Black in Antebellum South Carolina*. Columbia: University of South Carolina Press, 1973.

Smugglers before the Swedish throne: Political activity of free people of color in early nineteenth-century St Barthélemy

Ale Pålsson

ABSTRACT

The Swedish colony St Barthélemy, established in 1785 and under Swedish rule until 1878, was an attractive island for neutral transit trade and for a large number of free people of color, many of whom became naturalized Swedish subjects. As subjects under the Swedish crown, they sought political rights through petitions, stressing their place within the colonial system. Free people of color were also connected to the Greater Caribbean and the mobility of the free port allowed for inter-colonial networks. The Swedish Governor Johan Norderling compared the activity of free people of color in the Swedish colony with other colonies, as well as Haiti and the USA. For him, free people of color throughout the Caribbean were grouped as belonging to the same community. Thus, the examples of activity in other colonies exemplified the dangers of further political rights in the Swedish colony. He also used the Caribbean network to communicate with other French, Spanish, and Dutch governors about a revolutionary plot planned by free people of color. Yet despite being nodal points within a network for planning subversive plots, St Barthélemy was not a particularly radical space in terms of independence or antislavery, but rather a space facilitating subversive actions between empires.

On 31 July 1822 in the Swedish Caribbean colony, St Barthélemy Philippe Bigard and Samuel Mathews Balborda signed a document along with 26 other free men of color in which they complained about their unfair treatment by the Swedish governor Johan Norderling. This petition specifically protested that three free men had been whipped without a trial. Absent protection from the Swedish colonial system, there was from their view no legal distinction between their group and slaves.[1] In September of the same year, Bigard sent a letter to Balborda, informing him of a plan to capture Puerto Rico and offered him to lead a regiment of sharp shooters.[2] Governor Norderling discovered this plan however, and proceeded to send warnings of this plot to the governors within the vicinity. The petition and the plot may seem like fundamentally different political strategies, one pleading for political rights from a colonial master, the other taking them by force. Yet both of these were within the realm of political strategy for free people of color. Also, both the petition and the uprising demonstrated a differentiation between advocating for political rights of free men of color and for the abolition of slavery, and performed these actions outside of the gaze of the Swedish governor. In a time when free people of color were increasing numbers and influence in the Caribbean, how did the cosmopolitan environment of neutral free ports impact their political activity? In examining free men of color within the port of Gustavia in St Barthélemy, it will become clear how the Swedish colonial system could be used to reinforce and gain new political rights, yet the absence of colonial supervision and high mobility of people, goods, discourse, and information was beneficial for clandestine political activity within the larger Caribbean region, which often reflected the beliefs and interests of slave-owning merchants.

As maritime connections have become more prevalent in research on colonial history, seemingly insignificant and geographically small areas have garnered new interest to historians due to the outsized potential of single ports. In his impressive work on early modern Bermuda, Michael J. Jarvis concludes that, "We need to pay as much attention to economic, cultural, migratory cross-colonial contact between places on the periphery as we do to contact between periphery and core."[3] He has, in this work, shown how the small island of Bermuda had a vibrant history closely connected to events around the Atlantic world. Similarly, free ports have gained a new interest among Caribbean historians as connecting links within a Greater Caribbean network, as inter-colonial trade and movement has been shown as crucial aspects of Atlantic history. Linda M. Rupert explores the free port of Curaçao as an arena for not only economic, but also cultural and religious possibility. The loose control necessary to attract merchants and tolerate illicit commerce would also provide a cross-cultural milieu, as for example Jews escaping religious persecution were able to settle in free ports.[4]

Jeppe Mulich has created a model to consider free ports as inter-imperial microregions, which facilitated movement of people, goods, and information between imperial spaces. While such microregions were not isolated to the Caribbean, he refers to the Danish Caribbean as an example of how they functioned. Together with Lauren Benton, who has contributed greatly to a more nuanced perception of imperial sovereignty within the Atlantic, he argues that the early nineteenth century created ideal conditions for such spaces.[5] Atlantic trade had simultaneously increased in volume and become more controlled by especially the British, which created the need for avenues to escape the Royal Navy. New ideals of governance provided opportunities to create spaces outside of colonial control, with more liberal policies for religion, trade, and political community. Neutral free ports were exactly this: areas outside of control of larger imperial powers that could facilitate the increasing Atlantic trade to, from, and especially within the Caribbean.[6]

There is much to suggest that neutral free ports were of significance for the growing number of free people of color in the Caribbean, and especially for Haiti. In his article "Crisscrossing Empires", Julius Scott points to St Thomas especially as an example of the mobility of sailors and slaves within the Lesser Antilles during the late eighteenth century. Yet as his analysis points less toward the political language within St Thomas or Curaçao as how movement of people and information within an increasingly rebellious Caribbean could be conducted through these ports.[7] The role of free ports within a radical Caribbean may be even further understood through the research of Julia Gaffield. In her work on the quest for Haitian recognition after its revolution, she points to Dutch Curaçao and Danish St Thomas as areas where Haiti could continue to trade, despite being ostracized by the USA, Great Britain, and France. French agents were active in suppressing this commerce with the free ports, arguing that Haiti was excluded from the rules of neutrality, but merchants continued to trade. Discreet and never formally recognized, commerce with neutral free ports was essential to the Haitian economy.[8] While her focus remains on St Thomas and Curaçao, she mentions on occasion the Swedish colony St Barthélemy.[9] Much like the other islands, the Swedish neutral free port gave opportunity for free people of color to travel, trade, and connect with the surrounding Caribbean outside of the gaze of British and French forces, although they still suffered systematic oppression from the Swedish colonial leadership. Victor Wilson has recently researched St Barthélemy's smuggling and neutrality-based trading, showing the trade connections of the island to particularly North America, but also the Greater Caribbean.[10]

While free ports are acknowledged as economically important areas for Haiti and the South American republics due to their options of covert trading, little is known about the ideological sentiments of merchants in these ports, especially free people of color. By examining the political behavior of free people of color in St Barthélemy, we can understand not just the economic, but also the political relation they had toward the changing Caribbean world.

Neutral Scandinavian ports

Scandinavian colonialism in the Caribbean has often been regarded as an exception to more widely known exploits by the British, French, Spanish, and Dutch. Sweden and Denmark nevertheless established Atlantic colonies in the seventeenth and eighteenth centuries that were far more than side notes of European colonization. Denmark was more successful than Sweden in establishing colonies in West Africa and the Americas, and also established a colony in South Asia. In the Caribbean the Danes captured the island of St Thomas from the Dutch West India Company in 1666, and established a stable settlement in 1672. The Danes subsequently colonized the neighboring islands of St John and St Croix in 1718 and 1733, respectively.[11]

St Thomas was the second largest of these islands, but in the nineteenth century grew at an exceptional pace, increasing from around 500–700 whites from 1789 to 1797, after which it exploded to 2122 whites in 1815. However, the island's free population of color grew even faster, from around 150 in 1789, to 250 in 1797, to outnumbering whites with as many as 2284 in 1815. The slave population remained constant during this time, amounting to around 4500 people.[12] Evidence suggests that the sharp increase of free people of color in St Thomas was more of a result of immigration from other islands than manumission or natural increase.[13] Such sharp growth on St Thomas was closely connected to its status as a free port, where ships of all nationalities were free to move to and from the colony. As the French and Haitian Revolutions unfolded, Danish neutrality in many imperial conflicts gave the colony an opportunity to overcome its few plantations and produce profits through commerce.[14] For free people of color these free ports offered unique opportunities for trading and employment. In a survey of 221 able-bodied free men of color in St Thomas in 1802, 89 were not from the Danish West Indies. Of these, 69 came from Curaçao, St Eustatius, and other free ports. Half of the 221 free men possessed maritime artisan skills, such as carpenters or sail makers. There were also many free women of color migrating to the island, working as hucksters and shopkeepers.[15] There was no formal legal difference between port and country beneficial to free people of color, nor were free ports unattractive to white sailors. Yet port economies, geographically removed from plantations, were attractive for free people of color, and enabled formation of social communities.

Swedish began colonizing the Caribbean much later than the Danes. In 1784 Sweden acquired the island of St Barthélemy from France in exchange for trading rights in Gothenburg. Initially, Swedish diplomats negotiated with France for a larger island, such as Tobago, but settled for a much smaller island close to several different French, Dutch, British, Spanish, and Danish islands. Since St Barthélemy featured only 21 km^2 of mountainous terrain with limited fresh water, the island could not support sugar plantations. Instead, Swedish officials declared that the island's newly built harbor town Gustavia would be a free port, allowing trade from all nations and encouraging merchants to become naturalized Swedish subjects. Sweden, like Denmark, was neutral in many of the larger conflicts of the late eighteenth and early nineteenth century. Flying Swedish colors could allow a merchant to avoid trading restrictions between warring nations, as well as British contraband laws.[16] New Swedish subjects could either own or command ships under a Swedish flag, depending on how much they had paid for their naturalization papers. A 16-dollar fee gave an individual the right to command a Swedish-flagged ship, while 100 dollars secured the right to own a Swedish-flagged ship or warehouses on the island.[17] This naturalization process was specific to St Barthélemy and simpler than becoming a Swedish citizen in Europe. The inhabitants had to have lived on the island for a year or sailed in the service of Sweden. Upon naturalization, the new Swedes vowed to become residents on the island, while being free to travel to other islands. Several wealthy naturalized Swedes owned property on other islands as well as in St Barthélemy.

Neutrality and its access to constant trade was the ultimate reason for becoming a Swedish subject. As soon as the Napoleonic Wars ended in 1815, naturalization applications plummeted. Rival empires were quite suspicious of the new Swedes in St Barthélemy, which they commonly called a smuggler's den or pirate's cove and involved in illegal slave trade.[18] Officially, Swedish leadership was clear that all naturalized subjects should be considered as authentic Swedes and that all trade was carried out in accordance with lawful neutrality. In particular, commercial connections with Haiti angered the French, who attacked the island in 1807 looking for the trader William Israel. Israel, originally from the USA, had issued sea passes for at least two schooners to travel to Haiti.[19] "The governors of Curaçao to St. Thomas did outlaw trade Haiti in late 1804 and late 1805, respectively, but the prohibition on trade [...] remained largely on paper."[20] In the case of St Barthélemy, Swedish crown prince Charles Jean Bernadotte clarified the stance on trading with Haiti and rebellious Spanish colonies in his instructions to the new Governor Johan Rosensvärd in 1816:

> The friendship between the King and the King of Spain does not allow that St Barthélemy welcomes or encourages open trade with the Spanish colonies rebelling against their mother country. If these countries retain their independence, and the colony can derive real benefit from selling contraband through not officially allowed, but clandestine, voyages, the Governor is authorized to allow this, without the government [...]. The same applies for mercantile speculations with Saint Domingue, which cannot be openly permitted because of the peaceful relations between Sweden and France.[21]

So, while just as Gaffield states there was no intention to officially support Haiti as a state, the Swedish crown knew of and unofficially supported illicit commerce with Haiti and South American rebels.

While the population of the island included only 739 French subjects and slaves when the colony became Swedish in 1784, by 1812 its number had increased to almost 5500, of which almost 4000 lived in Gustavia. Practically everything in the city had been built from scratch, with building materials shipped from Sweden and construction labor by the slaves of remaining French subjects.[22] They also built forts, yet there was low Swedish military presence on the island, only amounting to a garrison of 50 soldiers and a local militia.[23] For the region the Swedish colony offered a greater degree of religious freedom, with Protestant, Catholic, and Methodist congregations co-existing. Swedish officials even provided money for establishing a Methodist chapel and Catholics held mass in the Lutheran church.[24] This stood in contrast to metropolitan Sweden's still strict Lutheran religious policies, and was a concession made in order to attract non-Lutheran and Jewish traders to the colony, as had been done previously in the free port town of Marstrand on the Swedish west coast.[25]

In Gustavia there were in 1812 1025 whites, 1038 free people of color, and 1818 slaves, but the countryside outside the port had 933 whites, just 90 free people of color and 588 slaves.[26] Free people of color in St Barthélemy clearly tended to live in the port rather than the countryside, probably due to the work offered within the city as peddler, port workers, sailors, and even as merchants. There are also suggestions that free women of color worked in the sex industry, for example when, "a party of White Gentlemen & Coloured Ladies had a Ball in this Island; No Coloured men were admitted."[27] Free people moving away from the small number of plantations of the interior was most likely also an important component, as well as the social community of free people of color within Gustavia. About 18% of the registered sailors in 1814–1815 were either slaves or free people of color. While not all did so, many free people of color like William Panilio, the owner of two ships, became naturalized Swedish subjects, a stipulation for conducting trade under the Swedish flag.[28] He and other free men of color would turn toward the Swedish state for support in seeking political rights in St Barthélemy.

Petitioning for equality

The form of government in St Barthélemy changed in 1811 with the reintroduction of a ruling council to which three members were to be elected from the local population alongside an additional four members who were appointed Swedish officials. This system had previously been implemented in St Barthélemy during its initial colonization in 1785. It was based on the *Raad* in St Eustatius from which many of the new Swedish subjects had relocated, both white and free people of color. St Eustatius had also been a free port, but had been declining since 1781, as a result of British and French attacks and occupations. Even though the elected members of the council were not able to form a majority and gain governmental control, nine free men of color petitioned in 1812 to be given the right to vote for these positions.[29] Many of these were small-scale merchants operating from St Barthélemy and born in, for example, St Kitts or St Martin, but achieved Swedish subjecthood through naturalization. Their request was however denied, with the belief in Stockholm that while it would seem improper to deny voting rights for property owning free people of color, "the common practices in the West Indies may be necessary, as deviation from this may, if not cause all the horrors of St Domingue, with the passing of time put all property in the hands of the free coloured."[30] It was unclear exactly how voting rights would either increase violence or decrease white-owned property, yet this was the basis for revoking political rights.

The question of voting rights would however return in 1821, when 23 free men of color signed and presented a new petition, asking for the right to participate in elections.[31] The governor of the time, Jonas Norderling, was strongly opposed to increasing the rights of free people of color, as "many in this caste are guilty of indecent conduct," especially when drinking wine.[32] In Stockholm however, the Colonial Department decided that free men of color would be given the right to vote for members of the council. What is interesting was the lack of discussion given to the issue in Sweden. The Colonial Department granted the right to vote without any justification or discussion. While this issue was important for both free people of color and the governor, it was met with disinterest in Sweden.

When put in colonial practice, this right was severely limited, besides the demands of property ownership and residence on the island placed on voters for the council already. Those seeking to vote were to report to the Swedish officials the day before the white population, and Swedish officials could disregard anyone deemed dangerous to the colonial regime. Their right to vote could also be disregarded if anyone could "bear testimony of irregular conduct."[33] When voting turnout for council members among free men of color was understandably low, Governor Norderling complained that they had "pretensions of voting on the same day of whites."[34]

In another petition that soon followed 28 free men of color complained about their treatment by Governor Norderling after three free men of color were whipped extrajudicially. They urged the authorities in Stockholm to enforce the due processes they were entitled to as Swedish subjects as part of the legal relationship between St Barthélemy and Sweden. They hoped the King would "not tolerate seeing a large class, called to fulfill all their duties as subjects, becoming the object of odious discrimination and contempt more damning than treating them as their own slaves."[35] As Melanie Newton has shown in petitions from Barbados, assertions of the limited rights of free people of color were often dependent on establishing a distance between themselves and slaves. If they were not treated differently from slaves, their freedom was an empty concept. These petitions were most likely written by a group of property and slave-owning free people of color, who considered themselves above the enslaved Afro-Caribbean masses.[36]

Understanding that they could not ask the governor to deliver this petition to Stockholm, they asked a visiting Swedish naval commander to ship it in secret to Stockholm on his return trip. The Colonial Department reprimanded the governor for his extrajudicial actions, seeing as the free men of color were a group "whose importance and civilization increased daily."[37] If they were not given legal political rights there was a risk that this group could seek to overthrow the Swedish colonial system. They were also important allies to have in the Caribbean:

> Political sense, and your local experience, should convince you Sir, that European sovereignty on these beaches will not last long against the superior number of the Negroes, if free people of colour are not interested in [...] the continuation of the system of slavery.[38]

In the mind of Swedish authorities, the same feelings of hatred and revenge that fueled the Haitian Revolution could brew in St Barthélemy. Whereas this nearby revolution had previously been invoked to justify the restriction of political rights, it was now invoked for the enforcement of legal rights as self-preservation.

The support from Sweden for free people of color should not be confused as a liberal sensibility for the plight of free Afro-Caribbeans. Rather, it was a way to appease free people of color, so as to not risk the stability of the colony. Most likely, the Colonial Department reasoned similarly in allowing free people of color to vote in council elections. The Swedish government generally ignored St Barthélemy and felt only enough responsibility to mitigate revolutionary impulses and avoid diplomatic incidents. In a colony rife with secretive trading and smuggling, the most efficient way to govern was generally to not pry into the business of its population. This may be why some free people of color favored free ports, as the hands-off governance of neutral nations gave more room to establish personal fortune.

However, even though the petition was sent to Sweden in secret, Governor Norderling was aware of it beforehand. He had discovered that a group of free men had met at the house of Carl Tybell, a Swedish captain. Tybell was part of *Sainte Clique*, a small group of native Swedes opposed to Norderling's leadership. There is little indication that these two groups were allied, though, as the *Sainte Clique* were more concerned with Norderling's corruption than his treatment of free people of color. Many of the free people of color shared last names with influential merchants in the ports, such as Anthony Vaucrosson, the son of St. Eustatius-born merchant Jean Jacques Vaucrosson. Samuel Balborda, who will reappear in this article, was, according to a list of petitioners in 1829, a 40-year old "mulatto" who worked as a broker.[39] This group likely represented a wealthier segment of the free population of color on the island. The governor suspected that the group of free men of color was meeting to draft a petition, saying:

> The fruit of this plot was a very humble request to Your Majesty, where I am accused of violating the rights of free people of colour by punishing a negro from the countryside to 24 strikes of the whip, as well as a scoundrel from the city with twelve.[40]

Norderling's defense was not that the petitioners lied, but that they and free people of color in general were unruly, untrustworthy and that the extrajudicial punishments were justified. For example, the first man punished was a courier to the country militia, but had refused to deliver a message, and had shoved the captain when the order was repeated. The second man had been talking to a woman of color through the grates of the jail. When a guard ordered him to leave, he had struck the guard with a stick. Norderling decided that a trial was not necessary, but that the men should be whipped for their offenses and then released.[41] Norderling did not isolate his mistrust to people of color in St Barthélemy, but also mentioned unruly behavior among people of color in St Kitts as well as in Charleston, South Carolina: "The spirit of men of color is very bad in the entire area."[42] As a white member of the Greater Caribbean community, he and the other Swedish governors were influenced by larger racist discourses, which certainly had impacts on their policy-making and worldview.

These various petitions were connected to each other, and paralleled similar petitions on neighboring islands. In the Danish West Indies 331 free people of color from all islands signed a petition in 1816 asking for stronger political and economic rights. They also complained about being punished without a fair trial, just as the Swedish free people of color did in 1822.[43] Also in this time free people of color in the British and French Caribbean submitted petitions for political rights, some with thousands of signatures.[44] Information spread quickly, especially in free ports like St Barthélemy and St Thomas. The actions of free men of color in St Barthélemy most likely inspired neighboring islands. Just a few years after free men of color were allowed limited voting rights, a petition came from the neighboring island of St Kitts, asking for the right to vote for and to be elected in the local assembly, as well as to act as jurors.[45] When considering that the islands were in frequent enough communication that letters to and from St Barthélemy generally passed through St Kitts, there is no doubt that the free population of color in the British colony had heard of this political shift in the Swedish colony and had perhaps inspired them to pursue similar actions. Knowledge of political rights under different colonial regimes spread across islands, not only in petitions but even more so in the newspaper of St Barthélemy.

Behind the print and on the paper

The local newspaper on St. Barthélemy, *The Report of Saint Bartholomew*, was founded in 1804 by the local judge, Anders Bergstedt. It was primarily meant to spread government information to people on the colony, as well as to discuss Swedish maritime neutrality within the Caribbean. Due to there being very few Swedish-speakers in St Barthélemy and many mariners coming from North America and anglicized islands such as St Eustatius and Saba, the newspaper was printed in English, with certain articles in French. However, after a tumultuous set of events in 1810 that culminated with a mutiny by the city militia, Bergstedt who was also the major of the militia, was exiled and the newspaper was discontinued. Limited publication would begin again in 1811, under unknown editorship. In 1812, the free man of color, John Allan, became the editor of *The Report* and would remain so until 1819. Allan was originally from Antigua and had just recently become a naturalized Swedish subject.[46]

Compared to the previous editorship, *The Report* became more political after Allan became the editor, especially with a major shift regarding the Haitian Republic. Allan was a frequent defender of Haiti, its rights to independence from France and the legitimacy of its rule and rulers:

> As virtue and talents belong to no particular complexion, and improvements are common to all who have industry to seek and to acquire them, it is of no little consequence that the MAN who is exercising the Sovereign Authority over a people destined, perhaps, before long to take an acknowledged rank among the nations of the Earth, is *virtuous and enlightened:* fitted alike to cultivate the arts of peace or to endure the turmoils of a Camp, inspiring by good faith and by a regard for justice, confidence in all with whom he has any intercourse or connection! Intelligent gentlemen (one of them a public character) who have lately returned from that country, and who speak in high terms of the hospitality and urbanity of the Government, corroborate and confirm this statement of things.[47]

Despite the ongoing civil war at the time, Haiti was depicted as a well-functioning state and Allan's capitalization of the word "MAN" indicated both an encouragement of people of color's humanity and the gendered political position Henry Christophe had as a man. Commerce and movement between Haiti and St. Barthélemy also served as evidence of stable Haitian governance at this time. Allan stated that although he did not have the room to reprint and translate the proceedings and documents of the council meeting at the Palace of Sans Souci on 21 October 1814 where King Henry Christophe argued for Haitian independence, it had "been generally circulated" and "no doubt been read with corresponding interest."[48]

This stood in stark contrast to the previous editorship of Anders Bergstedt, under whom the Haitian Revolution had been described as the mass slaughter of white people by merciless death squads.[49] A clear shift in description of Haiti can thus be seen between the two editors. Allan also printed other material concerning free people of color, such as a letter signed by free people of color in Dutch St. Martin to Governor Cantzlaar in 1816, expressing their rejoice at the return of Dutch rule, and that soldiers of color discharged by the British had been treated unfairly.[50] Furthermore, this article included an excerpt of Hannah More's "Slavery: A Poem" at the request of "Two Sambo's, sons of a virtuous solitary Man."[51] Allan was also supportive of South American revolutionaries, opposed to Napoleon and a strong believer in the freedom of the press.[52]

Yet with regard to slavery Allan's opinions were often ambiguous, as became evident following the British demand in 1814 for France to abandon the slave trade within five years. While never defending the slave trade, "the traffic in human flesh," he seemed to often argue that there were other issues of at least equal importance. On 13 August 1814, he asked if war was not as damaging to humanity and liberty as slavery, especially in consideration of British impressment policies:

> Is it more repugnant to the liberties of man, to take from his home, and separate from his wife and child, and translate him from rudeness, to a peaceful and industrious employment, an African! than it is to catch up a free born son of Europe or America, and without regard to whether he is of the same national description as myself, or for a moment consulting his disposition or motives of either affection or animosity to the party against which I am going to array him; force him from all his connections, and compel [sic] him to sustain a part in my quarrels, and share in conflicts where none of the merit and renown can belong to him, and where both are measured by the number of mangled bodies of the slain and wounded, with which the earth is made to groan.?[53]

He also reprinted the letter from the pseudonym "Creole" with a similar anti-military message, which also argued for the defense of private property from military capture, as well as one from "B.L.A. Creole of Guadeloupe," who argued that one nation should not have the power to inflict laws upon another and asks why the British does not demand that the Russian Emperor emancipates the serfs.[54] On 3 September 1814, Allan also asked how come "not one word [had] been uttered on that most abominable of all abominations, the revival and re-establishment of the inquisition in Spain."[55]

This partially represents a desire to allow a variety of opinions, whether from a liberal appreciation of debate or from a fear of alienating anyone of *The Report's* already quite few subscribers. To a certain degree, pandering to the interests of neutral merchants, for whom capture of ships by British privateers was a matter close to their hearts, could help sell sorely needed subscriptions. Yet even if Allan did this with a white readership in mind, it also suggests that Allan was more interested in promoting the virtue of established free men of color in Haiti and the Caribbean than arguing for increasing their number through the abolition of slavery.

The ambiguous relationship between *pardos* and South American revolutionaries could be similar to Allan's editorship, as well as the attitude of many free people of color during the early nineteenth century.[56] Allen was strikingly supportive of independence movements and democratic enfranchisement, eager to separate America from monarchy and its European colonial masters, philosophically guided by Enlightenment philosophy, yet non-committal about the abolition of slavery. There were no arguments at all for an independent St Barthélemy however, as the colony depended on Swedish neutrality and diplomacy in order to remain a viable marketplace. Yet this did not hinder political support for the establishments of new republics elsewhere in the Americas, including with a continuing slave society. Of course, there were many free people of color who abhorred and opposed slavery, yet most chose political activism for their own enfranchisement as a priority above equality with marginalized black populations.

Similarly, revolutionary operations organized and launched by free people of color in St. Barthélemy were closer to the revolutionary ideals of the South American republics than those of Haiti, in terms of the continuation of slavery. Even in revolts, free people of color at times valued equality between free men above freedom for all.

The Ducoudray-Holstein expedition

In August 1822, Governor Norderling suspected that free men of color in St Barthélemy were involved in a conspiracy. Considering the island's status as a free port and its trade connections to Haiti and South American revolutionaries, this was not an uncommon occurrence.[57] He had noticed that a schooner and two brigs had arrived in Gustavia, with arms and provisions. Norderling's initial suspicion was that they would be used to attack Guadeloupe, although he did not believe such a plan could be successful. Nevertheless, he reported his findings to Antoine Philippe de Lardenoy, governor of Guadeloupe, yet without clarifying his reasoning. In this letter Norderling also mentioned that once the schooner arrived people of color then left for St Kitts, St Eustatius, and St Martin "with an ambassadorial air."[58] Norderling's suspicion was correct, as there certainly was a network of resistance of people of color between British, Dutch, and French islands.

Norderling therefore arrested Philippe "Titus" Bigard, a free man of color "suspected of plotting a revolt against the whites on [Guadeloupe]" together with a group of accomplices.[59] Philippe was among those who had previously petitioned the Swedish king regarding extrajudicial punishments against free men of color. In a later report from October, Norderling mentioned that "one of [Bigard's] envoys to St Martin was arrested and put in jail for thirteen days" whose personal letters had been torn apart.[60] Norderling later gained testimony from Abraham Balborda, a man of color in St Martin. He claimed that Bigard had recruited his brother Samuel Balborda to join an attack force destined for Puerto Rico, and that it was Balborda who had torn up his letter. The fleet appeared to consist of "twenty four vessels fitted out from the Haytian Government, to make the Conquest of the Island of Portorico [with] four thousand five hundred Haytian Troop."[61] The size of the force heading to Puerto Rico fluctuated wildly in different reports, and officials later discovered that it had departed not from Haiti, but from the USA. These inaccuracies regarding the possible Haitian connection make more sense considering that Abraham's testimony may have been achieved through torture. Norderling suspected that the South American revolutionary General Henri Ducoudray-Holstein, of Prussian descent, was behind the plot and alerted Governor de Lardenoy and Governor de Linares of Puerto Rico of the impending attack.[62]

Holstein was previously an officer under Napoleon, but had left for America after having been imprisoned over accusations of treason. In America he served under Simón Bolívar in

Venezuela, but left after personal conflicts with Bolívar. After moving to Curaçao, he met a group from Puerto Rico that encouraged him to establish a new republic in their homeland, called Republica de Boricua, in reference to the original Taíno inhabitants of the island.[63] The proposed name change was most likely inspired by the recent change of Saint Domingue to Haiti, the island's Taíno name. Their proposed new republic would have no distinction between race, religion, and birthplace and would allow foreigners to become citizens. Yet their liberalism did not extend to the slaves of Puerto Rico, who were to remain enslaved to avoid the collapse of the plantation economy.

While their exact role is unclear, the brothers Louis and Philippe "Titus" Bigard were a part of this expedition to create a new Caribbean republic in Puerto Rico. They had also signed the petition for voting rights submitted in 1812, as well as the petitions in 1821 and 1822. They had consistently been involved in regional activism, as Abraham Balborda had signed a letter by free people of color in Dutch St Martin to Governor Cantzlaar in 1816 that had expressed their joy at the return of Dutch rule and had been reprinted in *The Report of Saint Bartholomew*.[64] Once again they exhibited an ambivalent relation toward slavery among free people of color, as although they supported radical struggle for free people of color and the construction of more progressive constitutions they did not necessarily strive for the abolition of slavery.[65] A census from 1835 showed that "roughly 40 percent of the slaveowners [in Gustavia were] free persons of colour."[66] While this number was quite possibly lower in 1821, it shows the interest that many free people of color had to continue slavery, despite their otherwise radical political opinions.

Prior to landing in St Barthélemy the ships had conducted preparations in Danish St Thomas. This was no coincidence, but speaks to the status free ports had in covert operations and transgressions against imperial borders. For example, just a few years before British expeditions in support of Bolívar had used St Barthélemy as a resting place while their ships regrouped. Some of their other ships had operated in St Thomas, where the Danish governor considered the island's trading relation to Puerto Rico too vital to jeopardize, and had thus chosen to warn the Spanish of this British expedition.[67] For both white and black radicals, as well as smugglers and pirates, the Scandinavian colonies were nodes of network connections, which they tried to keep covert. On these matters Scandinavian governors walked a tightrope between too much and too little restriction. Too much, and they risked losing trade to less restrictive colonies. Too little, and such activity on their islands could compromise Danish and Swedish diplomatic positions, not to mention risking an invasion and occupation. Ultimately, when the Ducoudray-Holstein expedition left Gustavia for Puerto Rico it encountered a storm. The ships diverted southward to Curaçao where they were arrested because Governor Norderling had uncovered their plot and warned regional officials.[68]

While fundamentally rivals, governors of different empires were known to help combat rebels and revolutionaries, and generally kept each other aware of political ferment on neighboring islands.[69] When abolitionist free men of color were prosecuted in Martinique in 1824 in what would be known as the Bissette Affair, Norderling copied the sentences for the Swedish Colonial Department.[70] He expressed clear suspicion that President Boyer of Haiti was behind recent disturbances in Martinique, but also forwarded a proclamation by Boyer that denied any Haitian involvement.[71] He was deeply suspicious of free people of color and while no disturbances occurred in St Barthélemy, he saw rebellions in Jamaica,

Trinidad, and the French Caribbean as foreboding signs of what might have awaited his own regime.[72] Yet he did not often overreact on his suspicions against free people of color, as doing so would have compromised Gustavia's unique status as a free port. Nevertheless, as a committee of merchants reported to the Swedish administration in 1819, St Barthélemy had been outdone by St Thomas since the Danish port had "a reputation for liberallity" and that "they knew how to relax not only in matter and amount, but what was still more hostile to us, in manner."[73] Although deeply distrustful toward free people of color, Swedish governors had no choice but to adopt a similar openness in governing St Barthélemy rather than sacrifice the economic benefits of having this politically active group on their island.

Conclusion

Whether they should be viewed as permissive meeting places for mariners, as hubs for information, trade, and political discourses, or as nineteenth century nests for piracy, slave trade, and covert operations, free ports such as Gustavia in St Barthélemy and Charlotte Amalie in St Thomas were certainly spaces for upward mobility by free people of color. Port cities were more popular for this growing class of subjects than the plantation societies in the rural Caribbean countryside. In Gustavia, much of this was because of Sweden's hands-off approach to colonial rule, their minimal military presence, and limited interventions by the mother country. This approach was not driven by a progressive Swedish political sensibility, but rather by a disinterest in colonial maintenance and receptiveness to the potential wealth generated by these classes of people. As long as the colony was profitable, stable, and not a diplomatic nuisance, authorities in Sweden were satisfied. Islands such as St Barthélemy thus offered a new start for people of who were recently freed from slavery, or who were encumbered by more restrictive racial hierarchies of neighboring colonies. This was even more the case for those who chose to become naturalized Swedish subjects, a status that opened doors to commerce as neutrals between belligerent nations. Through petitions to their colonial masters, they explored and even expanded their political rights and Swedish citizenship. While this was often successful, it was a path of compromise and offered unique opportunities compared to less permissive racial codes of neighboring empires, yet without even granting free men of color equal status to whites.

Their petitions for greater rights put them in parallel with nearby islands in the Caribbean, the frequency of which suggests a connective political activism in the region. The Ducoudray-Holstein expedition exemplifies how free people of color communicated and planned attacks across imperial borders and shows the connection islands such as St Barthélemy had to North America, Haiti, and the South American republics. This access to the Greater Caribbean provided opportunities for advancement of political rights, as experiences from different communities could be exchanged. However, it also meant that the radical actions of other free communities of color were tied to those groups in St Barthélemy, at least in the mind of Swedish officials. Rebellious actions in not only Haiti, but in many other islands were referred to in discussions of political rights for free people of color. While these examples were used both as proof that free people were not prepared for new political responsibilities, and that denying them rights within the colonial system could create chaos, it demonstrated that free people of color across the Greater Caribbean were part of a common political community.

Nevertheless, their political beliefs were complex. Among other examples, the Bigard brothers' involvement in the Ducoudray-Holstein expedition shows how many politically minded free people of color did not prioritize abolition of slavery as a near-term goal. While recognizing its backwardness and renouncing the horrors of the slave trade, many free people of color still retained an ambiguous relationship with the slave-based economy that mirrored many liberals in the Americas at the time. This was partially due to many of them being slave owners themselves. Many held pride in their freedom, and considered themselves as not only separate but better than the enslaved. For authorities in Stockholm, free people of color's tacit support of slavery was a reassurance that they would not create another Haitian Revolution, which was a constantly lingering fear. While there were trade connections between Haiti and St Barthélemy and support for its independence from France, the legitimacy of Haiti as an independent nation was a separate matter from the illegitimacy of slavery.

Free ports such as Gustavia were not radical political spaces or more egalitarian spaces as much as spaces with intentionally limited government control for expeditious, pragmatic purposes. While plantation colonies could have extensive systems of population control, free ports were often governed by looking the other way. This was useful for inter-colonial movement and establishing networks with for example Haiti, as well as for avoiding detection. Yet the general political discussions on the island among both white subjects and free people of color stressed loyalty to Sweden and its colonial system.

St Barthélemy was a space for sporadic and delimited progressive political attainment. Belonging to a neutral colonial power was after all the sole reason for Swedish naturalization, whether done by whites or free people of color. As this article demonstrates, Scandinavian free ports in the Caribbean were beneficial for a small but growing number of merchants of color, not because of a difference in attitude or identity, but as an escape from other more restrictive colonial governmental controls. This enabled the port to facilitate movement of information, people, and goods between Haiti and the rest of the Caribbean for the right price. While many ports were attractive to free people of color due to the need for workers and artisans and the absence of plantations, the significance of St Barthélemy was not necessarily how it connected to Sweden, but Sweden's pragmatic disconnection from the colony. This allowed for inter-imperial movement and mobility of goods, people, and information to the rest of the Caribbean. Swedish governance was not significant because of a liberal attitude toward free people of color, but because of a lack of enforcement of its laws. The absence of Sweden, rather than the presence, made Gustavia the port that it was with a unique free population of color.

Notes

1. Petition from G. C. Fabson, Thomas Gibbes, John Heyliger, et al., 31 July 1822. Swedish National Archives, Stockholm (hereafter SNA): St Barthélemy Collection (hereafter SBS), vol. 8:A.
2. Testimony of Abraham Balborda, 15 September 1822. SNA: SBS, vol. 8:A.
3. Jarvis, *In the Eye*, 464.
4. Rupert, *Creolization and Contraband*.
5. See, for example, Benton, *A Search for Sovereignty*.

6. Mulich, "Microregionalism and Intercolonial Relations," 72–94; Benton and Mulich, "The Space between Empires," 151–171.
7. Scott, "Crisscrossing Empires."
8. Gaffield, *Haitian Connections*, 23–50.
9. Ibid., 50, 115–116.
10. Wilson, *Commerce in Disguise*.
11. Dookhan, *A History of the Virgin Islands*, 34–45. For more research on the black population of the Danish West Indies, see Sebro, *Mellem afrikaner og kreol*; Simonsen, *Slave Stories*; Weiss ed. *Ports of Globalisation, Places of Creolisation*.
12. Hall, *Slave Society in the Danish West Indies*, 5. St Croix was the one most suited for plantations. Although it was the last Caribbean colony acquired by the Danes, it would become the most populated, with roughly 20,000–25,000 slaves, 2000 whites, and 1000–2000 free people of color between 1789 and 1815. St John had around 2000 slaves and 150 whites during this time, with free men of color increased from 15 to 271 between 1789 and 1815.
13. Hall, *Slave Society in the Danish West Indies*, 157.
14. Ibid., 21–23.
15. Ibid., 178–181.
16. For more information on the founding of Gustavia and the role of neutrality, see Wilson, *Commerce in Disguise*, 56–99; Müller, *Consuls, Corsairs, and Commerce*, 175–180.
17. "Ordinance of the Governor and Council on the Island of St Bartholomew relative to certain taxes & duties." *The Report of Saint Bartholomew*, 5 July 1804, no. 14.
18. McCarthy, *Privateering, Piracy and British Policy*, 31–32; Head, *Privateers of the Americas*, 78; Wilson, *Commerce in Disguise*, 157–161.
19. Wilson, *Commerce in Disguise*, 210–211.
20. Gaffield, *Haitian Connections*, 59.
21. Charles Jean Bernadotte's instructions to Governor Rosensvärd. Archives Nationales d'Outre-Mer, Aix-en-Provence (hereafter ANOM): Fonds Suédois de Saint-Barthélemy (hereafter FSB), images 238–239, vol. 325. Original quote:

    L'amitié, qui existe entre la Roi et la Roi d'Espagne ne permet point, que l'Ilse de St. Barthélemy accueille ou encourage un commerce ostensible avec les colonies Espagnoles en insurrection contre la Mère-Patrie. Si ces pays consorvent leur indépendance, et que par des voyes nullement avouées officiellement, mais clandestines, la colonie puisse retirer quelque avantage réel par un commerce interlope avec eux, le Gouverneur est autorisé de le permettre sous main sans que cependant le Gouvernement [...] Il en est de même des speculations mercantiles sur St. Domingue, qui ne peuvent pas être autorisées ouvertement à cause des rèlations de paix, qui subsistent entre la Suède et la France.

22. Hellström, *... åt alla christliga förvanter ...* , 55–56.
23. Hildebrand, *Den svenska kolonin St Barthélemy*, 64.
24. Hellström, *... åt alla christliga förvanter ...* , 70–72, 101.
25. Ibid., 52–53.
26. Lavoie, Fick, and Mayer, "A Particular Study of Slavery in the Caribbean Island of Saint Barthelemy," 384.
27. *The Report of Saint Bartholomew*, 21 August 1804, no. 19.
28. Wilson, *Commerce in Disguise*, 94–95.
29. Petition from Bigard, Bigard Jr., Chadwick et al., 19 February 1812. ANOM: FSB, images 41–43, vol. 128.
30. Protocol, 11, 1812. SNA: Statsrådsprotocoller, Handels och financeexpeditionen, Original quote:

    kanske fordrar Westindiens allmänna bruk för allt närvarande detta afseende, och en afvikelse därifrån skulle, om den ock ej föransakade alla de gruslígheter som på St Domingo, i tidens lopp möjligen föranleda dertill, att all fast egendom komma i fria Couleurtas händer.

31. Petition from Hodge, Balbordan, Falson et al. to the king. 5 March 1821. SNA: SBS, vol. 7:B. Original quote: "Ils se hatent de porter aux pieds du Trône lés témoignages de leur dévouement à Votre personne Sacrée, Ou Votre Dynastie, et à la Métropole."
32. Governor Norderling's report to Stockholm, 11 August 1821. SNA: SBS, vol. 7:B. Original quote: "[P]lusieurs de cette caste s'etant depuis rendus coupable d'une conduite peu decente".
33. Proclamation by Johan Norderling, 20 February 1822. ANOM: FSB, image 223, vol. 135. Original quote: "portent quelque témoîgnage contre la conduite régulière".
34. Report from Norderling to Wetterstedt, 6 March 1822. SNA: SBS, vol. 8:A. Original quote: "Ce sont des gens à prétentions … qu'ils eussent préféré de se legaliser, comme les blancs, le jour de l'election au Gouvernement."
35. Petition to the king from Falson, Gibbes, Heyliger, et al. 31 July 1822. SNA: SBS, vol. 8:A. Original quote: "ne souffrira pas qu'une classe nombreuse appellée à remplir tous les devoirs de sujets devienne l'objet d'une distinction odieuse et d'une mepris dáutant plus accablant qu'en les assimilant à leurs propres esclaves."
36. Newton, *Children of Africa in the Colonies*, 65–67.
37. Protocol from the Colonial Department, 7 December 1822. SNA: Pomeranian and Colonial Department (hereafter PCB), vol. B II:4. Original quote: "dont l'importance et la civilisation, tout les jours augmentant".
38. Protocol from the Colonial Department, 7 December 1822. SNA: PCB, vol. B II:4. Original quote:

    Une saine politique d'ailleurs, et votre experience sur les lieux, ont dû vous convaincre Monsieur, que la souveranite des Europeens sur ces plages loin ne saura être maintenû contre le nombe superieure des Negres, Si les gens de couleur libres […] ne se sontent assez intresses du […] concourir avex eux dans la continuation du systeme de esclavage.

39. List of petitioners. SNA: SBS, vol. 10:A.
40. Governor Norderling's report to Stockholm, 10 September 1822. SNA: SBS, vol. 7:B. Original quote:

    [L]e fruit de ce complot à ete une très humble requête à Votre Majesté, où je fuis, dit-on, accusé d'avoir enfreint les droits des gens de couleur libres en faisant punir un Negre de la campagne de vingt quatre coups de la Galôn, et un polisson de la ville de douze.

41. Governor Norderling report to Stockholm, 10 September 1822. SNA: SBS, vol. 7:B.
42. Governor Norderling report to Stockholm, 10 September 1822. SNA: SBS, vol. 7:B. Original quote: "L'esprit des gens de couleur est tres mauvais dans tout la voisinage."
43. Hall, *Slave Society in the Danish West Indies*, 169–174.
44. See Heuman, *Between Black and White*, 21–41; Murray, *The West Indies*, 79–80; Hartkopf, *Sweet Liberty*, 90.
45. Cox, *Free Colored in the Slave Societies*, 101–102.
46. Franzén, *Svenskstad i Västindien*, 63–69.
47. *The Report of Saint Bartholomew*, 10 December 1814, no. 173.
48. Ibid.
49. "Massacre in St. Domingo." *The Report of Saint Bartholomew*, 31 January, 1807, no. 108; *The Report of Saint Bartholomew*, 14 February 1807, no. 98. The article was reprinted from the New York Spectator, May 1806.
50. *The Report of Saint Bartholomew*, 23 March 1816: no. 230; "From the Dominica Chronicle." *The Report of Saint Bartholomew*, 11 January 1819, no. 346.
51. *The Report of Saint Bartholomew*, 26 January 1818, no. 315.
52. For support of the South American revolutionaries, see *The Report of Saint Bartholomew*, 23 November 1818: no. 340. For examples of references toward Napoleon, "Boney's Adventures." *The Report of Saint Bartholomew*, 16 December 1815: no. 217; *The Report of Saint Bartholomew*, 24 December 1814: no. 175; "Finale Song, For Bonaparte." *The Report of Saint Bartholomew*, 10 February 1816: no. 225. For comments on the freedom of press, see *The Report of Saint*

Bartholomew, 27 August 1814, no. 160; *The Report of Saint Bartholomew*, 24 September 1814, no. 164; "London, August 27th." *The Report of Saint Bartholomew*, 28 October 1819, no. 368.
53. *The Report of Saint Bartholomew*, 13 August 1814, no. 158.
54. *The Report of Saint Bartholomew*, 3 September 1814, no. 161; *The Report of Saint Bartholomew*, 26 November 1814, no. 171.
55. *The Report of Saint Bartholomew*, 3 September 1814, no. 161.
56. See Lasso, *Myths of Harmony*.
57. Wilson, *Commerce in Disguise*, 210–211, 233–235.
58. Copy of Norderling's letter to de Lardenoy, undated. SNA: SBS, vol. 8:A. Original quote: "Cela a l'air d'ambassades."
59. Norderling's report, 2 August 1822. SNA: SBS, vol. 8:A. Original quote: "soupçonnes de mediter une revolte contre les blancs dans les dites colonies."
60. Norderling's report, 15 October 1822. SNA: SBS, vol. 8:A. Original quote: "En av deras utskickade till St. Martins blef där fängslad och quarhållen i tretton dygn."
61. Abraham Balborda's testimony, 15 September 1822. SNA: SBS, vol. 8:A.
62. Letter from Norderling to de Lardenoy, 18 September 1822. SNA: SBS, vol. 8:A. He received responses from them on 14 October and 8 November 1822. Also found in SNA: SBS, vol. 8:A. As before, he had no explanation for his suspicions.
63. Soler, *Historia de la esclavitud*, 212.
64. *The Report of Saint Bartholomew*, 23 March 1816, no. 230.
65. See Alzamora, *Mayagüez*. The expedition, as well as Ducoudray's ideology, is also mentioned in Mongey, "Les vagabonds de la république," 75–78.
66. Lavoie, Fick, and Mayer, "A Particular Study of Slavery in the Caribbean Island of Saint Barthelemy," 391–393.
67. Hughes, *Conquer or Die!*, 44–55.
68. Alzamora, *Mayagüez*, 33–35.
69. Geggus, "Slavery, War, and Revolution," 20–21.
70. Sentence in the court of Martinique against Bissette, Volny, Fabien Delfille et al., 12 January 1824. SNA: SBS, vol. 9:A. For more on the Bissette affair, see Hartkopf, *Sweet Liberty*, f. 99.
71. Report by Governor Norderling to Stockholm, 15 February 1824; proclamation by President Boyer, 6 January 1824. SNA: SBS, vol. 9:A.
72. Letter by Governor Norderling to Count Wetterstedt, 9 October 1824. SNA: SBS; vol. 9:A.
73. Undated petition by Cock, Israel, Dinzey Jr. et al. SNA: SBS, vol. 6:B.

Acknowledgements

The research on which this article is based has been done in cooperation with Fredrik Thomasson (fellow at Uppsala University) and Victor Wilson (doctor at Turku University).

Disclosure statement

No potential conflict of interest was reported by the author.

ORCID

Ale Pålsson http://orcid.org/0000-0003-3883-867X

Bibliography

Alzamora, Federico Cedó. *Mayagüez: Capital de la República Boricua*. Mayagüez: Departamento de Arte y Cultura, 2010. Accessed August 26, 2016. http://mayaguezsabeamango.com/images/documentos/capital.pdf.

Benton, Lauren. *A Search for Sovereignty: Law and Geography in European Empires, 1400–1900*. Cambridge: Cambridge University Press, 2010.

Benton, Lauren, and Jeppe Mulich. "The Space Between Empires: Coastal and Insular Microregions in the Early Nineteenth-century World." In *The Uses of Space in Early Modern History*, edited by Paul Stock, 151–171. New York: Palgrave Macmillan, 2015.

Cox, Edward L. *Free Colored in the Slave Societies of St. Kitts and Grenada, 1763–1833*. Knoxville: The University of Tennessee, 1984.

Dookhan, Isaac. *A History of the Virgin Islands of the United States*. Kingston: Canoe Press, 1994.

Franzén, Gösta. *Svenskstad i Västindien: Gustavia på Saint Barthélemy i språk- och kulturhistorisk belysning*, Stockholm: Almqvist & Wiksell International, 1974.

Gaffield, Julia. *Haitian Connections in the Atlantic World: Recognition after Revolution in the Atlantic World*. Chapel Hill: University of North Carolina Press, 2015.

Geggus, David Patrick. "Slavery, War, and Revolution in the Greater Caribbean." In *A Turbulent Time: The French Revolution and the Greater Caribbean*, edited by David Barry Gaspar and David Patrick Geggus, 1–50. Bloomington: Indiana University Press, 1997.

Hall, Neville A. T. *Slave Society in the Danish West Indies: St. Thomas, St. John, and St. Croix*. Mona: The University of the West Indies Press, 1992.

Hartkopf, Rebecca Schloss. *Sweet Liberty: The Final Days of Slavery in Martinique*. Philadelphia: University of Pennsylvania, 2009.

Head, David. *Privateers of the Americas: Spanish American Privateering from the United States in the Early Republic*. Athens: University of Georgia Press, 2015.

Hellström, Jan Arvid. *" … åt alla christliga förvanter … ": En undersökning av kolonialförvaltning, religionsvård och samfundsliv på S:t Barthélemy under den svenska perioden 1784–1878*. Uppsala: Erene, 1987.

Heuman, Gad. *Between Black and White: Race, Politics, and the Free Coloured in Jamaica*. Westport, CT: Greenwood Press, 1981.

Hildebrand, Ingegerd. *Den svenska kolonin S:t Barthélemy och västindiska kompaniet fram till 1796*. Lund: Ph Lindsteds universitetsbokhandel, 1951.

Hughes, Ben. *Conquer or Die! Wellington's Veterans and the Liberation of the New World*. Oxford: Osprey, 2010.

Jarvis, Michael J. *In the Eye of All Trade: Bermuda, Bermudians, and the Maritime Atlantic World, 1680–1783*. Chapel Hill: University of North Carolina Press, 2010.

Lasso, Marixa. *Myths of Harmony: Race and Republicanism During the Age of Revolution, Colombia 1795–1831*, Pittsburgh: University of Pittsburgh Press, 2007.

Lavoie, Yolande, Carolyn Fick, and Francine-M. Mayer. "A Particular Study of Slavery in the Caribbean Island of Saint Barthelemy: 1648–1846." *Caribbean Studies* 28, no. 2 (1995): 369–403.

McCarthy, Matthew. *Privateering, Piracy and British Policy in Spanish America, 1810–1830*. Woodbridge: Boydell Press, 2013.

Mongey, Vanessa. "Les vagabonds de la république: les révolutionnaires européens aux Amériques, 1780–1820." In *Les empires atlantiques des Lumières au libéralisme (1763–1865)*, edited by Clément Thibaud, Federica Morelli, and Geneviève Verdo, 67–82. Rennes: Presses universitaires de Rennes, 2009.

Mulich, Jeppe. "Microregionalism and Intercolonial Relations: The Case of the Danish West Indies, 1730–1830." *Journal of Global History* 8, no. 1 (2013): 72–94.

Müller, Leos. *Consuls, Corsairs, and Commerce: The Swedish Consular Service and Long-distance Shipping, 1720–1815*. Uppsala: Acta universitatis upsaliensis, 2004.

Murray, D. J. *The West Indies and the Development of Colonial Government*. Oxford: Clarendon Press, 1965.

Newton, Melanie J. *Children of Africa in the Colonies: Free People of Colour in Barbados in the Age of Emancipation*. Baton Rouge: Louisiana State University Press, 2008.

Rupert, Linda M. *Creolization and Contraband: Curaçao in the Early Modern Atlantic World*. Athens: University of Georgia Press, 2012.

Scott, Julius S., "Crisscrossing Empires: Ships, Sailors, and Resistance in the Lesser Antilles in the Eighteenth Century." In *The Lesser Antilles in the Age of European Expansion*, edited by Robert L. Paquette and Stanley L. Engerman, 128–143. Gainesville: University Press of Florida, 1996.

Sebro, Louise. *Mellem afrikaner og kreol: Etnisk identitet og social navigation i Dansk Vestindien 1730–1770*. Lund: Lund University, 2010.

Simonsen, Gunvor. "Slave Stories: Gender, Representation, and the Court in the Danish West Indies, 1780–1820s." *PhD diss.*, Florence: European University Institute, 2006.

Soler, Luis M. Diaz. *Historia de la esclavitud negra en Puerto Rico*. San Juan: Universidad de Puerto Rico, 1953.

Weiss, Holger, ed. *Ports of Globalisation, Places of Creolisation: Nordic Possessions in the Atlantic World During the Era of the Slave Trade*. Leiden: Brill, 2016.

Wilson, Victor. "Commerce in Disguise: War and Trade in the Caribbean Free Port of Gustavia, 1793–1815." *PhD diss.*, Åbo Akademi, 2015.

Revolutionary narrations: Early Haitian historiography and the challenge of writing counter-history

Erin Zavitz

ABSTRACT
This article examines a selection of understudied nineteenth-century Haitian texts to illuminate how Haitians tensely narrated their country's foundational event and negotiated the challenge of constructing the first black nation-state in the Americas. The predominantly mixed-race male authors held their own biases and prejudices that were often informed by the same racialized labels they sought to overturn. Writing Haiti's history, specifically that of the revolution, exposed these biases as well as critical social divisions, most notably between an emergent Eurocentric élite and the majority of recently freed, uneducated former slaves who spoke no French. Despite appeals to unity and Haitians' Africanity, early narratives of the revolution disavowed or treated with ambivalence the role of former slaves and African-derived spiritual traditions in Haiti's founding. I trace this ambivalence towards or disavowal of the black majority through a corpus of understudied texts that represent specific interventions in Haiti's emerging national historiography. In particular, I focus on how five authors, Juste Chanlatte, Baron de Vastey, Hérard Dumesle, Thomas Madiou, and Beaubrun Ardouin, narrate the Haitian Revolution and grapple with the role or contributions of slaves/former slaves in the revolution and the influence of African-derived spiritual traditions. Their histories initiated a process of incorporating the black majority and African traditions into the official national imaginary, though on élite terms. For these authors, the predominantly black majority, while contributors to the country's founding, needed civilizing in order for Haiti to prosper and progress as a nation in the post-Enlightenment Atlantic World.

Haitian literary production began with the country's independence on 1 January 1804. As Jean-Jacques Dessalines, the first head of state, and his generals outfitted forts with canons they had seized from the French, government secretaries and printers began the process of establishing national publishing houses with former French printing presses. As members of the African Diaspora, Haitian authors seized this historic moment to counter the racialized images of Haiti and make Afro Americans people in the eyes of Enlightenment Europe.[1] Even as Haitian intellectuals embarked on a revolutionary project of writing black history, they struggled to overcome the legacy of colonialism and slavery and erase the gaping divisions between the political, military, and cultural elite and the urban and rural masses. Narrating the nation's history was as much an antagonistic and exclusionary process as it was a celebratory one.

Little attention has been given to how Haitians tensely narrated their country's foundational event.[2] Although the bicentennials of the French and Haitian Revolutions, the publication of Michel-Rolph Trouillot's *Silencing the Past: Power and the Production of History*, and the 2010 Haitian Earthquake have contributed to an ever-growing amount of scholarship on Haiti that has served to "unsilence" the revolution, these publications also create new silences. In particular, scholars have praised the revolution's radical promises and elided its post-1804 exclusionary elements and the construction of new social hierarchies.[3] To understand Haitian state making and the legacy of colonialism and slavery, we need to examine how Haitian historiographic traditions illustrate the colonial double bind nineteenth-century Haitian intellectuals faced.[4] Examining the exclusionary elements advances our understanding of postcolonial and post-slavery societies as well as the nineteenth-century Black Atlantic by reminding us that even the most radical event of the Age of Revolution contained conservative features.[5] In order to make Haiti appear civilized and worthy of nationhood to a European audience, these intellectuals excluded or highly censored the black majority of former slaves. Despite the tension, and the hostility the élite felt towards the Kreyòl-speaking masses, their histories initiated a process of incorporating the black majority and African traditions into the official national imaginary.

Africanity and universalism: emerging counter-histories of the revolution

The first histories of the revolution appeared during a moment of intense political division. The assassination of Jean-Jacques Dessalines in October 1806 led to a power struggle between Alexandre Pétion and Henry Christophe and the division of the country into two states. Writers associated with each ruler published pamphlets and tracts for Haiti's small French-literate élite and international audiences. The most important for historiographical developments are Juste Chanlatte and Pompée Valentin Vastey (Baron de Vastey) who both served in Christophe's government. Their texts circulated throughout the Atlantic World and even appeared in diplomatic negotiations. For example, Jean-Gabriel Peltier, Christophe's emissary in London sent a copy Juste Chanlatte's *Le Cri de nature* to Robert Peele as part of on-going efforts to win British recognition and illustrate "the improvement of civilisation in those quarters."[6] With these external audiences in mind, Vastey and Chanlatte constructed the first narratives of the revolution that defined Haitian independence as freedom from slavery and an end to French colonial rule. The experiences of the men and women the revolution freed played a limited role in their accounts.

Born circa 1766 in Port-au-Prince, Chanlatte was the mixed-race son of Pierre-Rémy (or Rémi) Chanlatte.[7] While very little is known about his youth, Juste grew up with politically and militarily active family members and received an education in France.[8] He returned to Saint-Domingue on the eve of the revolution and played a prominent role in the fight for racial equality in the West, earning the rank of Major General, and penning one of the revolution's most violent documents.[9] While Chanlatte left Saint-Domingue for parts of the revolution, by 1804 he had returned and was one of Jean-Jacques Dessalines' secretaries. Following Dessalines's assassination, Chanlatte emerged on the Haitian literary scene as a poet, playwright, and pamphleteer for Henry Christophe alongside Pompée Valentin Vastey. Under Christophe, Chanlatte published Haiti's first complete narrative of the revolution, *Le Cri de la nature*. After Christophe's death and the dissolution of his kingdom in northern Haiti in 1820, Chanlatte moved back to Port-au-Prince and took up a job with the republic's official paper, *Le Télégraphe*. He died there in 1828.[10]

Successively working for Dessalines's empire, Christophe's kingdom, and Boyer's republic, Chanlatte was the most politically versatile early Haitian author. His literary output illustrates an impressive adaptability both in terms of audience and genre. Nevertheless, Chanlatte's prose, poetry, and plays remain understudied. Literary scholar Chris Bongie in his article "The Cry of History: Juste Chanlatte and the Unsettling (Presence) of Race in Early Haitian Literature" is the first to rehabilitate Chanlatte's prose. He contends that *Le Cri de la nature* is a "counter-history" of the revolution that is the first to reveal "the absurdities of racial science and the ambiguities of Enlightenment thought."[11] Bongie offers an engaging discussion of the text's creation, contribution, and revision by French rhetorician A. J. Bouvet de Cressé in 1824. Bongie focuses on the absence/presence of race in the two editions and Chanlatte's "unmooring (black) identity from its racialized foundations."[12] Although Chanlatte's lack of racial terminology or color designations is a radical challenge to contemporary European notions of race, the absence of race in his narrative of the revolution occludes contributions of Haiti's black majority to the country's independence.

Chanlatte began his account with a critique of race to legitimate the revolution that established a model for later Haitian writers. Influenced by abolitionists, in particular Abbé Grégoire to whom the pamphlet is dedicated, Chanlatte rejected theories of black inferiority and white superiority through an argument for a universal human race; at the same time, he enunciated the first claim to Haitians' Africanity. He declared that "nous" (we) had accomplished great feats as evidenced by the "ruins" in "Egypt, India, and the Iberian Peninsula."[13] Here, Chanlatte connected Haitians to an African past and suggested a solidarity among colonial peoples. His "nous" referred not to a population defined by skin color but civilizations or societies outside Western Europe. Thus, the architectural feats of Iberia's Islamic rulers and the pyramids of ancient Egypt could all serve as examples of non-European accomplishments and progress.

Chanlatte's revelation of a glorious black past served to counter planters' arguments that blacks were inferior and without a history. He contended that to speak of "our" inferiority "was to legitimate, in a way, the actions of traders in human flesh and to lay down a justification for slavery."[14] In deconstructing the claims of slave traders and planters, Chanlatte was the first Haitian author to advocate for the unity of the human race. Three centuries of enslavement legitimated Haitian revolutionaries' rebelling against this immorality.[15] His argument of racial equality serves as an introduction to the revolution and as a vindication of Haitians' struggle against the French, "les tyrans de l'innocence."[16]

Chanlatte turned to the history of the revolution in the second chapter of *Le Cri de la nature*. Despite Chanlatte's anti-slavery frame, his word choice and chronology expose his ambivalence about the contributions of the black majority. First, though lacking dates, Chanlatte provided contextual details to locate the main events of his account from 1789 to 1803 with a specific focus on the War of Independence (1802–1803). Absent from his chronology are details of the 1791 slave revolt. While the three centuries of slavery served to explain the motivations for revolution, Chanlatte offered only a veiled reference to the slaves' actions: "The first blows were then struck against the hydra of slavery and this electrical current spread from one end of the island to the other."[17]

These attacks on slavery occur after the executions of Vincent Ogé and Jean-Baptiste Chavanne (February 1791) but before the arrival of the first civil commissioners (1792). "[F]irst blows" most likely refer to the slave revolts which began in northern Saint-Domingue and "this electrical current" to subsequent revolts as well as the confederations of *gens de couleur* in the South and West. Chanlatte's word choice celebrates the actions of all of Saint-Domingue's Afro-descended population in the struggle against slavery, yet does not distinguish between the actions of the free people of color and slaves. Equally absent is any discussion of African-derived spiritual practices (today Vodou) or the rebellion's leaders. The only individual he named in the chapter who had been a slave was Toussaint Louverture.

If Chanlatte rapidly passed over the details of the 1791 slave revolt, he dedicated considerable space to describing the atrocities committed by the French during the War of Independence. This focus was a rhetorical strategy common to early Haitian publications and a means to legitimate Haitian independence. Notably, Chanlatte did not assign the decision to turn against the French expedition to any of Haiti's early leaders. Instead, he contended, "So many unheard of barbarities and executions forced us [Haitians] to run to the woods, whence resonated our cries for vengeance."[18] Chanlatte's continual use of the pronoun us obscures any divisions among the insurgents; the narrative implies that all Haitians joined together in the struggle. His description of Haitians taking to the woods suggests the phenomenon of marronage and that it played a central role in, at least, the final phase of the revolution. Following Chanlatte's logic, it was only from the woods that the insurgents could unite and defeat the French. While he may have simply meant guerrilla warfare, he alluded to an experience of the enslaved. Nevertheless, similar to his discussion of attacks on slavery and the electric current of liberty spreading across the colony, Chanlatte's account only makes passing reference to Haiti's former slave population and their contribution to and experiences of the revolution. The enslaved majority are assumed to be part of Chanlatte's "nous" (us), which erases any pre-1804 social divisions similar to Haiti's first constitution that decreed all Haitians black.[19]

Chanlatte's fellow state publicist Pompée Valentin (né Jean-Louis) Vastey, the Baron de Vastey, was one of the most prolific early Haitian authors. Born in 1781 in the northern parish of Marmelade, Vastey's father was a Frenchman who rented land (*fermier d'habitation*), probably a coffee plantation, and his mother was a free woman of color from southern Saint-Domingue.[20] Vastey traveled to France for education and experienced at least part of the revolutionary period in the metropole.[21] In spite of his connections to France, Vastey returned to Saint-Domingue at some point during the revolution and, after independence, became an advocate for Christophe's Kingdom of Haiti (1811–1820), and an exponent of anti-French sentiment. However, after Christophe's stroke, suicide, and resulting power vacuum, southern president Jean-Pierre Boyer and his troops entered the city of Cap Haïtien and took Christophe's supporters prisoner; rebels had already killed his only surviving heir. On 18 October 1820, Boyer's troops executed Vastey because of his ardent support for Christophe.[22]

Vastey's death silenced an important black Atlantic voice. He published over half a dozen pamphlets and monograph-length works addressed to both foreign readers and Haitians, most often mixed-race men in Port-au-Prince and the South, whom he considered his brothers.[23] Vastey sought to legitimate the revolution and the government of his patron King Henry Christophe for both audiences. Literary scholars Chris Bongie,

Doris Garraway, and Marlene Daut have masterfully brought Vastey's texts back into scholarly study.[24] Their work illuminates the role of audience for Vastey, the circulation of his text in the nineteenth-century Atlantic World, and how geopolitical factors shaped his writing. In particular, Vastey's first publications coincide with the restoration of the French monarchy and renewed efforts by former French planters to reclaim (through invasion or other means) Haiti as a French colony.[25] More than Chanlatte, Vastey was an early proponent of Africanity as well as a vocal critic of colonialism and slavery. Bongie, Garraway, and Daut have expounded on these themes in Vastey's writings; however, less studied is his narrative of the revolution and representations of the black majority. In contrast to Chanlatte who obscured the diverse actions Haitian revolutionaries through a language of universalism, Vastey overtly discussed social divisions and employed racial labels in his account of Haiti's founding, yet failed to offer a substantially more inclusive narrative in which the enslaved were historical actors.

Among Vastey's numerous works, only the first chapter of his final publication, Essai sur les causes de la Révolution et des guerres civiles d'Hayti (1819), is entirely devoted to the revolution's history. Vastey's account opens with a demographic description of the colony's inhabitants to establish how colonialism divides and racializes individuals. He stated, "Prior to the revolution of 1789, the population of Haiti consisted of three distinct castes each of which was further subdivided according to the established prejudices of the Colonial System."[26] Vastey further emphasized the effects of colonialism through his use of racial labels (white, black, mulatto) to describe the social divisions of revolutionary Saint-Domingue. Vastey's terminology reveals the rivalries and alliances among the social groups as well as demands and contributions of each. This adds a layer of complexity that is absent in Chanlatte's narrative. These divisions are only resolved by Haitian independence. In the closing pages of the chapter, he exclaimed:

> At last, the veil of error and falsehood was torn away. Before the radiant sun of independence, factions dissolved like clouds from a strong wind; the atmosphere cleansed by victory, we began to breath the pure air of liberty and independence.[27]

The defeat of the French equalled an end to colonialism and slavery and all the prejudices and divisions those institutions spawned.

Vastey's narrative offers a triumphant ending with the erasure of all social divisions; yet, another racial label, nègre marron, illustrates how the legacy of colonialism and slavery haunt Haiti after 1804 and disavow the contributions of the black majority. Vastey contended that the French used the label fugitive slave "nègre marron" to degrade Haitians. For example, in reference to French negotiations, he declared that the French gave a free people "the epithets of evil savage and fugitive slave."[28] The label of maroon or fugitive slave belittled Haitians' status as people free from slavery and colonial rule. The term also signified lawlessness, the absence of civilization and government. Maroons were an external insult by the French to define Haitians as inferior but also an internal threat to Christophe's centralized state and economy. Literary scholar J. Michael Dash states, "[Vastey's] ideal, like that of his King, was that of a scientifically advanced modern state not the creation of a maroon culture based on the African village."[29] The Code Henry, which Vastey helped write, laid out labor rules and punishment for vagrancy, marronage by another name. The vagrants for Vastey and Christophe were the black majority, former slaves who did not share in the élite's economic vision of continuing sugar production.

Thus, for Vastey the label maroon held no patriotic meaning; rather it was a term given to vagabonds who threatened the functioning of the state, and, by extension, the maintenance of independence. This rhetoric placed the black majority at best in need of "civilizing" and at worst outside of the national community conceived of by intellectuals and the state.

Romanticists, slaves, and black history

The centralization of power in Port-au-Prince in the 1820s under the long rule of Jean-Pierre Boyer (1818–1843) fostered a flourishing of literary activity. Similar to the first generation of Haitian intellectuals, this new generation of authors saw themselves continually striving "to refute the contention that people of African descent could not govern themselves or develop a 'civilized' society."[30] Recording the history of Haiti remained an integral counter argument to the racialized images of the country in foreign publications. In contrast to Chanlatte and Vastey, the second generation of Haitian intellectuals constructed more nuanced narratives of the revolution that tentatively incorporated contributions of the black majority and acknowledged the influence of African-derived spiritual traditions.

Hérard Dumesle stood as a transitional figure between the close of the first decades of Haitian historiography and the boom of Haitian romanticism in the mid-nineteenth century. Dumesle's biography, like those of his predecessors, is quite sparse. He was born in 1784 in the southern port city of Les Cayes. Little is known about his childhood and his experience of the revolution. After independence, he had a short-lived military career fighting in Jean-Jacques Dessalines' invasion of Santo Domingo (1805) and later (1807–1810) for Alexandre Pétion's republic against Henry Christophe. Laying down his arms, Dumesle returned to Les Cayes where he served as a regional politician, writer, and editor of Les Cayes's first newspaper, *L'Observateur: Journal Périodique*.[31] Here, Dumesle continued the struggle for the republic with his pen, or, more exactly, printing press. Although a supporter of Pétion and the republic, Dumesle did not agree with Haiti's second president Jean-Pierre Boyer and became a leading opponent of Boyer's regime. A member of the revolutionary forces that overthrew Boyer in 1843, Dumesle eventually ended up in exile and died in Kingston, Jamaica in 1858.

His *Voyage dans le nord d'Hayti* (1824) is the first post-unification history and marks a crucial intervention in Haitian historiography: the inclusion of the August 1791 slave revolt. While literary scholars and historians have debated the authenticity of Dumesle's account and the details surrounding the 1791 slave revolt, in particular the Bois Caïman ceremony, few have examined his text in its entirety.[32] Literary scholar Carl Hermann Middelanis offers the only scholarly analysis of *Voyage dans le nord d'Hayti* in his article "Les Mémoires Fleurissent Dans Les Lieux Ruinés." Middelanis uses Dumesle's text to explore the paradoxes of audience, language, and sources inherent in early Haitian writing.[33] In particular, he contends that Dumesle's account of Bois Caïman celebrates the contributions of the black majority.[34] Thus, Dumesle's account breaks with the earlier writings of Chanlatte and Vastey and initiates a historiographic shift that later historians would further develop.

While Dumesle began his narrative of the revolution with mixed-race leader Vincent Ogé's failed 1790 uprising for the political rights of free people of color, the historical landscape of northern Haiti inspired him to include the role of enslaved men and women. He explained:

Near the middle of August 1791, fieldworkers, millworkers, and sugar house workers of several slave gangs gathered during the night. In the midst of a violent storm, in a thick forest that covered the summit of Morne Rouge, they devised a plan for a massive insurrection that they sanctified with a religious ceremony.[35]

Comparing Dumesle with earlier representations of the black majority's role in the revolution, it is apparent that his account is the most inclusive to date and serves to more fully integrate the enslaved into the narrative. The description of the ceremony acknowledges Haiti's cultural diversity and the influence of African-derived spiritual practices in the revolution. Moreover, Dumesle accompanied his prose with verses in French, translated into Kreyòl in the footnotes, of a speech given by the ceremony's leader (later designated as Boukman). Dumesle was the first Haitian author to use Kreyòl or mention Vodou. His account precedes the work by intellectuals associated with the later School of 1836. Like the next generation of authors, he tentatively acknowledged Haiti's majority culture and introduced an early wave of cultural nationalism that would be furthered developed by Haitian romanticists in the 1830s.

In 1825, a year after Dumesle's publication, King Charles X of France recognized Haiti in exchange for an indemnity. Haitian President Jean-Pierre Boyer sought to pay off the debt through agricultural exports. This placed a renewed stress on the Haitian peasantry and created divisions among the élite who did not all agree with Boyer's policies. Regardless, improved relations with France opened up new archives and sources for the creation of detailed accounts of the revolution. Moreover, the generation of men and women who had fought for Haiti's independence was aging, and intellectuals felt a renewed pressure to record their stories and the country's founding. While publications waned in the years immediately following recognition, the 1830s saw an increase in literary production.

The rise of Haitian Romanticism in the 1830s renewed interest in Haitian history and literature. Influenced by French Romanticism, Haitian authors turned to the folk or Haitian peasant for inspiration. Port-au-Prince based intellectuals such as Thomas Madiou and the brothers Ardouin (Céligni and Beaubrun) and Nau (Émile and Ignace) formed the School of 1836 and began incorporating Vodou and black peasant characters into their writings.[36] For example, Ignace Nau incorporated proverbs and terms in Kreyòl into his newspaper serials.[37] In "Un Episode de la Révolution: Contes Créoles," Nau provided a notes section for foreign readers where he translated terms, such as *abonosho*, *lambi*, and *caplata*, associated with Vodou, or what Nau called "la superstition."[38] Vodou was not an equal belief system with Roman Catholicism practiced by the Haitian élite, thus Nau referred to it as superstition. His definitions for foreign readers further denigrated Vodou. He explained *caplata* as "magician."[39] For post-Enlightenment European readers magician implied charlatan and devalued Vodou in their eyes.[40] Yet, the Kreyòl *kaplata* was a common term for Vodou priest "from the colonial period until the nineteenth century."[41] Although Nau and other members of the School of 1836 incorporated linguistic and spiritual elements of Haiti's black peasants, their work illustrates intellectuals' persistent ambivalence about the black majority, their contribution to the revolution, and Haiti's African-derived cultural traditions.

The final two authors, Madiou and Ardouin, were part of the School of 1836 and penned Haiti's first multi-volume, archival-based histories.[42] Although far from inclusive, the texts do introduce slaves as subjects (albeit in need of proper guidance from the gens de couleur). They also include representations of folk culture, especially early Vodou practices.

And, to capture the experiences of the black majority, they drew on written and oral sources. Madiou and Ardouin were ambivalent at best and often hostile towards the black majority. Nevertheless, they included the majority in their histories of the Haitian Revolution.

Thomas Madiou's initial volumes appeared in Port-au-Prince print shops in the late 1840s during the rule of black president-turned-emperor Faustin Soulouque, a political contemporary of Napoleon III. Madiou's history is a hybrid of Haitian intellectual traditions. Most notably, Madiou treated revolutionary leaders with a degree of neutrality and openly acknowledged the divisive nature of color. Moreover, he incorporated the actions of slaves into the revolutionary narrative. Maroons and rebelling slaves fought for liberty, often for centuries, and their actions contributed to Haiti's independence. Yet, he supported his class (the mixed-race élite) and argued that free people of color, whom he saw as culturally superior, provided a necessary supervisory role during the revolution.

Born in Port-au-Prince in 1814 to "fairly affluent" parents, Madiou grew up as part of Haiti's nascent elite.[43] Madiou attended schools in Angers, Nantes, Rennes, and finally Paris where he completed a law degree in the early 1830s. Like his contemporary Beaubrun Ardouin, Madiou drew upon his father's government connections and his own position as secretary to General Inginac (chief minister of Boyer's government) to support his research. Working for Inginac, Madiou traveled throughout Haiti and did research for his book, including interviews with aging revolutionary veterans.

In the three volumes that focus on the revolution, Madiou maintained the central argument of revolutionary narratives: Haitian independence was the only means to uphold the abolition of slavery and racial discrimination. Madiou added a corollary to his justification of independence. He stressed that Haiti's history was an account of "the African race transplanted in Haiti."[44] Like his predecessors, Madiou sought to narrate a black history at a time when Europeans and white Americans argued that Africans and African Americans had no history. Haiti served as international proof of blacks' capacity for self-rule and civilization.

In Madiou's history, the black masses could not be principal actors in the struggle for independence; instead, elite free men of color along with a select group of courageous and skilled former slaves led the revolution. He contended that the enlightened men of the West (free men of color) influenced the region's slaves and assisted in organizing and leading revolts. Madiou asserted:

> What a difference between the slave insurrection in the West led by free men of color and that of the North where the slaves were left to themselves! On one hand, order, respect for property, and not a single death. On the other hand, disorder, pillage, and frightful vengeance.[45]

Madiou based his argument for the beneficent leadership of free people of color and their "civilizing" influence on the (comparative) lack of property destruction in the uprisings around Port-au-Prince. The mixed-race élite included property owners and they had an interest in maintaining plantations during and after the revolution. The majority of Haiti's population before and after emancipation did not share the mixed-race élite's idea of maintaining the plantation system. Thus, while Madiou negatively characterized the northern slave rebels, he exposed social divisions that shaped the revolution and independent Haiti. For Madiou and his contemporaries the narrative of the revolution needed to present a certain image of Haiti's founding, one that could not include either pillaging slaves or ex-slaves who remained neutral in the final war of independence. He implied that only select men could lead and govern Haiti which excluded the black majority who lacked (European) customs and education.

Though Madiou did not assign full agency to the enslaved, he offered the first chronology of slave resistance, which humanized the enslaved and made them contributors to the struggle for freedom and independence. Madiou began in the late-seventeenth century with the revolt of Padrejean, "the first important revolt of the Blacks, in whom the feeling of freedom germinated."[46] Although the French put down the revolt, Madiou's word choice recast slaves as active participants in the anti-colonial struggle that he dated from 1492. First, he referred to slaves as blacks, removing the colonial label that demarcated their status. Second, he claimed the rebelling blacks sought freedom. Madiou made an anachronistic move here: his reference to freedom meant not simply an escape from slavery but the principle of liberty as it came to be defined in the Age of Revolutions. Madiou continued this characterization with subsequent slave revolts and presented the enslaved as men who could understand and strive for the revolutionary principles of 1789.

Madiou aptly integrated colonial slave resistance into his narrative. The August 1791 revolt and its leaders proved more challenging. Notable is the absence of the Bois Caïman ceremony.[47] Madiou, who did not shy away from including sensational details on cultural practices and local beliefs, only mentioned a meeting of leaders on the night of 14 August 1791. He recounted:

> On the night of August 14, 1791, 200 representatives of slave gangs from the Northern province gathered at the Lenormand plantation. There, a colored man read from an alleged royal decree in which the king accorded the slaves three days off a week. It was decided that the 22 of this month the rebellion would begin.[48]

Madiou secularized the first meeting and removed any spiritual influence. The presence of an unnamed colored man, who may or may not have been a slave, reading a fake royal decree demeans the role of the enslaved and their motivations. They were not the central actors here, and they planned a revolt simply based on a rumor.

Madiou's description is noteworthy because Dumesle, who also most likely conducted interviews, included a ceremony in his 1824 publication, and less than a decade later Madiou's contemporary, Beaubrun Ardouin, described a meeting and ceremony based on his brother Céligny's unpublished research. While the circle of Haitian intellectuals was quite small, Madiou may not have had access to Dumesle's text nor Céligny's work.[49] Perhaps he had not read Haitian accounts of the ceremony and thus did not include it. Moreover, Madiou's interviewees were most likely mixed-race officers who neither participated in Bois Caïman nor wanted to acknowledge the contributions of former slaves to their country's founding.[50]

In addition to limited sources or interviewee bias, the absence of the ceremony is illustrative of Madiou's and the élite's anti-Vodou stance. Previous scholars have commented on Madiou's personal judgments and his need to present a "respectable" (superstition and sorcery-free) Haiti.[51] For example, Kate Ramsey contends that in the mid-nineteenth-century foreign visitors constructed an idea of "vaudoux," which included "'fetishism,' sorcery, and black magic," as "proof of Haiti's lapse into barbarism."[52] The omission of Bois Caïman was perhaps a response to these foreign accounts. Moreover, Madiou's harsh criticism of the rebels' practices further delineated a line of respectability between the slaves and educated free men of color. In August 1791 and other revolts, Madiou described the slave leaders' reliance on superstition and the advice of sorcerers and magicians.[53] Despite Madiou's disdain, he admitted that these beliefs inspired troops. He wrote almost in wonder of the power of Hyacinthe, an insurgent leader from the West: "Hyacinthe ran throughout the rows of slaves armed with a bull's tail, saying I could send back bullets." Madiou's awe is joined with a feeling of regret for the lives lost due to ignorance of European weaponry. He lamented:

> Insurgents grabbed the canons, and embraced them. They were killed without ever letting go. Others dug their arms into the canons to stop the balls, and addressing their comrades in arms cried: "Come, come we've got them!" The canons fired and body parts scattered everywhere.[54]

Madiou's portrayal of slaves places them in the center of the narrative as initiators in the anti-colonial struggle, though one doomed to fail without guidance from the élite. Although slaves desired liberty, their early revolts did not succeed because they lacked the inspiring principles of the French Revolution and the guidance of free people of color. Moreover, their actions during the Haitian Revolution suffered from a combination of the ignorance in which slavery kept them and their reliance on "primitive" African traditions like sorcery and superstition. Black leaders who rose above these nefarious influences, such as Toussaint Louverture and Jean-Jacques Dessalines, struggled with the legacy of colonialism and slavery. Madiou excused their actions because they had grown up in slavery and contended race was not a factor. Overall, though, his representations of gens de couleur and slaves demonstrate the importance of cultural hybridity. He contended it was only through alliances and exchanges between the Afro-descended population that the revolution succeeded and Haiti would succeed. Nevertheless, these exchanges were frequently one-sided. They focused on the black majority's adoption of European customs and values, symbols of their and, by extension, the nation's progress and civilization.

Madiou's histories appeared at the same time as the mixed-race élite's political machine's politique de doublure came crashing down.[55] Faustin Soulouque (an illiterate former slave) consolidated power in his own hands and proceeded to arrest and execute many of the men who had "elected" him to office, including friends and family of the final author examined here, Beaubrun Ardouin. Ardouin escaped death because he was serving as a diplomat in Paris. After the news of his half-brother Céligny's death he remained in Paris, now an exile. A witness to the ridicule of Haiti and its "primitiveness" in the foreign press, Ardouin decided to write his own history of Haiti to counter foreign perceptions and correct flaws in Madiou's account.[56] To reach French readers, Ardouin's 11 volumes were all published with in Paris, in contrast to Madiou who published in Haiti.

Beaubrun Ardouin was also of mixed European and African descent. In contrast to Haiti's early authors, Beaubrun and his brothers were self-educated. They grew up in the Nippes region and experienced the final years of the revolution from this small southern port. Beaubrun did not remember the war between Toussaint Louverture and André Rigaud (1799–1800) or the invasion of the French (1802–1803), which happened during his earliest years. Nevertheless, the results of both campaigns impacted the family, particularly Louverture's confiscation of his father's property in 1800. The family's memories of the war and suppression of Rigaud supporters tempered Ardouin's vision of Haiti's history. Moreover, Ardouin's father's politics impacted his career in independent

Haiti.[57] Like Madiou, Ardouin benefited from his father's alliances and found employment with various state offices including the national printer. A supporter of Pétion and his successor Boyer, Ardouin quickly rose in the republican government of Port-au-Prince. Through his own position and his father's relationships with revolutionary generals, Ardouin had access to national archives and the ability to interview key figures in the Haitian Revolution.[58]

In the opening lines of his introduction, Ardouin eloquently expressed the desires of a postcolonial historian. He explained, "I wanted to just try and examine from the point of view natural to a Haitian, and in opposition to the countless foreign authors who had themselves considered this history from their perspective."[59] Similar to the first generation of authors and his peers, Ardouin declared that Haiti's history needed to be written by Haitians because history had a didactic value and passed along lessons to the next generations (*Etudes*, 1:3). Ardouin expounded, when these lessons were properly presented, they could unite the citizenry, increase patriotism, and educate the masses (*Etudes*, 1:16).

In spite of his hostility towards Madiou, Ardouin arrived at similar claims in support of mixed-race leadership and viewed the western free men of color as slaves' "natural protectors" (*Etudes*, 1:204). Although Ardouin applauded the work of free people of color, he made one of the largest contributions to integrating the black majority in the revolution's history. His narrative offers the most detailed discussion of the Bois Caïman ceremony. Ardouin credited his brother Céligny for the account (*Etudes*, 1:226). Céligny explained his source was Paul Aly, a subordinate of Toussaint Louverture, who in 1841 was a Haitian military officer in Santo Domingo.[60] Céligny named the leaders, all "the most intimate friends" of Louverture and, like Hérard Dumesle, proposed there was a meeting and ceremony, though the two accounts differ on location and date (*Etudes*, 1:229). For the Ardouins and Dumesle the organization of the uprising included a religious element, whereas Madiou described only a secular meeting. Moreover, the Ardouin brothers were the first Haitian authors to depict Boukman as a priest. There is a significant distinction in how each brother described him, though.

Beaubrun claimed that his entire section on Bois Caïman came from his brother's unpublished work (*Etudes*, 1:226). In volume 1 of *Etudes* (1853) he wrote, "Boukman also had recourse to the magical influence of fetishism" (*Etudes*, 1:299). In contrast, Céligny's book, posthumously published by his brother in 1865, used a different adjective: "Boukman also had recourse to the terrible."[61] David Geggus suggests that Beaubrun changed his brother's text when he incorporated it into his 1853 history. It is equally likely, given the historical context of each publication, that Beaubrun used Céligny's original text in 1853 but altered it before it went to press in 1865. Three major changes had occurred by 1865 that could have influenced the harsher judgment implied by the replacement of "magical" with "terrible." One, the Vatican finally recognized Haiti in 1860 and French priests arrived in 1864 to take over religious and educational instruction. Two, at the same time the priests arrived a notorious case of cannibalism was passing through the Haitian court system, "l'affaire de Bizoton." If foreign visitors were already employing images of sorcery and cannibalism to illustrate Haiti's return to black savagery, the Bizoton affair did not help improve this image. Lastly, the new mixed-race president Fabre Geffrard passed legislation that further criminalized Vodou practices in 1864.[62] Beaubrun returned to a Haiti in which the élite were far more suspicious of popular beliefs and intent on eliminating them than they had been in 1841 when Céligny wrote the Bois Caïman account.

Fetishism was an obstacle in Haiti's march to becoming a civilized nation. Thus, Beaubrun may have changed the adjective in the 1865 printing to match the new anti-Vodou sentiments.

Ardouin's portrait of Bois Caïman is just part of his interpretation of slaves' role in the revolution. Similar to Madiou, he also constructed a genealogy of resistance to illustrate that slaves were capable of understanding the idea of liberty. Ardouin asserted, "up to the time of the Saint-Domingue revolution, the blacks [slaves] proved time and again that the love of liberty was as powerful in them as in other men."[63] Unlike Madiou, he began the tradition with a Taino rebel, cacique Henry (Enriquillo).[64] Ardouin extended the love of liberty to other oppressed people and connected Haiti's struggle for freedom to the desire to avenge the island's first native population (*Etudes*, 1:217). The capacity of slaves and other oppressed peoples to desire freedom and liberty made them human in Ardouin's narrative and demonstrated their potential for becoming allies in the revolution.

Nonetheless, like Madiou and earlier authors, Ardouin hesitated to assign the slaves full agency. This reluctance is most apparent in his discussion of Bois Caïman, which included a detailed analysis of the various reasons for it.[65] Ardouin suggested that former members of Ogé's band, who hid themselves in the mountains, helped organize the revolt.[66] Using his brother Céligny's interview with Aly (Louverture's subordinate), Ardouin also contended that Toussaint Louverture played a central role in organizing the revolt, though on behalf of the royalists of Cap Français.[67] These two assertions illustrated Ardouin's larger arguments regarding the role of free people of color as revolutionary guides. Moreover, his description reveals an ambiguous notion of slave agency. He resolved, "the slaves took advantage of all the groups' intentions to serve them as auxiliaries, as instruments."[68] Here the slaves both take advantage of the situation but also serve as the instruments of the royalist planters and free people of color. Ardouin's contradiction obscures slaves' actions but also acknowledges the complex web of motivations and rivalries of revolutionary Saint-Domingue.

Ardouin's portrait of the rebelling slaves presents an additional contradiction: the celebration of Haitians' (biological) African heritage and denigration of African culture. Similar to Madiou his narrative includes descriptions of early Vodou practices. Through his characterization of Boukman and other insurgent leaders like Halao, as well as the Congo bands, he condemned these traditions and their primitiveness, yet not African ancestry.[69] Through (European) education, Afro-descendants could become civilized and progressive. In a later volume, he eloquently explained the postcolonial dilemma:

> For it must be said once and for all, in the past, as now, the mulatto and black of this country had accepted and must always accept with pride their African origins and not be ashamed in the face of colonial prejudices. They had and still have to vigorously suppress all the ideas, all the practices born of the barbarism of Africa that are irreconcilable with the civilization of the people.[70]

Ardouin captured the contradiction of nineteenth-century Haitian intellectuals. They were of African descent and justified in their literary combat their existence to a world dominated by European and American racism and imperialism. Haitian authors celebrated the achievements of black men in the revolution. However, to refute white publications, they had to work within the contemporary Eurocentric rhetoric that defined civilization and progress according to European norms. Thus, Ardouin's vehement anti-Vodou stance and his characterization of African culture as barbarous and uncivilized are attempts to champion Haiti's civilization by distinguishing the African culture as less and less Haitian.

Conclusion

These first generations of authors composed histories of Haiti's founding which articulated the themes of anti-colonialism and anti-slavery and celebrated the unity of Haitians as Afro-descendants. These postcolonial histories were framed by internal factors including social divisions both inherited from the colonial past and newly created by independence. Beyond such domestic issues, Haiti's position as a post-slavery state run by men of African descent in a world of colonialism, racism, and slavery meant Haitian authors faced barriers that their American and French counterparts did not when narrating their nation's founding. Bearing witness on the international scene became important rhetorical strategies to both narrate the revolution and justify Haiti's founding. Equally pressing was the need to present Haiti as a civilized country. Mixed-race authors faced the additional challenge of narrating the contributions of the black majority and the influence of African-derived traditions. The publishing boom of the mid-nineteenth century left an origin story that ambivalently integrated the enslaved. In particular, Ardouin and Madiou detailed a history of resistance that incorporated slaves into the national narrative. The focus, though, remained on mixed-race men and the chosen black leaders (heroes) who are in the archive. It would take the crises of the early-twentieth century (U.S. Occupation and First World War) to overturn the Eurocentric hierarchy of culture and create a space to rehabilitate and celebrate African culture alongside Haiti's French cultural heritage.

Notes

1. Gates, *Figures in Black*, 25 and Daut, *Tropics of Haiti*, 421.
2. David Nicholls spearheaded English-language scholarship on Haitian intellectual and political history in his seminal publication, *From Dessalines to Duvalier*. He argued that race, meaning Haitians' shared African descent, served to unite Haitians, while color, specifically the designations mulatto and black, divided the population and ultimately harmed the country's development. The most comprehensive response to Nicholls's black and mulatto legends is Marlene, Daut's *Tropics of Haiti*. Daut claims Nicholls's legends are an extension of these nineteenth-century racialized accounts that "blame nineteenth-century Haitians rather than the legacy of colonialism and slavery, or even the continuing threat of French invasion in the two decades after independence for the country's 'racial' divisions" (Daut, 22). In place of Nicholls's legends, she contends that publications that circulated in the Atlantic World racialized the revolution and portrayed it as an act of "'mulatto/a' revenge rather than for 'black' freedom" (Daut, 4–5).
3. Garraway, "Empire of Freedom," 3–4 and Bongie, *Preface*, 3.
4. Figueroa, *Prophetic Visions of the Past*, 13.
5. Johnson, *The Fear of French Negroes*, 175.
6. Peltier to Peele [sic], London, 27 June 1810. The National Archives, Kew (hereafter TNA): War Office, 1/79/407.
7. Chanlatte's date of birth is generally given as 1766. Max Bissainthe claims he died at age 60 in 1828, which would make his birth year 1768: Bissainthe, *Dictionnaire de bibliographie haïtienne*, 59.
8. For more on Chanlatte's family, see Geggus, "The Changing Faces of Toussaint Louverture," footnote 10; *Haitian Revolutionary Studies*, 301, note 71.

9. Madiou, *Histoire d'Haïti*, 1:130. Following the British invasion of 1793, Chanlatte sided, at least temporarily, with the occupation forces that controlled the west through the mid-1790s. With the withdrawal of the British and consolidation of French republican control under Toussaint Louverture, he apparently fled to the U.S.
10. Berrou and Pompilus, *Histoire de la littérature haïtienne*, 1:25.
11. Bongie, "The Cry of History," 811.
12. Ibid., 833.
13. "L'Inde, l'Égypte et la péninsule d'Espagne conservent encore quelques restes du glorieux passage de leurs ancêtres ... " Chanlatte, *Le Cri de la nature*, 7. James Sidbury has noted a similar use of Egypt in the Anglophone Black Atlantic, see Sidbury, *Becoming African*, 42, 73.
14. "Désavouer en nous l'unité d'espèce, poser en fait notre infériorité morale, c'était légitimer en quelque sorte le traffic des vendeurs de chair humaine et constituer en principe le droit de l'esclavage." Chanlatte, *Le Cri de la nature*, 9.
15. Ibid., 11.
16. Ibid., 17.
17. "Dès lors l'hydre de l'esclavage reçut les premières blessures, et cette impulsion électrique se communique d'un bout de l'île à l'autre," Chanlatte, *Le Cri de la nature*, 29.
18. "Tant de barbaries, d'exécutions inouïes nous ayant forcés de nous jeter dans les bois, le cri de la vengeance a résonné de toutes parts," Chanlatte, *Le Cri de la nature*, 53.
19. "Article 14," Haiti, *Constitutions of the World*.
20. "Acte de Baptême," Jean Louis Vastey, 29 March 1788, quoted in Daut, "From Classical French Poet," 36. An earlier Haitian source, Vastey's own grandson, Haitian author Oswald Durand, recounted the arrival of his great-grandfather from France in 1769, see Durand, "Tournée Littéraire," 403–404.
21. Daut, "From Classical French Poet," 37.
22. Madiou, *Histoire*, 6: 127–129 and Nicholls, "Pompée Valentin Vastey," 129.
23. For specific appeals to a Haitian audience, see Vastey, *Le Cri de la Patrie*, 5; *A Mes concitoyens haïtiens*, 6, 15; and *Le Cri de la conscience*, 14.
24. Bongie, trans. *The Colonial System Unmasked*; Daut, "The 'Alpha and Omega' of Haitian Literature"; Daut, "From Classical French Poet to Militant Haitian Statesman"; and Garraway, "Empire of Freedom."
25. Bongie, "'Monotonies of History'," 82 and Garraway, "Empire of Freedom," 12.
26. "Avant la révolution de 1789, la population d'Hayti se divisait en trois castes distinctes qui se subdivisaient entre elles suivant les préjugés établis par le Système Colonial," Vastey, *Essai sur les causes*, 3.
27. "Le voile de l'erreur et du mensonge s'était enfin déchiré: au soleil radieux de l'indépendance, toutes les factions se dissolvèrent comme un vent impétueux disperse les nuages; notre atmosphère épurée par la victoire, nous commençâmes à respire l'air pur de la liberté et de l'indépendance!" Vastey, *Essai sur les causes*, 38.
28. " ... un lui donnant les épithètes de sauvages malfaisans et de nègres marrons," Vastey, *Le Cri de la conscience*, 17.
29. Dash, "Before and Beyond Negritude," 531.
30. Ramsey, *The Spirits and the Law*, 63.
31. The paper included sections on politics, current events, and literature and espoused similar pro-republic ideology. It appears to have only run for one year, 1819.
32. For a discussion of Bois Caïman and the historiographical debates surrounding it, see Geggus, *Haitian Revolutionary Studies*, 81–92. Recent controversy over Bois Caïman surfaced following the 2010 earthquake when American televangelist Pat Robertson claimed the ceremony was a pact with the devil.
33. Middelanis, "Les Mémoires," 100–101.
34. Ibid., 111.
35. "Vers le milieu du mois d'août 1791, les cultivateurs, manufacturiers et artisans deplusieurs ateliers se réunirent pendant la nuit, au milieu d'un violent orage dans une forêt épaisse qui

couvre le sommet du morne rouge, et là formèrent le plan d'une vaste insurrection qu'ils sanctifièrent par une cérémonie religieuse," Dumesle, *Voyage*, 85.

36. Trouillot, "En Faveur d'une Littérature Indigène," 84.
37. Trouillot, *Les Origines Sociales*, 122 and Charles, "Les Contes Créoles," 87.
38. Nau, "Un Episode," 15 December 1836, 8 and Zavitz, "Encountering Creole genesis," 90–91.
39. Nau, "Un Episode," 15 December 1836, 8.
40. Ramsey, *The Spirits and the Law*, 5.
41. Hebblethwaite, *Vodou Songs*, 246.
42. A third historian, Joseph Saint-Rémy also wrote three histories of the revolution in this time period; however, I have chosen to focus on the interventions of Madiou and for this piece.
43. Pressoir, Trouillot, and Trouillot, *Historiographie d'Haïti*, 137.
44. "la race africaine transplantée en Haïti," Madiou, *Histoire d'Haïti*, 1:iii.
45. "Quelle différence entre cette insurrection des esclaves de l'Ouest dirigés par les affranchis, et celles des esclaves du Nord, livrés à eux-mêmes! D'une part l'ordre, le respect des propriétés, pas un assassinat; d'une autre part, désordre, pillage et affreuses vengeances." Madiou, *Histoire*, 1:132.
46. "Ainsi fut éteinte cette première révolte importante de Noirs chez lesquels naissait le sentiment de la liberté." Madiou, *Histoire*, 1:27.
47. Geggus, *Haitian Revolutionary Studies*, 83.
48. "Dans la nuit du 14 Août 1791, 200 députés des ateliers de la province du Nord se réunirent sur l'habitation Lenormand. Là, un homme de couleur leur donna lecture d'un prétendu dècret, par lequel le roi leur accordai trois jours de liberté par semaine. Il y fut décidé que le 22 du même mois l'insurrection serait générale." Madiou, *Histoire*, 1:93. For Madiou's discussion of what he terms superstitions and fetishes: see *Histoire*, 1:96–98, 131–133, 234–235.
49. Beaubrun Ardouin admitted in his history that Dumesle's book was extremely rare in Haiti, thus Madiou may not have ever read it (*Etudes*, 3:528, note 1). In Madiou's first edition, Dumesle's name is never referenced, nor for that matter Dalmas's, the first French publication based on eyewitness accounts of the uprising.
50. Madiou, *Histoire*, 1:xiii.
51. Nicholls, *From Dessalines*, 88; Dayan, *Haiti, History, and the Gods*, 9; and Ramsey, *The Spirits and the Law*, 62–63.
52. Ramsey, *The Spirits and the Law*, 80.
53. Madiou, *Histoire*, 1:96, 131, 234.
54. Ibid., 132.
55. Politics of the understudy was a system in which the élite, frequently lighter-skinned, would select a black presidential candidate who would rule as a puppet. Having a black president would appease the majority of Haitians while also giving the mixed-race élite control to run the government and support their interests.
56. For details on international reactions to Soulouque, see Hoffmann and Middelanis, *Faustin Souluque d'Haïti*.
57. Trouillot, *Beaubrun Ardouin*, 11–12.
58. Ibid., 15.
59. "J'ai voulu seulement essayer de l'examiner au point du vue naturel à un Haïtien, et par opposition à tant d'autres étrangers qui ont eux-mêmes considéré cette histoire à leur point de vue." Ardouin, *Etudes*, 1: 1. Subsequent references to this volume will appear in textual parentheses.
60. Ardouin, *Essais*, 16, n6. Dumesle placed the event in "the middle of August," while Céligny Ardouin gave the specific date 14 August (Dumesle, *Voyage*, 85; Ardouin, *Essais*, 17).
61. Ardouin, *Essais*, 17.
62. Ramsey, *The Spirits and the Law*, 83.
63. " … jusqu'à l'époque de la révolution de la colonie française, les noirs prouvèrent, de temps à autre que l'amour de la liberté était aussi puissant en eux que parmi les autres hommes," Ardouin, *Etudes*, 1:220.

64. Earlier authors had also recounted the story of Enriqullo, see Prévost's, *Relation des glorieux évenemens*, xv–xxi and Vastey's, *Le Système colonial*, 10–12.
65. These passages are also a fascinating example of Ardouin's breadth of sources and his methodology of quoting at length from sources to demonstrate competing viewpoints, see Ardouin, *Etudes*, 1: 220–231.
66. Ardouin, *Etudes*, 1:220.
67. Ibid., 1:226–227.
68. "les esclaves profitèrent des dispositions de tous les partis à se servir d'eux comme des auxiliaires, des instrumens[sic] … ", Ardouin, *Etudes*, 1:232.
69. For Halaou's description see Ardouin, *Etudes*, 2:352; Ardouin presented the Congos as "ignorant bands," *Etudes*, 5:374.
70. "Car il faut le dire une fois pour toutes, si à ces époques reculées, comme aujourd'hui encore, le mulâtre et le noir de ce pays ont dû et doivent toujours accepter avec fierté leur origines africaines, ne pas en rougir devant les préjugés coloniaux, ils ont dû et doivent encore réprimer vigoureusement toutes ces idées, toutes ces pratiques née de la barbarie de l'Afrique et inconciliables avec la civilisation du peuple." Ardouin, *Etudes*, 2:362.

Acknowledgements

I am grateful to Brenden Kennedy, Robert Taber, and Charlton Yingling for their insightful feedback on earlier versions of this article. I am also indebted to the two anonymous reviewers' comments. All translations are my own.

Disclosure statement

No potential conflict of interest was reported by the author.

Funding

Research for this article was supported by the American Philosophical Society [Franklin Grant] and the University of Montana Western.

ORCID

Erin Zavitz http://orcid.org/0000-0002-1144-290X

Bibliography

Ardouin, Beaubrun. *Études sur l'historie d'Haïti suivies de la vie du général J.M. Borgella*. Paris: Dezobry et Magdeleine, 1853–1860.
Ardouin, Céligny. *Essais sur l'histoire d'Haïti*. Port-au-Prince: Chez T. Bouchereau, 1865.
Berrou, Raphaël, and Pradel Pompilus. *Histoire de la littérature haïtienne: illustrée par les textes*. Port-au-Prince: Éditions Caraïbes, 1975–1977.

Bissainthe, Max. *Dictionnaire de Bibliographie Haitienne*. Metuchen, NJ: Scarecrow Press, 1973.

Bongie, Chris. "'Monotonies of History': Baron de Vastey and the Mulatto Legend of Derek Walcott's 'Haitian Triology'." *Yale French Studies* 107 (2005): 70–107.

Bongie, Chris. Preface to the *Colonial System Unmasked*, by Pompée Valentin Vastey, 1–10. Liverpool: University of Liverpool Press, 2014.

Bongie, Chris. "The Cry of History: Juste Chanlatte and the Unsettling (Presence) of Race in Early Haitian Literature." *Modern Language Notes* 130, no. 4 (2015): 807–835.

Chanlatte, Juste. *Le Cri de la nature*. Cap Haïtien: Chez P. Roux, Imp. de l'Etat, 1810.

Charles, Christophe Philippe. "Les Contes Créoles d'Ignace Nau." In *Isalina ou Une Scène Créole*, edited by Christophe Philippe Charles, 87–91. Port-au-Prince: Editions Choucoune, 2013.

Dash, J. Michael. "Before and Beyond Negritude." In *A History of Literature in the Caribbean: Volume 1 Hispanic and Francophone Regions*, edited by Albert James, Julio Rodriguez-Luis, and J. Michael Dash Arnold, 529–546. Amsterdam: J. Benjamins, 1994.

Daut, Marlene L. "From Classical French Poet to Militant Haitian Statesman: The Early Years and Poetry of the Baron de Vastey." *Research in African Literatures* 43, no. 1 (2012): 35–57.

Daut, Marlene L. "The Alpha and Omega of Haitian Literature': Baron de Vastey and the U.S. Audience of Haitian Political Writing." *Comparative Literature* 64, no. 1 (2012): 49–72.

Daut, Marlene L. *Tropics of Haiti: Race and the Literary History of the Haitian Revolution in the Atlantic World, 1789–1865*. Liverpool: Liverpool University Press, 2015.

Dayan, Joan. *Haiti, History, and the Gods*. Berkeley: University of California Press, 1995.

Dumesle, Hérard. *Voyage dans le Nord d'Hayti ou revelations des lieux et des monumens historiques*. Imp. du Gouvernement: Aux Cayes, 1824.

Durand, Oswald. "Tournée Littéraire." *Haïti Littéraire et Sociale* (20 September 1905), 403–404.

Figueroa, Víctor. *Prophetic Visions of the Past: Pan-Caribbean Representations of the Haitian Revolution*. Columbus: Ohio State University Press, 2015.

Garraway, Doris. "Empire of Freedom, Kingdom of Civilization: Henry Christophe, the Baron de Vastey, and the Paradoxes of Universalism in Postrevolutionary Haiti." *Small Axe: A Caribbean Journal of Criticism* 16, no. 3 (2012): 1–21.

Gates, Henry Louis, Jr. *Figures in Black: Words, Signs, and the "Racial" Self*. New York: Oxford University Press, 1987.

Geggus, David. *Haitian Revolutionary Studies*. Bloomington: Indiana University Press, 2002.

Geggus, David. "The Changing Faces of Toussaint Louverture: Literary and Pictorial Descriptions." John Carter Brown Library. Accessed April 2013. http://www.brown.edu/Facilities/John_Carter_Brown_Library/toussaint/index.ht.

Haiti, Imperial Constitution. (1805). *Constitutions of the World*. http://www.modern-constitutions.de/nbu.php?page_id=02a1b5a86ff139471c0b1c57f23ac196&show_doc=HT-00-1805-05-20-fr.

Hebblethwaite, Benjamin. *Vodou Songs in Haitian Creole and English*. Philadelphia, PA: Temple University Press, 2012.

Hoffmann, Léon-François. *Haitian Fiction Revisted*. Pueblo, CO: Passeggiata Press, 1999.

Johnson, Sara. *The Fear of French Negroes: Transcolonial Collaboration in the Revolutionary Americas*. Berkeley: University of California Press, 2012.

Madiou, Thomas. *Histoire d'Haïti*. 1847–48. Reprint. Port-au-Prince: Henri Deschamps, 1988–1991.

Middelanis, Carl Hermann. "Les Mémoires fleurissent dans les lieux ruinés: Le *Voyage dans le Nord d'Hayti* ou les paradoxes de l'historiographie d'une jeune Nation." *Ethnologies* 28, no. 1 (2006): 99–118.

Nau, Ignace. 1836. "Un Episode de la révolution: connte créole." *Le Républicain*, December 15.

Nicholls, David. "Pompée Valentin Vastey: Royalist and Revolutionary." *Revista de Historia de América* 109 (1990): 129–143.

Nicholls, David. *From Dessalines to Duvalier: Race, Colour and National Independence in Haiti*. 2nd ed. New Brunswick, NJ: Rutgers University Press, 1996.

Pressoir, Catts, Ernst Trouillot, and Hénock Trouillot. *Historiographie d'Haiti*. Mexico, DF: Instituto Panamericano de Geografía e Historia, 1953.

Prévost, Julien. *Relation des glorieux événemens qui ont porté Leurs Majestés Royales sur le trône d'Hayti*. Cap-Henry: R. Roux, 1811.

Ramsey, Kate. *The Spirits and the Law: Vodou and Power in Haiti*. Chicago, IL: Chicago University Press, 2011.

Sidbury, James. *Becoming African in America: Race and Nation in the English Black Atlantic, 1760–1830*. New York: Oxford University Press, 2007.

Trouillot, Hénock. *Beaubrun Ardouin: L'homme politique et l'historien*. Port-au-Prince: Instituto Panamericano de Geografía e historia, 1950.

Trouillot, Hénock. *Les Origines sociales de la littérature haïtienne*. Port-au-Prince: Éditions Fardin, 1962.

Trouillot, Hénock. "En faveur d'une littérature indigene." In *Isalina ou une Scène Créole*, edited by Christophe Philippe Charles, 68–86. Port-au-Prince: Editions Choucoune, 2013.

Trouillot, Michel-Rolph. *Silencing the Past: Power and the Production of History*. Boston, MA: Beacon Press, 1997.

Vastey, Valentin Pompée (Baron de). *Le Système colonial dévoilé*. Cap-Henry: P. Roux Imp. du Roi, 1814.

Vastey, Valentin Pompée (Baron de). *A Mes concitoyens haïtiens*. Cap-Henry: Chez P. Roux, 1815.

Vastey, Valentin Pompée (Baron de). *Le Cri de la conscience*. Cap-Henry: Chez P. Roux, 1815.

Vastey, Valentin Pompée (Baron de). *Le Cri de la patrie*. Cap-Henry: Chez P. Roux, 1815.

Vastey, Valentin Pompée (Baron de). *Essai sur les causes de la révolution et des guerres civiles d'Hayti*. Sans-Souci: L'Imprimerie Royale, 1819.

Zavitz, Erin. "Encountering Creole genesis in the Haitian Press: Massillon Coicou's fin-de-siècle feuilleton 'La Noire'." In *La Española – Isla de Encuentros*, edited by Jessica Barzen, Hanna L. Geiger, and Silke Jansen, 87–98. Tübingen: Narr Francke Attempto, 2015.

A case of hidden genocide? Disintegration and destruction of people of color in Napoleonic Europe, 1799–1815

Margaret B. Crosby-Arnold

ABSTRACT
Migration, social mobility, and integration of new populations in late eighteenth-century Europe resulted in an expansion of diversity, which contributed to abolition and culminated in full civil rights between 1791 and 1799. This revolutionary experiment in equality faced both domestic and multinational opposition, which led to the genocidal purge of diversity in Europe and the wider world during the Napoleonic Era.

Monsieur le Préfet, a few particular and temporary circumstances led to the refusal of passports to people of color requesting to return to St. Thomas or St. Domingue. At present, however, there are only disadvantages without any benefits to keeping these people in France. They are a corruption to the purity of European blood and most are dependent on the government. As a result, you are kindly instructed that there should be no obstacles whatsoever in your *département* preventing the departure of people of color, of any age or sex, that want to return to the island of St. Domingue or that of St. Thomas.[1]

Marked by global, economic, civil, and total warfare rolled into one, the French Revolutionary and Napoleonic wars raged continuously from the slave insurrections of the 1790s through at least the last battles in the second week of August 1815, when British forces invaded Guadeloupe, to secure "the French colonies in the West Indies to the Crown of France."[2] Taking into account the Napoleonic expeditions to the sugar islands in 1801 and the genocidal warfare that ensued, the Treaty of Amiens (1802) cannot be considered a peace. "Mass killings and atrocities were so widespread," Philip Dwyer writes, "that they would appear to be an integral if not an accepted part of warfare during the Revolutionary and Napoleonic periods."[3] The warfare of total extirpation that had been reserved for enslaved insurgents in the colonies reversed sail to be applied against the market populations of Europe. In the aftermath of such horrors, Europe was strewn with a variety of voluntary and involuntary migrants, displaced persons, refugees, and as the 7 March 1817 circular indicates, entirely unwanted populations that the post-war French empire continued to see as threatening the "purity of European blood."

The circular, issued by the *Secrétaire d'État*, responded to numerous requests from *département* officials about what to do with leftover populations of color, many still held in so-called *dépôts*. While the history of diversity is just organizing as a subfield, a growing body of scholarship points toward diversity in the *longue durée* of metropolitan

European history.[4] The question, then, is what catastrophic event occurred to cause the virtual disappearance of these global populations? This article seeks to bring a hidden genocide out of the shadows of forgotten historical and collective memory, one that commenced almost immediately with the *coup* of November 1799 that propelled Napoleon Bonaparte to power. People of color were a heterogeneous population that was ever more broadly defined by an increasing dictatorial and imperial regime to encompass all *non-blancs*, *blancs* not quite culturally *blanc* enough and even their sympathizers, often referred to as *Negrophiles*. Napoleonic imperialism had as its aim the construction of a new Europe, at the heart of which, I argue, was a violent mission of to purge diversity of color. Like the First Empire's legal codes, *lycées* and monuments, this project of sociopolitical engineering survived well beyond the Battle of Waterloo.[5]

What constitutes genocide?

The most obvious catastrophe that led Raphaël Lemkin to conceptualize "genocide" was Nazi Germany's attempted annihilation of Jewish populations.[6] His conception and analysis of genocide was, however, much broader and, as the title of his book *Axis Rule in Occupied Europe* indicates, genocide was more than the particular, horrific violations and mass-violence against Jewish populations. While Jews were "one of the main objects of German genocide policy," the peoples of occupied Europe on the whole were also objects of that policy, and Lemkin pointed toward the implementation of German administrative, police, law, court, property, finance, and labor systems across the occupied regions.[7] "A group," as Samantha Power writes, "did not have to be physically exterminated to suffer genocide."[8] Rather, as Lemkin explained:

> It is intended rather to signify a coordinated plan of different actions aiming at the destruction of essential foundations of the life of national groups, with the aim of annihilating the groups themselves. The objectives of such a plan would be disintegration of the political and social institutions, of culture, language, national feelings, religion, and the economic existence of national groups, and the destruction of the personal security, liberty, health, dignity, and even the lives of the individuals belonging to such groups. Genocide is directed against the national group as an entity, and the actions involved are directed against individuals, not in their individual capacity, but as members of the national group.[9]

For those populations subjected to genocide in the extreme – "a process of liquidation" – mass-killing was only one dimension of the physical technique (77–78). This also included physical debilitation, achieved through starvation, discrimination in feeding and/or endangering of health through deprivation of basic needs, such a blankets, adequate clothing or medicine, and forced labor (87–88).

While Lemkin emphasized the importance of a biological element, this had to do with the attainment of national superiority. Genocide was more destructive than injuries suffered during warfare and would leave the German people "stronger than subjugated peoples after the war even if the German army [was] defeated" (81). Policies of genocide were characterized by absorption, forced cooperation, and despoliation. Effected through the destruction of a given national pattern and imposition of a German one, absorption aimed "at the complete assimilation of a given area with the political, cultural, social, and economic institutions of the Greater Reich" (8–9). By forced cooperation, he meant, "full economic cooperation and, in part, as to certain groups, political cooperation as well" (9). Despoliation involved targeting a zone for purposes of economic exploitation, namely "raw materials, food and labor" (9). Administration could be direct, or through the placement of Reich commissioners, military commanders or co-opting of local officials. "Because the aims of the German occupation [were] not limited to military considerations, but [were] directed toward the integration of the occupied countries into the 'New European Order' under German hegemony," local laws were incompatible with this aim (25). Accordingly, genocide's social technique was accomplished through the abolition of local laws and law courts and the imposition of German law and law courts, including Germanization of the judicial language and bar (83).

Lemkin identified six additional techniques of genocide. The political technique was the destruction of local institutions of self-governance through the imposition of German forms and could include obliterating symbols of former national character by tearing down commercial signs and/or inscriptions on buildings. Rigid control of cultural expression, including education, language, and media were representative of the cultural technique. The economic technique, "[t]he destruction of the foundations of the economic existence of a national group," as he wrote, "necessarily brings a crippling of its development, even a retrogression" (85). In occupied countries of "people of non-related blood," biological techniques of depopulation were pursued, including the adoption of measures designed to decrease birthrates (86). The religious technique included the destruction of religious leadership, pillaging and destruction of church property and/or the attempt to disrupt religious influences in occupied zones, and, finally, there was the moral technique of encouraging and/or inducing populations to self-destructive forms of behavior (89–90).

Unfortunately, Lemkin's broad understanding was obscured by what scholars of critical genocide studies have identified as the problem of "the Twentieth-Century Core with the Holocaust both foregrounded and backgrounded."[10] Lemkin, however, was "keenly interested in colonial genocides," viewing "colonialism as an integral part of a world history of genocide."[11] In contrast to the limited perspective of holocaust studies, critical genocide scholars have recovered Lemkin's broader conception and revolutionized understanding of genocide.[12] As a result, critical genocide studies has become a robust new field of research, with the history of genocide encompassing almost every period of history, region of the world and current of intellectual thought.[13]

A genocidal general, economic crisis, and wars of expansion

I have detailed a broader conception of genocide because, outside of critical genocide studies, there is a tendency to cling to the limited notion of physical annihilation. There remains a reluctance to call a spade a spade and acknowledge that the global power that was Napoleonic France committed genocide, not only in its possessions beyond Europe's shores, but also across occupied Europe where French administration was imposed and resistance to same resulted in retaliatory massacres. As Ben Kiernan argues, it is anachronistic not to recognize the occurrence of genocide in earlier periods, because early moderns operated with an understanding of genocide as a crime against humanity, even though they termed it variously, "holocaust," "crimes against humanity," "extermination," "extirpation," "annihilation," and/or "driving out by force."[14] At the same time, in his important studies on the Napoleonic Era and violence, Philip Dwyer makes it clear that "[t]here is no room for doubt that massacres were widespread and deliberate." [15] After the taking of Jaffa in March 1799, the army under Napoleon's command force-marched between 2400 and 3000 prisoners to the beach and slaughtered them.[16] Amongst the soldiers, a "traffic in young women" soon ensued in exchange for various other looted objects.[17] The resulting disorder did not lead to the protection of the women, but rather Napoleon ordered that they be brought to the hospital courtyard, where "they were promptly executed by a company of chasseurs." Yet, and undoubtedly out of an abundance of caution, even Dwyer stops short of suggesting genocide.

"All genocides have been contested," and, as René Lemarchand writes, there have always been those "willing to deny the undeniable."[18] Dancing around the obvious is a form of silence about what we may properly call the Napoleonic Genocide. It is a problem because it serves the purposes of denialism, "an extreme form of myth-making," where mythologies "promote revisionist assessments that stop short of denial."[19] "Revisionism," according to Lemarchand, "puts a radically new construction on the motivations and circumstances of genocidal violence," and "[m]ore often than not the presumed victims turn out to be the *génocidaires*, or else there are perpetrators on both sides, the result being double genocide."[20] As it relates to the reinstatement of slavery, Philippe Girard suggests that "to understand Bonaparte's seeming abrupt policy shifts in 1799–1802, one should [...] stay clear of a philosophical, racial, or ethnical approach to the emancipation debate."[21] Rather, he argues that the Consulate "was a pragmatic, post-ideological regime that strove to leave behind the conjectural disputes associated with the earlier phases of the French Revolution and to focus on what was politically and militarily feasible."[22] In "Caribbean Genocide," the population resisting re-enslavement becomes the *génocidaires*.[23] After detailing what the commander of the Saint Domingue expedition, Charles Leclerc, described as a "war of extermination," Girard concludes that "the atrocities committed in 1802–1803 constitute a blot on the French imperial record," but contrary to some historians' claims, they emerged locally in response to military setbacks rather than as part of a policy of extermination designed in Paris.[24] Napoleon was not responsible for the atrocities, because per Girard, he "made no call for the eradication of the population of color."[25] The atrocities in Girard's opinion did not "destroy in whole or in part" a racial group as set forth in Article 2 of the Genocide Convention.[26] It is "impossible to determine the number of people killed by the French with any precision," he writes. It is "difficult," according to Girard, to assess "intent" on the basis of "hyperbolic statements" by Leclerc or his successor, Donatien-Marie-Joseph Rochambeau, and, finally, it is not genocide because "the perpetrators of the atrocities were defeated."[27]

Part of the problem as it relates to failing to recognize genocide as part and parcel of Napoleonic imperialism stems from our narrow understanding of economic entanglement. With the publication of Kevin O'Rouke and Jeffrey Williamson's seminal study, *Globalization and History*, there is general agreement amongst economists and economic historians that expanding migration, cultural transfer, and transmission of diseases points towards the existence of a soft globalization in the eighteenth century.[28] Since then, ample research has shown that price convergence was already a factor in the early modern period, and globalization, marked by the integration of markets and trade, was also full-blown in the economic sense.[29] Atlantic history, according to Alison Games, is better understood as "a *slice* of world history," where "the Atlantic can offer a useful laboratory within which to examine regional and global transformations."[30]

"Virtually everywhere one looks in the Atlantic world in the early modern period," as Peter Coclanis argues, "one finds other worlds impinging on and often shaping developments."[31]

The Atlantic economy was entangled in a global economy, the whole of which by 1789 – in many of its facets – was dependent on the coerced cultivation of critical colonial commodities by enslaved populations of African descent in the Americas. In 1789 Amsterdam, the purchase of coffee produced in the French colony of Saint Domingue outstripped even purchases from Dutch Guiana, and, where coffee production had once been centered in the Middle East, 80% of the worlds coffee now came from the Americas.[32] "By the 1770s," according to Steven Topik, "French coffee from St. Domingue was replacing Yemini competitors in the Ottoman market of Cairo because it was cheaper, even [though] it had to cross the Atlantic and the Mediterranean."[33] By the second half of the eighteenth century the global coffee market – dominated by the French – was integrated; "prices now were quite stable from month to month and fairly comparable between Java and the Americas."[34]

Between 1733 and 1755, French colonial commodity production doubled, and, by 1730 as Richard Harding writes, "French sugar had driven British sugars out of the valuable European re-export market."[35] Between 1730 and 1790, the amount of French sugar returned to French ports jumped from 60 to 180 million pounds annually.[36] While Britain consumed the sugar that it produced between its home market and its colonies, "the *raison d' être* of the whole French sugar business was the re-export trade."[37] By the 1770s, 70% of French sugar was re-exported. Indeed, some 87–95% of all sugar arriving in Marseille between 1740 and 1775 was re-exported to Alpine Italy, the Italian Peninsula, Spain, and the Levant.[38] From the second quarter of the eighteenth century, French trade in the Levant overtook European competitors, and French sugar and coffee supplanted the older Egypt trade in these commodities. In 1686, England held 43.4% of the Istanbul trade to Venice's 2.6%, while France, with only 15.7% was still well below the 38.3% held by the Dutch. This had changed radically by 1750. France's share increased to 65.1% compared to 15.2% going to the British, 3.4% to the Dutch and 16.3% to Venice. Even more telling of the importance of the trade in critical colonial commodities from the Caribbean, before 1769, textiles, chiefly from Languedoc, accounted for 80% of French exports to the Levant. In the 1780s, textile exports declined to 40%, while West Indian sugar and coffee exports to the Levant increased to 30% and the dyestuffs indigo and cochineal grew to 15%.[39]

The economic centrality of the re-export trade meant that the slave uprisings in Guadeloupe and Saint Domingue in the 1790s were tantamount to an economic Armageddon, contributing to a deadly confluence of economic disaster, where the British had the goods and were desperate for a share greater share of the global market, especially after the loss of the North American market, while the French had the market, but no goods to supply demand. This economic reality is of critical importance for understanding why people of color were singled out, from the beginning of Napoleonic rule, as objects of Napoleonic Genocide. As Levene explains, extermination is most likely to occur when the oppressed under circumstances of hyper-exploitation revolt against their oppressors, "leading to the latter's retributive over-kill."[40] The deadly confluence of economic disaster also meant that the only way the French could retain dominance of global markets was, militarily, to occupy them to keep the British out. More than any other single factor, this explains the path of French troops, not only during the Napoleonic period, but also from the beginning of the French Revolutionary wars, and it meant that the diverse populations of the occupied markets of Europe or the eastern Mediterranean were also vulnerable to genocide.

Napoleon was acutely aware of France's situation and the economic *raison d'être* of the "revolutionary" wars before he came to power in 1799. The goal of expedition to Egypt was imperialism and economic exploitation of the region. Already in 1797, Talleyrand argued that the future "lay in colonial expansion – that is, in colonizing new lands with French citizens."[41] He felt a need to replace the colonies lost in the Americas with ones closer to home, namely, in Africa. "It was largely, because Bonaparte, with the support of Talleyrand" pressured the Directory that the expedition was approved, and, notably, over the objections of Jean-François Rewbell, who had authored the amendment of 17 May 1791 that extended full civil rights to free people of color.[42]

It is evident from Napoleon's various communications as head of the *Armée d'Orient* that he operated with a worldview bound-up with economic imperialism and hyper-exploitation. From Jaffa, just days after the bloody beach massacre, Napoleon wrote a detailed account of his exploits to the Executive Directory on 13 March 1799, closing with the comment that "the Army of the Republic is mistress of all Palestine."[43] Back in Cairo by the end of June, he wrote the *Chérif* of Mecca that "in the next season," he hoped that the *Chérif* would "send a large quantity of ships loaded with coffee and goods from India."[44] The same day, he wrote to the Sultan of Darfur, asking that he "please send by the first available caravan, 2,000 strong and energetic, black slaves (*esclaves noirs*), over the age of six."[45]

Peculiar republicans and strange bedfellows

On the fifth anniversary of Abolition, Étienne Laveaux told a crowd assembled in Paris: "In our colonies everything is French," and "[t]his system of absolute unity makes our disconcerted enemies go pale with rage."[46] The French experiment in colorblind liberty, equality, and fraternity was not perfect, and many resisted it. Nevertheless, civil equality was state policy between 1791 and 1799. The National Convention did more than abolish slavery on 4 February 1794. "In consequence," it decreed, "that all men, without distinction of color, residing in the colonies are French citizens and will enjoy all the rights assured by the Constitution."[47] It was not just an emancipation decree, but a civil rights act that brought people of color, including freemen, under the umbrella of equal civil rights protected by the state. Ratified by popular vote, the 1793 constitutional document held that "all men are equal by nature and before the law," and declared "resistance to oppression is the consequence of the other rights of man."[48] The importance of this for people of color cannot be emphasized enough. First, it was a complete rejection of natural – essentialized – difference, and, second, it allowed for constitutional repatriation of those freedmen who had borne arms of resistance against pre-emancipation France. In international perspective, however, recognition of the right to resistance lent legitimacy and justification, not only to pre-emancipation armed resistance of slaves in the revolutionary French Caribbean, but also to any that had occurred in the past or might in the future beyond the sovereign domains of France. While the Constitution of the Year III (1795) altered the form of government, creating the Directory, it confirmed colorblind, egalitarian policies. Its general provisions provided for "no superiority among citizens other than that of public functionaries, and that only in relation to the performance of duties."[49]

Colorblind liberty in the French world made peculiar republicans and strange bedfellows of sworn enemies in a quarter-century long period of insurrection and warfare. As a result of sharing the island, Spain was "enmeshed in the revolutionary unraveling" of Saint Domingue "from the start."[50] While officials initially remained neutral, taking a wait-and-see approach, they soon received overtures of alliance from leaders of the slave insurgency in the neighboring French colony. Curiously, the slave owning power that was the Spanish monarchy chose to ally with enslaved insurgents in hopes of defeating the French Republic, and as Ada Ferrer writes, "the slave revolution of August 1791 was now, in mid-1793, almost entirely at the service of Spain."[51] In the meantime, "behind the Jeffersonian Republican rhetoric of revolution" in the USA, there emerged "an increasing fear of both the revolutionary ideology and the social reality of France and Saint Domingue in the late 1790s and early 1800s."[52] When news of slave revolution in Saint Domingue reached his desk in 1791, Governor Effington of Jamaica declared "a common cause" with planters of the French colony and sent naval assistance.[53] Publicly, the British pointed toward the opening of the Scheldt River in 1792 by French occupation forces and other "causes" to justify joining the First Coalition, but the British Navy peeled a course across the Atlantic to the riches of the French Caribbean, where they offered protection for the property rights of slaveholders. In September 1793, British expeditionary forces disembarked in the most lucrative of France's colonial possessions, to a courteous welcome in Jérémie and Môle Saint Nicolas. By 1798 the British expedition to Saint Domingue faced total defeat at the hands of the freedman Toussaint Louverture and his largely self-emancipated troops.[54]

As usual, General Thomas Maitland could be counted upon to relay the situation and its consequences in raw terms. In September 1799, he wrote to George III on the necessary measures to protect the "valuable island" of Jamaica to "ensure the failure of any attempt that may be made against it, either by open force or concealed intrigue."[55] His Majesty was already aware of the measures "adopted there with a view to keep the Negro Chief Toussaint in such a disposition toward the British government as may ensure his not countenancing any attack on the island of Jamaica."[56] "The principle and sole object […] for which any connection was even entered into with that black Chief," he wrote in seething terms, "was merely as a precautionary measure […] to secure the island of Jamaica against attack," and whether or not the arrangement was "strictly adhered to" was immaterial.[57] In the meantime, it was the plight of the governor of Jamaica to keep Louverture appeased, regardless of any "degradation in holding any connection with a Negro."[58] Such ruse diplomacy would have to be kept up until fortune presented a better option of getting rid of the evils of what Maitland variously called the "revolutionary System of France" and the "French mania."[59]

In this climate of international hostility, two very different visions of French empire began to collide in 1798–1799.[60] In contrast to abolitionists like Laveaux, the Minister of the Navy, Étienne Eustache Bruix attempted the disintegration and, arguably, destruction of revolutionary soldiers of color serving in Europe. Born in Saint Domingue, Bruix got his maritime start on a French slaver, before rising through the ranks and serving in the expedition to Egypt. Billeted in deplorable conditions on French coastal island of Aix, more than 60 soldiers submitted a complaint to the Martiniquean representative of color to the Council of Five Hundred, Étienne Victor Mentor. "We are active military servicemen," they opened their complaint, and "we have not even touched half of our pay."[61] In addition to withholding their pay, suddenly, they were "not allowed to go to the mainland without permission from the Minister of the Navy at Rochefort, while white soldiers go there on the simple approval of the island's commander."[62] "Since the 3 Prairial Order" of Bruix, they continued:

> It is painfully clear that we are being frowned upon and treated badly. All of our comrades pray that you will look into their unhappy condition. We are nude, without clothing, subjected to tyranny, and deprived of the right to go to Rochefort to purchase little necessities that we are forced to pay crazy prices for here. When we arrived, we were billeted in tents with little straw and infested with vermin and insects. Winter is approaching and we are already freezing in the cold. You see for yourself the many men who have been crippled in the service of the Republic. If we are not going to Guadeloupe this year, please see to it that we are not reduced to this state over the winter because we are dying like flies here. Knowing your zeal, Citizen Representative, and your love for your fellow citizens, the black and of color officers of the Pedro naval unit submit their complaint to the Executive Directory about the humiliating separation from whites and request that they should be allowed to serve with their fellow soldiers in the armies of the Republic without discrimination.[63]

In March of 1799, Mentor published the soldiers' complaint in his own protest treatise, where he indentified Bruix as a "*créole et grand planteur de St. Domingue.*"[64] He successfully convinced the government to reject the disintegration, but, by early November, he was out of power, when he, the deputy from Saint Domingue, Pierre Thomany, and other representatives of color were effectively disintegrated from government by the *coup*.

Objects of state-sponsored genocide: People of color

The political disintegration and destruction of people of color came so swiftly that it is difficult to imagine that it was not an intended outcome or even a motivating force behind the *coup*. Talleyrand and Pierre Louis Roederer were men who secured the support of Emmanuel Joseph Sieyés and instigated the overthrow of the government. All three men and others who would become key figures the new regime were members of the circle of Ideologues within the French National Institute.[65] Napoleon, as Dwyer details, "was brought into the conspiracy not because he was one of the few military men available with enough prestige to influence a large proportion of the army, but because he was seen to be in tune with these Ideologues."[66] With a few exceptions, scholars have argued that the Ideologues represented the politics of a moderate left.[67] While scholars have argued that in seeking the development of a rational political and social science, Ideologues were driven by a desire for social control, this has not been contextualized in the highly contentious debates and ongoing political conflicts over the abolition of slavery and the extension of full civil rights to populations of color.[68]

Roederer hailed from a wealthy family of glass manufacturers around the Trois-Évêches in the annexed region of Lorraine. He was an owner of the *Journal de Paris*, founded the *Journal d'Économie* in 1796 and, with Sieyès made up the political economy section of the French National Institute. He was, according to Kenneth Margerison, an early industrial capitalist who emphasized the primacy of commerce and industry and championed the rights of property owners, while Johan Menichetti argues that his "social conservatism is undeniable."[69] Ownership of human chattel was a specific property right that Roederer sought to protect. In the 10 December 1796 edition of his *Journal d'Économie*, he railed against the abolition of slavery. "The hateful and hated commissioners sent to American," he complained, were "tasked with the implementation of disastrous laws, more deadly for the Negroes than the horrors of slavery that they were the victims off."[70] "These laws were made by atrocious tyrants, exchanging the extermination of free men for the freedom of slaves," and should be revoked. "The legislature never should have been so hasty to alter the laws concerning the slaves," as it had proven disastrous for French global commerce.[71]

One oft-overlooked difference between the governments of the Directory and Consulate is that the later was all *blanc*, and purging diversity was part of the intended outcome of the *coup*. Within weeks, Napoleon arranged for a dinner with planters from Saint Domingue.[72] Although his wife made repeated requests, the new regime did nothing to procure the release of the celebrated general of color, Thomas Alexandre Dumas, when he was taken prisoner in the Kingdom of Naples. Treated with "with utter contempt" by Napoleon, he was left to languish from malnourishment, that left him blind in one eye.[73] Other leaders of color were purged, including Mentor, Thomany, and Louverture, while a number of pro-slavery officials assumed positions of power and influence. Former *indendant* of ancient-regime Saint Domingue, François Barbé-Marbois was appointed to the newly formed Council of State. In 1801, Bruix was also appointed to the Council of State. From a family that grew wealthy of the Atlantic trade in LeHavre, Jacques François Begouen, the most prominent deputy in the early Revolution to deploy economic necessity in defense of slavery and the slave trade, was appointed in 1803.[74]

On Christmas 1799, Napoleon wrote a series of communications that offer some indication, not only of intent, but also suggest that he and his advisors had already developed a coordinated plan to purge and destroy diversity. The first action was the *coup*. The second involved the abrogation of the protective public laws through the proclamation of the 1799 Constitution. It reinstated colonies in the place of what had been *départements*, not only signaling a disintegration of French national feelings, but destroying the path of self-governance for people of color. A day later, Napoleon wrote an address to the citizens of Saint Domingue, reading: "Citizens, a constitution that could not survive against so many violations of it is replaced by a new pact intended to strengthen liberty."[75] "Article 91," he announced, "holds that the French colonies will be ruled according to special laws."[76] Encoding the language of essentialism, he argued that the "decision derives from the nature of things and the difference in climates."[77] Next, he issued a Christmas *Arrêté*, ordering Julien Raimond, "*homme de couleur*," to return to Saint Domingue, specifically "for the reestablishment of agriculture," and that the statement "[b]rave blacks, remember that only the French people recognize your liberty and equality of rights" be inscribed on the uniforms of the colonial national guard.[78] The distinction between "blacks" and "French people," not only marked a hardening of racialized difference but the disintegration of people of color as French nationals and exclusion from the modern French nation-state.

Intent was also evident in France's diplomatic relations with Britain, and Napoleon was the fortune that Maitland had alluded to. In another letter written the day after Christmas, Napoleon made peace overtures to George III. "The war that has ravaged four regions of the world for eight years, shall it be eternal," he asked.[79] "Why are the two most enlightened nations of Europe, more powerful and stronger than required for their independence and security," he wrote, "sacrificing commercial good, domestic prosperity and the happiness of families for dreams of grandeur in vain."[80] France and England had become the source of "exhausting misfortune for all peoples" and civilized nations wanted "the end of a war that engulfed the entire world."[81] The overture was rebuffed, pointedly, on New Years Day 1800, and George III refused direct communication. Instead, a reply from Foreign Secretary, William Grenville, went to Talleyrand. Grenville emphasized that the original causes of the war had not "ceased to operate."[82] The "system" that led to France's "present miseries" enveloped Europe in "tedious and distinctive warfare, commenced and prosecuted [...] on principles long since unknown to civilized nations."[83] So long as that "system," which had disrupted the "stability of property" and "social order" prevailed in France, there could be no peace. References to "system," "social order," and "stability of property" were encoded terms signifying the problem of colorblind liberty in the French world.[84]

Multilateral cooperation

Scholarly opinions vary on when and why Napoleon chose to send the expedition to Saint Domingue. Dubois points toward the news of Louverture's "takeover of Spanish Santo Domingo" and promulgation of "Saint Domingue's 1801 constitution."[85] Girard argues that "the fear that Louverture might declare independence, not dissatisfaction with the 1794 emancipation law, is the most convincing explanation for Bonaparte's decision to remove him from office."[86] Yet, Article 77 of the 1801 constitution charged Louverture with presenting it "for the sanction of the French government" and it closed twice with the statement: *"la République Français une et indivisible."*[87] More significantly, the expeditions to reinstitute slavery in French Guiana and Guadeloupe were approved as early as 10 May 1800.[88] Serious planning for what was called the "reconquest" of Saint Domingue extended as far back as May of 1800, more than a year before Louverture's taking of Santo Domingo and the promulgation of the 1801 constitution. An early "Note on the Projected Expedition to Saint Domingue" of 23 May 1800 was attached to a 26 May 1800 report from the Minister of War to the First Consul. Titled *"Expédition Secrète prepare à Brest"*, it argued that "the division destined for Saint Domingue should not be commanded by "white officers," but rather by the "many black or mulatto officers" in the French armed forces.[89] Finally, in his letter to Louverture, where he rejected the colonial constitution's provision for colorblind equality, Napoleon argued that its "contents were contrary to the dignity and sovereignty of the French people, of which only a portion of Saint Domingue is a part."[90]

The program for the disintegration and destruction of people of color was marked by an unprecedented level of multilateral cooperation between enemy powers, nearly two years before the formal "Peace" of Amiens. Almost every power in the neighborhood knew about the impending Leclerc expedition except the intended victims. Napoleon's aide wrote to Louverture on 5 November 1800, that the republic would soon announce a new convention ending the Quasi-War (1798–1800) with the USA.[91] The substance of Napoleon's letter to Talleyrand in October of 1801 indicates considerable international cooperation in the planning stages of the expeditions to end the liberty, equality, and fraternity of people of color. A number of the vessels in the expedition would go to Jamaica, while Spain contributed six vessels that would leave Brest with the French squadron.[92] Three additional ships and four frigates would depart from Cadiz. "Destroying the new Algiers organized in the Americas," Napoleon closed his letter, "is in the interest of civilization."[93] In an additional letter the same day, he asked Talleyrand to write as soon as possible to Spain's Minister of Foreign Affairs and "inform him of the departure of an army to subdue the black rebels in Saint Domingue" and asked that a request be made to the general commander of Havana for assistance in rallying "the whites of the Spanish nation against Toussaint's blacks."[94] "With regards to the government of the blacks that I intend to annihilate in Saint Domingue," Napoleon wrote to Talleyrand on 13 November 1801, "I am less guided by commercial and financial considerations than by the need to stamp out, everywhere in the world, every species of the germs of anxiety and unrest."[95]

This was an important characteristic of the climate when, in 1801, the new Prime Minister, Henry Addington reopened peace deliberations with France. He agreed with Talleyrand that the "interests of the two governments is exactly the same – to destroy Jacobinism, especially, that of blacks."[96] As Addington's Secretary of State for Foreign Affairs, Baron Hawkesbury negotiated the Treaty of Amiens. Various interest groups wrote to him during the negotiations. Following a meeting with interested parties in London, on 27 October 1801, John Turnbull wrote on behalf of "planters, merchants and others" concerned with the Dutch settlements.[97] It was

> ardently to be wished for that arrangement might be made for the different governments to maintain and support and if necessary to aid and assist each other in maintaining and supporting the most correct and proper subordination among the Negroes in all the colonies to which they shall or may belong.[98]

Disintegration of people of color was therefore an international demand, and it appears to have been a secret condition of the "peace." France kept the British government informed about every aspect of the planned Leclerc expedition. In a report detailing the events, Captain Purvis of the ship *Royal George* wrote that a French schooner out of Brest approached their ship, when they were three leagues from the island of Ushant. An officer came on board "very particular in his inquiry where Admiral Cornwallis was."[99] The French officer insisted on delivering the dispatches to Cornwallis personally. "In the course of conversation," Purvis reported,

> he said the combined fleet were to sail for the West Indies very soon, and that he understood the dispatches with which he was charged, related to that circumstance, and therefore he must wait off Ushant until he had an opportunity to deliver these personally to the English Admiral, that he might return with his answer.[100]

According, to Cornwallis' note, after being stranded by unfavorable winds, he was able to meet up with the *Royal George* and receive the dispatches from the commander of Brest, Admiral Villeret-Joyeuse.[101] On 2 November 1801, Cornwallis wrote that the aid-de-champ had indicated that "more than twenty sail of the line" would leave from Brest and that more ships leaving "from Rochefort with the troops, were likewise going to the West Indies."[102] He attached a detailed report of the French expeditionary forces, which showed one thousand planned troops as well as Spanish ships to sail. All these materials were forwarded in a letter from Cornwallis to the Admiralty Office on 4 November 1801.[103]

It was not long before news of the planned expedition spread through informed British circles and, here, again cooperation becomes clear. Maitland wrote to advise Addington on the probable situation of Saint Domingue when the "French force [arrived] from Europe."[104] Even if Louverture were gotten rid of, he lamented that "the black power would still exist."[105] The British might suggest to the French in the "strongest terms," that if "they adopt the line of more coercion" they may succeed, "but," he emphasized, "without exterminating [a] great part of the present Negroes who they possess [this] will be of little use."[106] In an 1802 letter to Addington, James Stephen noted the strangeness of the sudden friendship between France and Britain.

> But if [Louverture], and the people of St. Domingo in general, were weak enough to believe Great Britain, sincerely disposed to favor the cause of negro freedom in the West Indies, they must be already convinced of their mistake. They have seen the bar of our naval hostilities removed from the coasts and the harbors of France in order that naval armaments might proceed against them; before notice of the Peace, should put them on their guard; and this not only while they were observing strict neutrality towards us, but while our quarrel with the Republic was not yet definitively ended. They will know that the British Cabinet chose even to encounter some national anxiety rather than not acquiesce in a measure hostile to the Negroes of St. Domingo.[107]

Leclerc wrote to Napoleon stating baldly that he was waging a "war of extermination" in Saint Domingue.[108] The mass drownings, including but not limited to that of 1200 troops of the 6th colonial demi-brigade, mass hangings, the destroying of food crops, mass executions by firing squads, and other inventive methods were more than atrocities.[109] It was genocide, and it was not confined to the colonial dominions. The disintegration and destruction of people of color was not accidental, but entirely intentional. As the story of the Haitian War of Independence is well known, the rest of this article concentrates of Napoleonic Genocide against people of color in the European theater.

Napoleonic genocide in the European theater

There was a specious ratcheting-up of false charges and propaganda against people of color on both sides of the Atlantic. François Kerverseau had spent many years as an administrator in the French Caribbean. From his position in Spanish Santo Domingo, he built a vast intelligence network that kept him informed about what was happing in neighboring Saint Domingue, and he emerged as one of Napoleon's best informants.[110] Bruix was also among Kerverseau's correspondents in France.[111] In 1797 before the *coup*, Kerverseau and Pierre de Leborgne co-authored a report, accusing Andre Rigaud of treason, but with the *coup* of 1799, Kerverseau's new target of defamation was Louverture.[112] Ultimately, his problem was with people of color in positions of distinction, a sentiment that he shared with Napoleon. Writing to his brother, Joseph Bonaparte, Napoleon wrote of peace and prosperity in Guadeloupe, but that "a mulatto was appointed as head of the colony," and therefore, "three vessels, four frigates and 3,000 good infantry men" had departed "to disarm the blacks and reestablish enduring tranquility."[113] In December of 1801, the *Société des Observateurs de l'Homme* hosted "talks 'On legislative errors which have been the principal cause of the decadence of certain powers' and 'On the origin of the word 'slave'."[114] By 1803, they were offering a twice-weekly lecture series on "The Natural History of Man," which specifically focused on "the different races of the human genus […] [and] the physical and moral characters which distinguish them."[115] As a member of the *Société*, Napoleon was known to attend its events.

It was, however, in the Council of State meetings concerning the promulgation of a civil code that the specific technique of deportation was discussed. The deliberations began in earnest in mid-July of 1801 and Napoleon, as First Consul, presided over the sessions. In the 22 July 1801 session, the Council took up general promulgation matters. Giving his understanding of the purpose of "civil laws relative to persons," Napoleon mentioned, first, the establishment of the "status of everyone in civil society."[116] Both leading jurist, Jean Portalis and Jean Jacques Cambacérès, suggested a delay between the promulgation and effective date of the code, arguing that it would help inspire public confidence and respect for all laws. Roederer was quick to shut down this line of argument and leaned on the Constitution to support Napoleon's absolute legislative authority, citing: "The First Consul promulgates the laws."[117] To establish any delay was "ridiculous." Antoine Boulay, president of the legislative section of the Council of State, raised the question of a delay for the colonies, but Napoleon responded that the laws would "be declared enforceable on the day of arrival."[118] He "invited" the editors "to vote with the councilors of state," and given his constitutional authority to appoint and dismiss the members of the Council of State and other ministers, it comes as no surprise that delay was rejected.[119]

In the 4 August 1801 deliberations, Napoleon suggested that it might be a good time to consider the status of deportees, "hypothetically," and assume that "they will be reunited on a vast expanse of land where they will form a colony."[120] Could "they be deprived of civil life outside their place of deportation," but rendered civil life, only "in the country where they would be deported?"[121] Such comments offer an indication that the regime was anticipating massive deportations. These sections of the transcript are full of references to the "condemned" and *mourir civilement*." Tronchet responded that "formerly, banishment for life from French territory carried with it civil death."[122] It would only be "exile" if the only effect were relegation to a specific region. In his usual blunt terms, Emmanuel Crétet commented that the "civilly dead" can "never be heard;" "if he is deported, he is absent; if escaped, sentenced in absentia."[123] A brumairian through and through, he was in the critical colonial commodities trade before the Revolution and would go on to serve as Director of the Bridges and Roads, Governor of the Bank of France in 1806 and Minister of the Interior from 1807 until his death in 1809.

The consequence of permanent banishment from French territory and/or the stamp of deportation would be civil death, but if the history of massacres in Jaffa and elsewhere are any guide, there was little to suggest that the government under Napoleonic dictatorship would be willing to take on the expense of nourishing deportees. Civil death, especially for people of color, was a prelude to the physical technique. In a report to the consuls in 1802, the Director of the Ministry of the Navy and Colonies, Denis Decrés, suggested that by deportation as "perpetual detention," the condemned face a "slow, but certain death."[124] Napoleon, the consuls, the councilors of state as well as a host of lesser officials knew what they were doing and they cranked up the mechanism of state to get genocide done abroad and at home. In accordance with the Order of 31 July 1801, the Gendarmerie corps were enlarged more than fourfold to 16,500 men with an increase in the number foot corps and some 2500 brigades total.[125] The expansion was accompanied by a push to "weed out undesirable men," and officer commissions now had to come directly from Napoleon.[126] Frenchmen of color were especially targeted for weeding out of elite military service of all kinds. "Throughout the period of the Napoleonic regime," it was the Gendarmerie that "fulfilled a multitude of roles within the *départements* of France and the Empire, and with the armies."[127]

Full drafts of the proposed civil code were in wide circulation in 1801, and it reiterated the exclusively *blanc* French identity that was initiated in the 1799 Constitution. Under Article 2 of the Constitution, citizenship depended on the ability to domicile in France:

> Every man born and residing in France fully twenty-one years of age, who has caused his name to be inscribed upon the civil register [...] and has since lived for one year upon the soil of the Republic, is a French citizen.[128]

Book I of the Civil Code, "Of Persons," set forth that "every Frenchman shall enjoys civil rights," but, again, French legal personality was dependent on the capacity to domicile in metropolitan France.[129] "Every individual born in France of a foreigner, may, during the year which shall succeed the period of his majority, claim the quality of Frenchman," but as Article 9 stipulated, this was "provided, that if he shall reside in France" or "give security to become domiciled in France and establish himself there within a year."[130] Unless one possessed the legal capacity to domicile in the continental territory of metropolitan France, one could not possess French identity or, accordingly, civil rights. Also, in the code's sections on Persons, there are provisions for the loss of the "quality of Frenchman" for those "who have borne or shall bear arms against their country."[131] First, this was retroactive, and, second, would have applied to many soldiers of color who had first fought for racial liberty in the 1790s and/or were serving with Louverture. It was also made explicitly clear that "sentences to punishments," that resulted in the deprivation of civil rights "shall imply civil death."[132]

The "Peace" of Amiens was signed on 25 March 1802. Having left Brest on 1 December 1801, the Leclerc expedition arrived in Saint Domingue in early February 1802, more than a month before the Peace was signed. On 20 May 1802, two measures were confirmed in the Consulate "legislature." The first was a *Loi de promulgation du traité d'Amiens*. The second was the *Loi relative à la traite des noirs et au régime des colonies*, which not only reinstituted slavery, but destroyed colorblind liberty as a condition of the Peace. Article 1 reads: "In the colonies restored to France in fulfillment of the Treaty of Amiens of 6 Germinal Year X, slavery shall be maintained in conformity with the laws and regulations in force prior to 1789."[133] Under Paragraph 3: "The trade in the blacks and their importation into the said colonies shall take place in conformity with the laws and regulations existing prior to the said date of 1789."[134]

Even more ominous signs of ill will followed in a series of disenfranchising laws and policies. On 6 April 1802 Napoleon issued an *Arrêté* naming Bruix to a new committee concerned with the organization of a colonial judiciary and "to the fix the estate of blacks."[135] On 27 April 1802, he wrote to Cambacérès about the new committee and of his intentions to issue a law "barring blacks from the continental territory of the Republic."[136] Attachments included a proposed law requiring colonial administrators to put together a list of individuals who were free before Abolition and requiring blacks to produce documents proving that they were emancipated before 1793. Local colonial laws were abrogated. While it stipulated all those who had fought to defend the Republic were to maintain their freedom, this did not bear out in practice as evident below. He further called for a vigorous revival of the slave trade and that all slaves procured through this revived trade, "arriving in Martinique and Saint Domingue shall be treated in the same manner as the were in all other European colonies before 1789."[137]

Apparently, the new committee did not need to meet long and, in fact, it is likely that decisions had already been made before it was set up. On 13 Messidor an X (2 July 1802) Napoleon issued the *Arrêté portant defense aux noirs, mulâtres et autres gens de couleur d'entrer sans autorisation sur le territoire continental de la République.*[138] Under Article I, foreigners were barred from bringing any "black, mulatto or other person of color of one or the other sex" into the "continental territory of the Republic." Article II banned any "black, mulatto or other person of color of one or the other sex [...] to enter the continental territory of the Republic," for any reason unless they were in service or had special permission. Lacking the ability to domicile in France, on mass, citizens of color in the French world were put to civil death. With no legal personality, no rights or civil remedies, effectively they were made dead to the French state, not to be heard from in the words of Crétet. Physical genocide was now possible.

It is clear from the "deportation" files scattered between national, departmental, and municipal archives that surveillance, harassment, and deportation were already occurring when Napoleon spoke of it in the Council of State's deliberations, as an 1801 file on the "Deportation of 132 individuals to the Seychelles" in the Indian Ocean suggests.[139] A 14 August 1802 Report from the Bureau of Colonies within the Naval Ministry detailed the deportation of seventy individuals, almost half of whom were re-deported to the Sultanate of Anjouan.[140] According to François-Louis de Magallon, there was a great deal of concern and excitement about the arrival in the colony of "these individuals who had been rejected from the breast of France in December of 1800."[141] At first they were kept on the frigate and corvette that had transported them, but after they were disembarked, some of them were found to be of "atrocious character," allegedly engaged in "provoking the blacks to revolt" and expressing their opposition to the Napoleonic regime.[142] After consulting the colonial assembly, which demanded the deportation of "these very dangerous individuals," Magallon had 33 of the deportees re-deported to Anjouan and the rest to Mahé.[143] The corvette, *Le Belvoir*, was expedited and the 33 were transported to Anjouan.

Apparently, Magallon had written to the Sultan, with whom the colony maintained commercial relations, asking that they be humanly treated. Yet, a plea, dated 18 May 1802, seemingly to anyone who might read it was written by deportees Jean Baptiste Antoine Lefranc, Pierre Nicholas Chretien, Charle Somois, and Rene Joly on behalf of the 33 men re-deported to Anjouan suggest otherwise.[144] Although promised that they would be treated "with kindness and humanity," they wrote that, "during the three months that we have been in [Anjouan], we have not been given the rations necessary for our subsistence, despite the repeated request that we have made."[145] An *État* on the 70 deportees showed that of the 34 who were re-deported to the largest of the Seychelles islands, Mahé, most, ranging in ages from 38 to 62 were still alive. Six men died and six had managed to escape. By contrast, with the exception of four men who had managed to escape, people of color sent to Anjouan died. There were 29 men listed on the deceased list and Joly and Chretien were among them.

Most of the deportation, however, was to islands just of the French coast and again the tragic saga of the 60 soldiers billeted on Aix Island was a harbinger of things to come. The expedition from French Guiana was approved by Napoleon no later than early May. On 26 June 1800 list of women and children deportees from Guiana, held in the "*dépôt* on Aix

Island" was, a generated.[146] It shows 81 deportees, women and girls, exclusively. Seven of the children were not receiving rations and it is not clear whether this was because they were too young or some other reason. As early as 1799, a file was generated on deportations to Oléron island. Again, the *État des deportés* suggest many deaths, and many of these people were older, in there 40s, 50s, and 60s, in contrast to the Anjouan deportees. In the file, there is an "Extract of the Deliberations of the Consuls of the Republic," of the so-called "republic one and indivisible," dated 6 September 1800.[147] It was the text of another *Arrêté* by Napoleon. Under Article 1, "individuals condemned to deportation who are currently in Guiana are to be transferred to the island of Rhé and Oléron as soon as possible [and] kept under the surveillance of the Prefect of Charente Inferior."[148] Deportees were brought from South America to a *dépôt* of the coast of France, a fate that many people of color would face. At the same time, people of color from Bordeaux were also purportedly slated for Oléron and the special census of people of color from 30 Messidor an 10, produced only 17 days after the 13 Messidor law banning people of color from France, had a combined total of some 531 souls.[149]

Contrary to what scholars have suggested, after 1803 Napoleon did not abandon his imperial ambitions in the Americas and turn his attention, exclusively, to the Continental System in Europe. As late as 6 August 1806, he wrote to Decrès requesting a report on Saint Domingue and plans for how he intended to reestablish French authority.[150] Thus, the genocide that continued in Europe after the formal declaration of independence in Haiti (Saint Domingue) on 1 January 1804, continued to be bound-up with economic imperialism. In an additional report, Kerverseau was still clamoring for the public to be made conscious of the crimes of people of color and calling for the nourishing of an "explosion of hate," in such a way that the "burning and eruption of the volcano" would be inevitable.[151] Either the "monster" would be exterminated or the "body," namely the French or more broadly the European body. It is next to this comment that one finds in tiny initials "NB." Indeed, overly confident that his program of re-enslavement would be successful, Napoleon wrote to the Emperor of Russia on 23 May 1802. "Finally," he wrote, "we have re-conquered our colony of Saint Domingue, but it was not without great difficulty."[152] "I hope," he continued, "that we may soon begin to supply Europe with colonial commodities."[153] This mission of economic imperialism based on the hyper-exploitation of people of color, required their absolute subjugation and, effectively, Napoleon was prepared to stand by an ultimatum of absolute subjugation or death.

"Deportation" continued throughout the Napoleonic years to the degree that there were still people to deport. A 20 July 1807 letter from Decrès to the Admiral Prefect of the 4th Maritime *arrondisement* in Nantes lends a sense of this state-sponsored genocide. "I have been informed," the Minister chastised, "that in contravention of the government Order of 2 July 1802 many *noirs, mulâtres et autres gens de couleur* of both sexes have been allowed to enter the continental territory of the Empire and remain without difficulty."[154] "This state of affairs," he continued, "is contrary to the intentions of His Majesty."[155] After a lengthy explication on the details of the law, the Admiral Prefect was ordered to locate and compile a list of any people of color in his area and take steps for their deportation. Decrès wrote, specifically, that no exceptions could be made "in favor of *noirs et autres gens de couleur* who had been engaged in the service of France." He closed warning the Admiral Prefect that he expected his *"plus rigoureuse"* execution of his directive.[156]

In 1806, a telling dispute erupted between the *Munitionnaire-Général*, Vanderbergh, in the new *départements* of Golo and Liamone (Corsica) and the Prefect over non-payment for bread. Vanderbergh was forced to write a report justifying a "supply of 1472 rations of bread" to the black deportees on the island of Elba.[157] In it, he indicated that people of color and others had been deported "continually," "during the years 9, 10, 11, 12 et 13" for holding in *dépôts*, not only in Corsica, but "on the Island of Elba and in Marseilles."[158] When he requested payment from the Prefect, he had refused indicating that there was no budget for this provision. The matter generated a report in the Interior Ministry. In addition to those deported from Saint Domingue, there were many civilian residents of France. Under Article 8 of an *Order* of 13 Friaries an 11 (4 December 1802), the deportees were put to public works and, under Article 11, they were to be fed bread.[159] It is clear from the record that neither Crétet nor anyone in the War Ministry was prepared to appropriate funds to cover the cost of nourishment.

The manner in which Louverture and Jean Baptiste Belley died is informative here. Louverture was starved at Fort du Joux prison in 1803, and similarly, Belley was imprisoned in the Belle-Île fortress in 1802 and died there in1805. An early letter from the Minister of War to the Minister of the Interior of 5 June 1803 indicated that persons of color of *"fonctions supérieures"* were in *dépôts*.[160] These included, not only Annecy, who had served in the National Convention, but also Jean-Baptiste Mills, who had been the first *mulâtre* member of the National Convention.[161] According to a September of 1808 letter even the *Régiment Royal Africain*, which had seen considerable duty in Central Europe and Italy, had been deported and held in the Corsica *dépôt*.[162] A 21 September 1807 letter to the newly appointed Minister of the Interior, Crétet, reported that deportees in all *dépôts* were fed *"une seule ration de pain pour jour."*[163] On 13 February 1805, the Prefect of the Department of Liamone, Arrighi, reported the transfer of 127 people of color of the 1st and 2nd Companies.[164] There were 55 souls in the 1st Company, all born in Guadeloupe. Thirty-six were put to public works on bridges and roads, three in the town, six as domestics and there were seven cripples and two in clasps according to Arrighi's report of 13 February 1805. There were 72 souls in the 2nd Company, 60 from Guadeloupe, the rest from Saint Domingue. Thirty-two were set to the bridges and roads, 12 to fortifications, 20 domestics, four in town and there was one cripple and one was in clasp. In September of 1808, responding to the request for an *"état nominatif des hommes de couleur de la 1st et 2nd companie,"* from Décres, the Prefect reported that only 24 were left and that, as a consequence of their "subsistence," half of these were too ill to work.[165]

To look again to what transpired on the local level to ordinary men and women of color, by the fall of 1803, the environment was so difficult that the Chief Magistrate in Nantes wrote that a "large number of people of color" were "requesting passports for the United States of America."[166] These were denied, and, instead, the Commissioner General of the Police "recommended the exercise of very strict surveillance of all individuals of color; their relations with foreign countries should above all be the object of your attention."[167] On the 29th, the Police Commissioner responded, that in response to the Chief Magistrate's recommendation, new measures were to be taken "relative to people of color."[168] On the same day in 1803, Prefect Letourneau issued a general *circulaire* to all police commissioners in his department to take another detailed census of all people of color in their districts, noting in addition to their names, the work, length of domicile in France, age, and any other observations of character.[169]

One such list from 4 February 1805 gives a sense of who was left of these purported threats to the security of the Empire.[170] François and Aimé Valentin, ages 16.5 and 12.5, were *quarteron* students from Senegal, working for a merchant named Benis. Just underneath them were Jean and Paul Benis, also students, but these were sons of Benis. We can assume that Benis was "*blanc*" as his name does not appear in the formal census. All were shown residing together in Nantes. Augustin Appau, age 32 and Louis Simon, age 34, were both wig-makers and the observations indicated that the "very honest" Augustin was married and the father of three children. Louis Labielais had been a Chief of a Brigade and was living with his wife, their children and a niece. Pierre Aldiquir was a "mulatto" ex-Justice of the Peace, shown living with his son François. Alexander Chatelot, age 41, was a carriage driver (*roulier*) originally from America, who was married to Thérèse Barillon, a "*femme Blanche*" with two children. Charles Bicou was a day laborer, "married to a *femme Blanche*," and Rose Benet, was a dressmaker originally from St. Lucia. Two of the seven domestics, it was observed, had served in the French army, fighting at battles in Holland and Marengo. It must be underscored that the names on the 1805 list were new names. Only six of the people on the 1802 census lists appeared on the 1805 list, the others had simply vanished.

Targeted again in Bordeaux in 1805, Bouer, Daugard, Albert, Deville, and Henriette Martel signed a letter of protest to the Prefect of the Gironde. It indicated that they had learned of the letters he was circulating around his "bureau," unjustifiably attacking the "morality" of "*jens* [sic] *de couleur*."[171] The next day, the Prefect responded with an angry letter to the Chief of Police, that opened, simply, "five deportees" which a meant a trip to a *dépôt* off the coast of France and, for many, slow but certain death.[172] Eleven years later, in 1816, the French government was still issuing requests to local officials on the state of people of color held in *dépôts*. The request again generated a series of letters in Bordeaux. Only 14 people were on the *État nominatif*.[173] All had been held for at least 10 years, with one exception who had been in for 20. What is worse, these people of color were not permitted to remain in France, but were transported to Senegal in accordance with the 13 Messidor order.[174] This was in Bordeaux, which during the period of eighteenth-century diversity had once hosted a population of color as large as 3600 including, not only residents, but temporary residents from the colonies, Africa and elsewhere.[175] There was also no change in policy in 1824, when there was yet another request for a census and removal, still appealing to the 13 Messidor order, was issued. There were two people in Nantes.[176]

Hiding and denying genocide/missing important links

"In post-genocidal society where current regimes are built on a past generations genocides," the editors of *Hidden Genocide* suggest that "this often entails hiding genocides from historical memory through law, public memorials or state education policy."[177] Napoleon was keenly interested in all three, both domestically and imperially in occupied Europe.[178] Massacres were not just acts of mass-violence or mass-killing or even just massacres; they were part and parcel of genocide. Even where mass-violence is discussed under another name, in the substance, of these studies it becomes evident that the physical technique of genocide was already an element of Napoleon's conquests and retreats before he rose to power in November of 1799.[179] It should therefore be less surprising that full-blown genocide erupted. Arguably, the specific targeting of people of color allowed for the honing of genocidal techniques that were spread throughout occupied Europe, including but not limited to the eradication of whole towns on the Italian and Spanish peninsulas, across German-speaking Central Europe, and in Russia. General Louis-Florimond Fantin des Odoards "did not even count Spain among the countries of Europe but rather described it as an 'African country' 'by its blood', its morals, its language, its manner of living and fighting.'[180] "This," Dwyer suggest, "is perhaps why some French officers were calling for a 'war of extermination' as the only possible means of assuring complete dominance of the Peninsula."[181] It was also the case, however, that the worst atrocities seemed to be in the European zone where the worshiping of the Black Madonna was common.[182] What happened in the notorious sieges of Badajoz, where an eighteenth-century traveler reported "numerous families of Negroes and Mulattos are settled in this country between Badajoz and Zafra?"[183]

A number of the leading administrators posted to occupied Italy and elsewhere in Europe were veterans of Caribbean colonial administration and wars. These included Jacques de Norvins and the notorious Moreau de Saint-Méry, both of whom viewed the populations of the Italian peninsula, under their control, through colored lenses.[184] Norvins had been Leclerc's private secretary for the expedition to Saint Domingue, before becoming first lieutenant in the *Corps des gendarmes d'ordonnance* in occupied Mainz. He, then, served Jérôme, a figure of French imperialism that, in his capacity as king of the satellite of Westphalia, was almost universally despised by German liberals for the rest of the century. Napoleon handed down a "constitution" in 1807, and it was published in the *Moniteur wesphalien*, the official periodical of the occupying French, founded by Norvins. He was later made secretary of the puppet Council of State of Westphalia, named *Chevalier de l'Empire français* in 1808 and by1810 he was director general of the police in the ex-Papal states. Saint-Méry followed up his study of Saint Domingue with one concerning the populations of occupied Italy, and, in the words of Broers, he "did more than import prejudices from the New World to the Old," setting "much of what he found in his Italian corner of the Old World well below parts of the New."[185]

Napoleonic Genocide, was not limited to the physical technique, but, in its full-blown form, appeared in the various facets identified by Lemkin and was a policy of militarized civilizing in occupied Europe and elsewhere. Indeed, the proclaiming and administration of the Kingdom of Westphalia is perhaps an example *extraordinaire* of the attempted complete assimilation of an area through direct administration and application of, at least, political, social, and cultural techniques. The imposition of *le cinq codes*, with the Code Napoleon bearing the Emperor's name, became a major source of discontent in the occupied German lands.[186] Jacob Grimm "'hated' the French law, which threatened to destroy German jurisprudence."[187]

The language of exclusion based on skin color found in the circular opening this article, however, is clear, and the modern ideology of race was crystallized as part and parcel of Napoleon's integration of and it appears that state sponsored genocide was the essential technique of its introduction. Notably, it was not the national blood of France alone that the circular referenced, but a supranational myth of Europe's primordial essence, linked to the "purity of European blood." The experiences and questions surrounding the position of people of color during the period cannot be untangled from eighteenth-century global economic entanglement, especially since their struggle to escape hyper-exploitation resulted in genocide. So devastating was the cultural and physical extirpation of people of color from the continental territory of the First French Empire and its sphere of influence that the history of diversity in metropolitan Europe writ large has been virtually expunged from collective memory and remains marginalized, if not forgotten altogether in mainstream historiography. As critical genocide scholars have argued, "the ferocity of the excesses of mass murder and genocide have too frequently been matched by the denial of these atrocities or, perhaps worst yet, genocides have seemingly been hidden, lost in the interstices of history and human discourse."[188] Paradoxically, the fact that diversity in the *longue durée* of European history – inclusive of Asian, African, and Native American diasporas as well as German, Polish, Scottish, Irish, and Italian ones – has been stripped out of historical memory offers evidence of the occurrence of genocide and suggests the need for more research on the history of diversity in Europe.

Notes

1. *Circulaire du 7 Mars 1817, N° 46510 sur les hommes du couleur*. Archives Nationales, Paris (Hereafter AN): F/7/9816.
2. "Whitehall, November 20, 1816," *The London Gazette*, Part 2 (London, 1816), 2226. Early insurrections: Moitt, "Slave Resistance"; Garrigus, "Coming Fame."
3. Dwyer, "Makes Me Shudder," 383.
4. Europe: Debrunner, *Presence*; Earle and Lowe, eds., *Black Africans*; Queija and Stella, eds., *Negros, Mulatos*; Honeck, Klimke, and Kuhlmann-Smirnov, eds., *Germany Black Diaspora*; Boulle, *Race*; Peabody, *No Slaves*; Coller, *Arab France*; Palmer, *Intimate Bonds*; Tozzi, *France's Army*; Heuer, "One-Drop"; Byrd, *Captives*; Gerzina, *Black London*; Reiss, *Black Count*, Hondius, "Blacks Early Modern Europe."
5. Aaslestad and Joor, eds., *Napoleon's Continental*; Dwyer and Forrest, eds., *Napoleon and Empire*; Planert, ed., *Napoleon's Empire*; Broers, "First Napoleonic"; Broers, *Napoleonic Imperialism*; Kagan, *End*; Bell, *Total War*; Rowe, *Reich*; Lafon, *Andalouise*; Woolf, "Napoleon Europe."
6. Schaller and Zimmerer, "Lemkin," 449 and Power, *Problem*, 31–46.
7. Lemkin, *Axis*, 78 and 7–74.
8. Power, *Problem*, 43.
9. Lemkin, *Axis*, 79. Hereafter quoted parenthetically.
10. Irvin-Erickson, La Pointe and Hinton, "Introduction," 5.
11. McDonnell and Moses, "Lemkin," 501–2. See also: Stone, *Historiography*, Totten and Jacobs, eds., *Pioneers*.
12. Moses, "Founding"; Jones, *New*; Stone, *Historiography*; Gellately and Kiernan, eds., *Specter Genocide*.
13. Bloxham and Moses, eds., *Genocide Studies*; Moses, ed., *Empire, Colony*; Hinton, ed., *Annihilating*; Kiernan, *Blood*; Levene, *Rise West*; Levene, *Genocide Nation*, Weitz, *Century Genocide*; Power, *Problem*; Hinton, La Pointe and Irvin-Erickson, Hidden, "Introduction"; Provost and Akhaven, *Confronting*.
14. Kiernan, "Anachronistic," 530–548.
15. Dwyer, "Violence," 120.
16. Dwyer, "Makes Me Shudder," 382.
17. Ibid., 399.
18. Lemarchand, *Forgotten*, 12.
19. Ibid.
20. Ibid.
21. Girard, "Bonaparte," 598.
22. Ibid.
23. Girard, "Caribbean."

24. Girard, "Haitian," 145.
25. Ibid.
26. Ibid.
27. Ibid.
28. O'Rourke and Williamson, *Globalization*, 109.
29. Dobado-González, García-Hiernaux, and Guerrero, "Integration."
30. Games, "Atlantic History," 748.
31. Coclanis, "Atlantic World," 728.
32. Topik, "Coffee," 28–29.
33. Ibid.
34. Ibid.
35. Harding, "War," 297; Crouzet, "Angleterre et France," 264.
36. Stein, "French Sugar," 6.
37. Ibid, 9.
38. Ibid., 9–12.
39. Eldem, *French Trade*, 68–89.
40. Levene, *Genocide*, 13.
41. Dwyer, *Napoleon: Path*, 337.
42. Ibid.; Popkin, *All Free*, 37–38.
43. Bonaparte au Directoire exécutif, 13 March 1799. In *Correspondence de Napoleon I* edited by Vaillant. (Hereafter CdeN) 5, 362.
44. Bonaparte au Chérif de la Mecque, 30 June1799. CdeN 5, 490.
45. Bonaparte au Sultan de Darfour, 10 June 1799. CdeN 5, 490.
46. Dubois, "Troubled," 297.
47. Abolition of Slavery Decree, 4 February 1794.
48. Constitution Year I.
49. Constitution Year III.
50. Ferrer, *Freedom's*, 83.
51. Ibid.
52. Newman, "American," 83; Horne, *Confronting*.
53. Geggus, "British," 289.
54. Geggus, *Slavery*.
55. General Maitland to George III, September 1799. The Baring Archive, London, Northbrook Papers, NP1.A7
56. Ibid.
57. Ibid.
58. Ibid.
59. Ibid.
60. Dubois, "Troubled," 296–297.
61. Mentor, *Dernier Mot D'Étienne Mentor*.
62. Ibid.
63. Ibid.
64. Ibid.
65. Staum, "Individual."
66. Dwyer, *Napoleon: Path*, 477.
67. Staum, "Individual"; Jennings, "Déclaration"; Polowetzky, *Bond Never*; Dwyer, *Napoleon: Path*, 47–48.
68. Staum, "Individual," 411.
69. Margerison, *Roederer*; Menichetti, "Roederer," 21.
70. Roederer, "Analyse," 228.
71. Ibid.
72. Dubois, "Haitian," 23.
73. Girard, *Slaves*, 46; Reiss, *Black Count*, 264–80.

74. Députés extraordinaires du Commerce, *Réflexions sur Le Commerce* (1790). Archives de la ville du Havre: F/2/ Révolutionnaire.
75. Bonaparte aux Citoyens de Saint Domingue, 25 December 1799. CdeN 6, 42.
76. Ibid.
77. Ibid.
78. *Arrêté*, 25 December 1799. CdeN 6, 42–43.
79. Bonaparte to George III, 25 December 1800. The National Archives, London (Hereafter TNA): Foreign Office (Hereafter FO)/27/56.
80. Ibid.
81. Ibid.
82. Grenville to Talleyrand, 1 January 1800. TNA: FO/27/56.
83. Ibid.
84. Ibid.
85. Dubois, *Avengers*, 253.
86. Girard, "Bonaparte," 603.
87. *Constitution de Saint Domingue* (1801).
88. Bonaparte au Forait, Minister de la Marine et Colonies, 10 May 1800. CdeN 6, 264.
89. *Rapport fait au premier Consul par le Ministre de la guerre, 6 Prairial an 8 de la République*. Service Historique de la Défense à Vincennes, B7/1 – Saint-Domingue.
90. Bonaparte au Louverture, 18 November 1801, CdeN 7, 322.
91. Bonaparte's aide au Louverture, 5 November 1800. CdeN 6, 498–499.
92. Bonaparte au Talleyrand, 30 October 1801. CdeN 7, 307–308.
93. Ibid.
94. Bonaparte au Talleyrand, 30 October 1801. CdeN 7, 308–309.
95. Bonaparte au Talleyrand, 13 November 1801. CdeN 7, 319–322.
96. Dubois, *Avengers*, 255–6.
97. Turnbull to Hawkesbury, 27 October 1801. TNA: FO/27/65.
98. Ibid.
99. Purvis report, 23 October 1801. TNA: FO/27/65.
100. Ibid.
101. Cornwallis note, 28 October 1801. TNA: FO/27/65.
102. Cornwallis note, 2 November 1801. TNA: FO/27/65.
103. Cornwallis to Admiralty, 4 November 1801. TNA: FO/27/65.
104. Maitland to Addington, 26 November 1801. TNA: FO/27/65.
105. Ibid.
106. Ibid.
107. Stephen, *Sugar Colonies*. 81.
108. Girard, "Atrocities," 139.
109. Ibid.
110. Girard, *Slaves*, 37–38.
111. Ibid., 356.
112. Kerverseau and Leborgne, *Rapport Fait Au Gouvernment*.
113. Bonaparte au Joseph Bonaparte, 7 January 1802. CdeN 7, 360.
114. Stocking, *Race*, 17.
115. Ibid.
116. *Procés-Verbaux du Conseil D'État*, 3.
117. Ibid.
118. Ibid.
119. Ibid., and Emsley, *Gendarmes*, 56–57.
120. *Procés-Verbaux du Conseil d'État*, 69.
121. Ibid.
122. Ibid.
123. Ibid.

124. *Rapport aux Consuls de la République* par le Ministre de la Marine, Bureau des Colonies, 1802. Archives Nationales d'Outre Mer, Aix-en-Provence (Hereafter ANOM): Generalites (Hereafter Gen)/667/2855.
125. Emsley, *Gendarmes*, 56–57.
126. Ibid.
127. Ibid.
128. Constitution Year VIII.
129. Civil Code (1804).
130. Ibid.
131. Ibid.
132. Ibid.
133. *Loi relative à la traite des noirs et au régime des colonies*. In Bulletin Des Lois De La Republique 192, 329–30. Paris: Imprimerie de la République, an 11. Archives Départementales de Seine-Maritime, Rouen (Hereafter ADSM): K/RA/2.
134. Ibid.
135. *Arrêté*, 6 Avril 1802. CdeN 7, 430.
136. Au Consul Cambacérés, 27 Avril 1802. CdeN 7, 444–445.
137. Ibid.
138. *Arrêté portant défense aux noirs, mulâtres et autres gens de couleur d'entrer sans autorisation sur le territoire continental de la République*. In Bulletin Des Lois De La République 219, 815–816. Paris: Imprimerie de la République, an 10. ADSM: K/RA/2.
139. Déportation de 132 Individus aux Seychelles, 1801. ANOM: Gen/626/2730.
140. Rapport des Marine: Bureau des Colonies, 26 Thermidor an 10. ANOM: Gen/626/2730.
141. Ibid.
142. Ibid.
143. Ibid.
144. Appel De Iisle D'Anjouan le 28 Préréal an 10 de la République francaise, 28 Prairial an 10. ANOM: Gen/626/2730.
145. Ibid.
146. Liste des femmes et enfants de couleur provenant de dépôt de l'Ile D'Aix, 7 Messidor an 8. ANOM: Gen/634/2743
147. Extrait des Registres des Délibérations des Consuls de la République, 19 Fructidor an 8. ANOM: Gen/634/2743.
148. Ibid.
149. Liste générale gens de couleure qui sont actuellement à Boardeaux, 30 Messidor an 10. ANOM: Gen/634/2743.
150. Napoleon au Vice-Admiral Decrès, 6 Août 1806. CdeN 8, 46.
151. Kerverseau, François, "Observations politiques et militaries sur la Colonie de St. Domingue," 30 Brumaire an X. AN: AF/4/1213.
152. A L'Empereur de Russie, 23 Mai 1802. CdeN 7, 473–474.
153. Ibid.
154. Ministre de la Marine et des Colonies au Admiral Préfet du 4th Arrondisement Maritime, 20 July 1807. Archives Départementales du Loire-Atlantique, Nantes (Hereafter ADLA): 4M/521.
155. Ibid.
156. Ibid.
157. Munitionnaire-Général au Minster de la Intérieur, 18 July 1806. AN: F/15/3498.
158. Ibid.
159. Rapport au Son Excellence le Ministre de l'Intérieur, undated. AN: F/15/3498.
160. Ministre de la Guerre au Minstre de l'Intérieur, 16 Prairial an 11. AN: F/15/3498.
161. Ibid.
162. Au Ministre de l'Intérieur, 5 September 1808. AN: F/15/3498.
163. Au Ministre de l'Intérieur, 21 September 1807. AN: F/15/3498.
164. Préfet du Département du Liamone au Minstre de l'Intérieur, 24 Pluviôse an 13. AN: F/15/3498.

165. Préfet du Département du Liamone au Minstre de l'Intérieur, 17 September 1808. AN: F/15/3498.
166. Le Grand-Juge, Ministre de la Justice au Commissaire general de Police à Nantes, 25 Ventôse an 12. ADLA: 4M/521.
167. Ibid.
168. Commissionaire général de Police au Grand-Juge Ministre de la Justice, 19 Ventôse an 12. ADLA: 4M/521.
169. Circulaire aux Commissaires de police. ADLA, 4M/521.
170. État Nominatif des hommes de couleur Existant à Nantes, 15 Pluviose an 13. ADLA: 4M/521.
171. Au Monsieur le Préfet, 12 Pluviôse an 13. Archives Départementales de la Gironde, Bordeaux (Hereafter ADG): Préfet de Gironde, Mesures de Sureté contre les nègres (Hereafter PDMS): C/1162.
172. Préfet au Ministre Chef de Police, 13 Pluviôse an 13. ADG: PDMS: C/1162.
173. État nominatif des hommes de couleur detenus au Fort du Hâ et à l'Hôpital, 15 January 1816. AN: F7/9816.
174. Ministre Secrétaire d'État de la Marine et des Colonies au Ministre Secrétaire d'État de la Police Général, 21 May 1816. AN: F7/9816.
175. Saugere, *Bordeaux*, 291.
176. Préfecture de la Loire-Inférieure au le Ministre de l'Intérieur, 4 March 1824. AN: F/7/6947.
177. Irvin-Erickson, La Pointe and Hinton, "Introduction," 5.
178. Lyons, *Napoleon Bonaparte*; Broers, *Napoleonic Empire*.
179. Bell, *Total War*; Broers, *Napoleonic Empire*; and Dwyer, "Violence"; Girard, "Haitian."
180. Dwyer, "Violence," 125.
181. Ibid.
182. Scheer, "Majesty."
183. Dillon, *Travels*.
184. Broers, *Napoleonic Empire*, 228–9.
185. Ibid.
186. Crosby, *German*, 68–72.
187. Ibid., 70.
188. Irvin-Erickson, La Pointe and Hinton, "Introduction," 4.

Acknowledgements

The author is grateful to God for the insight, her husband for support, Howard University Provost's Office for grants, Sara Danielsson and Rob Tabor for comments and suggestions, and French archivists and staff.

Disclosure statement

No potential conflict of interest was reported by the author.

References

Aaslestad, Katherine, and Johan Joor, eds. *Revisiting Napoleon's Continental System: Local, Regional and European Experiences*. New York, NY: Palgrave Macmillan, 2015.

Bell, David. *The First Total War: Napoleon's Europe and the Birth of Warfare as We Know It*. Boston, MA: Houghton Mifflin, 2007.

Bloxham, Donald, and A. Dirk Moses, eds. *The Oxford Handbook of Genocide Studies*. Oxford: Oxford University Press, 2010.

Boulle, Pierre. *Race et Esclavage dans la France de l'Ancien Régime*. Paris: Perrin, 2007.

Broers, Michael. *The Napoleonic Empire in Italy, 1796–1814: Cultural Imperialism in a European Context?* New York, NY: Palgrave Macmillan, 2005.

Broers, Michael. "The First Napoleonic Empire, 1799–1815." In *Nationalizing Empires*, edited by Stefan Berger and Alexei Miller, 99–134. Budapest: Central European University, 2014.

Byrd, Christopher. *Captives and Voyageurs: Black Migrants Across the Eighteenth-Century British Atlantic World*. Baton Rouge: University of Louisiana Press, 2008.

Civil Code of France. (1804). Accessed 5 May 2017. http://www.napoleon-series.org/research/government/c_code.html.

Clarence-Smith, W., and Steven Topik. *The Global Coffee Economy in Africa, Asia and Latin America, 1500–1989*. Cambridge: Cambridge University Press, 2003.

Coclanis, Peter. "Atlantic World or Atlantic/World?" *William and Mary Quartrely* 63, no. 4 (2006): 725–747.

Coller, Ian. *Arab France: Islam and the Making of Modern Europe, 1798–1831*. Berkeley: University of California Press, 2011.

Constitution of the Year I and Constitution of Year III, reprinted in Stewart, John. *A Documentary Survey of the French Revolution*. New York, NY: Macmillan, 1951.

"Constitution de la colonie française de Saint-Domingue." Rare Book Division, New York Public Library. (1801). New York Pubic Library Digital Collections. Accessed 5 May 2017. http://digitalcollections.nypl.org/items/99988061-a1fb-5c37-e040-e00a18066d37.

Crouzet, François. "Angleterre et France au XVIIIe siècle: Essai d'analyse comparée de deux croissances économiques." *Annales. Histoire, Sciences Sociales* 21, no. 2 (1966): 254–291.

Debrunner, Hans. *Presence and Prestige: A History of Africans in Europe before 1918*. Basel: Basler Afrika Bibliographien, 1979.

Département philosophie, Bibliothèque nationale de France. (1799) *Dernier Mot D'Étienne Mentor, Représentant du Peuple, a Étienne Bruix, Ministre de la Marine et des Colonies* [Paris, 21 Ventôse an VII]. Bibliothèque nationale de France. Accessed 5 May 2017. http://gallica.bnf.fr/ark:/12148/bpt6k5843546p.

Dillon, John Talbot. *Travels Through Spain*. Dublin, 1781.

Dobado-González, Rafael, Alfredo García-Hiernaux, and David Guerrero, "The Integration of Grain Markets in the Eighteenth Century: Early Rise of Globalization in the West." *The Journal of Economic History* 72, no. 3 (2012): 671–707.

Dubois, Laurent. "'Troubled Waters': Rebellion and Republicanism in the Revolutionary French Caribbean." In *The Revolution of 1800: Democracy, Race and the New Republic*, edited by James Horn, Jan Ellen Lewis, and Peter S. Onuf, 291–308. Charlottesville: University of Virginia Press, 2002.

Dubois, Laurent. *Avengers of the New World: The Story of the Haitian Revolution*. Cambridge, MA: Harvard University Press, 2004.

Dwyer, Philip. "'It Still Makes Me Shudder': Memories of Massacres and Atrocities during the Revolutionary and Napoleonic Wars." *War in History* 16, no. 4 (2009): 381–405.

Dwyer, Philip. "Violence and the Revolutionary and Napoleonic Wars: Massacre, Conquest and the Imperial Enterprise." *Journal of Genocide Research* 15, no. 2 (2013): 117–131.

Dwyer, Phillip, and Alan Forrest, eds. *Napoleon and His Empire: Europe, 1804–1814*. New York, NY: Palgrave Macmillan, 2007.

Dwyer, Phillip. *Napoleon: The Path to Power*. New Haven, CT: Yale University Press, 2008.

Earle, Thomas, and Kate Lowe, eds. *Black Africans in Renaissance Europe*. Cambridge: Cambridge University Press, 2005.

Eldem, Edhem. *French Trade in Istanbul in the Eighteenth Century*. Leiden: Brill, 1999.

Emsley, Clive. *Gendarmes and the State in Nineteenth-Century Europe*. Oxford: Oxford University Press, 2002.

Ferrer, Ada. *Freedom's Mirror: Cuba and Haiti in the Age of Revolution*. New York, NY: Cambridge University Press, 2014.

France and its Governments, the Napoleon Series. "Constitution of the Year VIII." The Napoleon Series. Accessed 5 May 2017. http://www.napoleon series.org/research/government/legislation/c_constitution8.html.

Games, Alison. "Atlantic History: Definitions, Challenges and Opportunities." *American Historical Review* 111, no. 3 (2006): 741–757.

Garrigus, John. "'Thy Coming Fame, Ogé! Is Sure': New Evidence of Ogé's 1790 Revolt and the Beginnings of the Haitian Revolution." In *Assumed Identities: The Meanings of Race in the Atlantic World*, edited by John Garrigus and Christopher Morris, 19–45. College Station: Texas A and M Press, 2010.

Geggus, David. "The British Government and the Saint Domingue Slave Revolt, 1791–1793." *English Historical Review* 96, no. 379 (1981): 285–305.

Geggus, David. *Slavery, War and Resistance. The British Occupation of Saint Domingue, 1793–1798*. Oxford: Clarendon Press, 1982.

Gellately, Robert, and Ben Kiernan, eds. *The Specter of Genocide: Mass Murder in Historical Perspective*. Cambridge: Cambridge University Press, 2003.

Gerzina, Gretchen. *Black London: Life Before Emancipation*. New Brunswick, NJ: Rutgers University Press, 1995.

Girard, Philippe. "Napoleon Bonaparte and the Emancipation Issue in Saint-Domingue, 1799–1803." *French Historical Studies* 32, no. 4 (2009): 587–618.

Girard, Philippe. "Caribbean Genocide: Racial War in Haiti, 1802–4." *Patterns of Prejudice* 39, no. 2 (2005): 138–161.

Girard, Philippe. "French Atrocities during the Haitian War of Independence." *Journal of Genocide Research* 15, no. 2 (2013): 133–149.

Girard, Philippe. *The Slaves Who Defeated Napoleon: Toussaint Louverture and the Haitian War of Independence, 1801–1804*. Tuscaloosa: University of Alabama Press, 2011.

Harding, Richard. "The War in the West Indies." In *The Seven Year's War: Global Views*, edited by Mark Danley and Patrick Speelman, 293–324. Boston, MA: Brill, 2012.

Heuer, Jennifer. "The One-Drop Rule in Reverse? Interracial Marriages in Napoleonic and Restoration France." *Law and History Review* 27, no. 3 (2009): 515–548.

Hinton, Alexander, ed. *Annihilating Difference: The Anthropology of Genocide*. Berkeley: University of California Press, 2002.

Hinton, Alexander, Thomas, LaPointe and Douglas, Irvin-Erickson, "Introduction." In *Hidden Genocides: Power, Knowledge, Memory*, edited by H. Alexander, T. LaPointe and D. Irvin-Erickson, 1-20. New Brunswick: Rutgers University Press, 2014.

Hondius, Dienke. "Blacks in Early Modern Europe: New Research from the Netherlands." In *Black Europe and the African Diaspora*, edited by Darlene Clark Hine, Trica Danielle Keaton, and Stephen Small, 29–47. Urbana: University of Illinois Press, 2009.

Honeck, Mischa, Martin Klimke, and Anne Kuhlmann-Smirnov, eds. *Germany and the Black Diaspora Points of Contact, 1250–1914*. New York, NY: Berghahn Books, 2013.

Horne, Gerald. *Confronting Black Jacobins: The United States, the Haitian Revolution, and the Origins of the Dominican Republic*. New York, NY: Monthly Review Press, 2015.

Johnson, Sara. *Fear of French Negros: Transcolonial Collaboration in the Revolutionary Americas*. Berkeley: University of California Press, 2012.

Jones, Adam. *New Directions in Genocide Research*. London: Routledge, 2012.

Kagan, Frederick. *The End of the Old Order: Napoleon and Europe, 1801–1805*. Cambridge, MA: Da Capo Press, 2006.

Kerverseau, François, and Pierre Leborgne. *Rapport Fait Au Gouvernement, Sur Saint-Domingue*. Paris: Chez Pain, 1797.

Kiernan, Ben. "Is 'Genocide' an Anachronistic Concept for the Study of Early Modern Mass Killing?" *History* 99, no. 336 (2014): 530–548.

Kiernan, Ben. *Blood and Soil: A World History of Genocide and Extermination from Sparta to Darfur.* New Haven, CT: Yale University Press, 2007.

Lafon, Jean-Marc. *L'Andalouise et Napoléon: Contre-Insurrection, Collaboration et Résistances dans le Midi de l'Espagne, 1808–1812.* Paris: Nouveau Monde Éditions, 2006.

Lemarchand, René. *Forgotten Genocides: Oblivion, Denial and Memory.* Philadelphia: University of Pennsylvania Press, 2011.

Lemkin, Raphael. *Axis Rule in Occupied Europe.* Washington, DC: Carnegie Endowment for International Peace, 1944.

Levene, Mark. *Genocide in the Age of the Nation State.* New York, NY: Palgrave Macmillan, 2005.

Levene, Mark. *Rise of the West and the Coming of Genocide.* London: I. B. Taurus, 2005.

Margerison, Kenneth. *P.–L. Roederer: Political Thought and Practice during the French Revolution.* Philadelphia, PA: American Philosophical Society, 1983.

McDonnell, Michael, and A. Dirk Moses, "Raphael Lemkin as Historian of Genocide in the Americas." *Journal of Genocide Research* 7, no. 4 (2005): 501–529.

Menichetti, Johan. "Pierre-Louis Roederer: La Science sociale au Conseil d'État." *Napoleonica La Revue* 16, no. 1 (2013): 17–48.

Moitt, Bernard, "Slave Resistance in Guadeloupe and Martinique." *Journal of Caribbean History* 25, no. 1 (1991): 136–159.

Moses, A. Dirk, ed. *Empire, Colony, Genocide: Conquest, Occupation, and Subaltern Resistance in World History.* New York, NY: Berghahn Books, 2008.

Moses, A. Dirk, "Revisiting a Founding Assumption of Genocide Studies," *Genocide Studies and Prevention* 6, no. 3 (2011): 287–300.

Newman, Simon. "American Political Culture and the French and Haitian Revolutions." In *Impact of the Haitian Revolution in the Atlantic World*, edited by David Geggus, 72–91. Columbia: University of South Carolina Press, 2002.

O'Rourke, Kevin, and Jeffrey G. Williamson. *Globalization and History: The Evolution of a Nineteenth-Century Atlantic Economy.* Cambridge, MA: MIT Press, 1999.

Palmer, Jennifer. *Intimate Bonds: Family and Slavery in the French Atlantic.* Philadelphia: University of Pennsylvania Press, 2016.

Peabody, Sue. *"There Are No Slaves in France": The Political Culture of Race and Slavery in the Ancien Régime.* New York, NY: Oxford University Press, 1996.

Planert, Ute, ed. *Napoleon's Empire: European Politics in Global Perspective.* New York, NY: Palgrave Macmillan, 2016.

Polowetzky, Michael. *A Bond Never Broken: The Relations Between Napoleon and the Authors of France.* Rutherford, NJ: Fairleigh Dickinson University Press, 1993.

Popkin, Jeremy. *You Are All Free: The Haitian Revolution and the Abolition of Slavery.* Cambridge: Cambridge University Press, 2010.

Power, Samantha. *A Problem from Hell: America and the Age of Genocide.* New York, NY: Perennial, 2003.

Procés-Verbaux du Conseil D'État Contenant La Discussion du Projet de Code Civil, Annèes IX et X. Paris: Imprimerie de La Rèpublique, 1803–04.

Provost, René, and Payam Akhavan, eds. *Confronting Genocide.* New York, NY: Springer, 2011.

Queija, Berta, and Alessandro Stella, eds. *Negros, Mulatos, Zambaigos: Derroteros Africanos en los Mundos Ibéricos.* Sevilla: Escuela de Estudios Hispano-Americanos, Consejo Superior de Investigaciones Científicas, 2000.

Reiss, Tom. *The Black Count: Glory, Revolution, Betrayal, and the Real Count of Monte Cristo.* New York, NY: Crown Trade, 2012.

Roederer, Pierre Louis. "Analyse des Actes de l'Autorité Publique." In *Oeuvres du Comte P. L. Roederer, 6*, edited by Pierre Roederer, 227–229. Paris: Typographie de Firmin Didot Fréres, 1853.

Saugere, Éric. *Bordeaux: Port négrier.* Biarritz: J & D, 1995.

Schaller, Dominik, and Jürgen Zimmerer, "Raphel Lemkin, the 'Founder of the United Nation's Genocide Convention' as an Historian of Mass Violence." *Journal of Genocide Research* 7, no. 4 (2005): 447–452.

Scheer, Monica. "From Majesty to Mystery: Change in the Meanings of Black Madonnas from the Sixteenth to Nineteenth Centuries." *American Historical Review* 107, no. 5 (2002): 1412–1440.

Staum, Martin. "Individual Rights and Social Control: Political Science in the French Institute." *Journal of the History of Ideas* 48, no. 3 (1987): 411–430.

Stein, Robert. "The French Sugar Business in the Eighteenth Century: A Quantitative Study." *Business History* 22, no. 1 (1980): 3–17.

Stephen, James. *The Crisis of the Sugar Colonies or An Enquiry into the Objects and Probable Effects of the French Expedition to the West Indies and their Connection to the Colonial Interests of the British Empire... In Four Letters to the Right Hon. Henry Addington, 1802*. Washington, DC: Negro Universities Press, 1969.

Stocking, George. *Race, Culture and Evolution: Essays in the History of Anthropology*. Chicago, IL: Chicago University Press, 1982.

Stone, Dan, ed. *The Historiography of Genocide*. New York, NY: Palgrave Macmillan, 2008.

Topik, Steven. "The Integration of the World Coffee Market." In *The Global Coffee Economy in Africa, Asia and Latin America, 1500–1989*, edited by William Clarence-Smith and Steven Topik, 21–49, Cambridge: Cambridge University Press, 2003.

Totten, Samuel, and Steven Jacobs, eds. *Pioneers of Genocide Studies*. New Brunswick, NJ: Transaction, 2002.

Tozzi, Christopher. *Nationalizing France's Army: Foreign, Black and Jewish Troops in the French Military, 1715–1831*. Charlottesville: University of Virginia Press, 2016.

Vaillant, J. *Correspondence de Napoléon I; publée par ordre de l'empereur Napoléon III, V, VI, VII and XIII*. Paris: Plon, 1858–70.

Weitz, Eric. *A Century of Genocide: Utopias of Race and Nation*. Princeton, NJ: Princeton University Press, 2015.

Woolf, Stuart. "Napoleon and Europe revisited." *Modern and Contemporary France* 8, no. 4 (2000): 469–478.

West meets east: Mixed-race Jamaicans in India, and the avenues of advancement in imperial Britain

Daniel Livesay

ABSTRACT
At the turn of the nineteenth century, small numbers of elite, mixed-race Jamaicans traveled to India in order to improve their financial and social statuses. They did so by joining the East India Company Army, or by working as lawyers and civil servants. This global movement – starting in Jamaica, continuing to Britain, on to India, and oftentimes back to Britain – allowed these individuals to reposition their identity as East Indian nabobs, rather than as West Indian elites. By divorcing themselves from an enslaved, African past, they could live more effectively as white Britons. But, as anti-black prejudice escalated at the end of the eighteenth century, it became much more difficult for Jamaicans of color to undertake this journey successfully, as well as to reframe their identities.

With a fresh haircut, and sporting a new blue coat, James Taylor showed himself off to his uncle Robert's family.[1] They were eager to see how he looked in preparation for his interview with the East India Company Army later that day. Robert had worked tirelessly to secure the meeting, and invited James to London in the days leading up to it. The request also finally allowed the family to meet James, who had been attending school in Yorkshire from an early age. They bonded immediately, and Robert declared that the young man was "a favorite with us all."[2] But the visit was not entirely jubilant. Everyone in the home worried obsessively about the interview, not because of James's qualifications, but because of his heritage. Although he had spent most of his life in England, James was born enslaved in Jamaica, the child of Robert's brother John and a mixed-race woman named Polly.[3] This fact automatically disqualified him from joining the Company's Army, which had ruled five years earlier that it would no longer accept cadets with any African ancestry.[4] James had been manumitted, and his father sent him to Britain largely in preparation for an opportunity such as this, and so the family continued forward and decided to lie to the Company. Despite the risks of being discovered, they falsified reports about his baptism, and swore that both of his parents were European.[5] But James's complexion, at least according to Robert, was dark enough to arouse suspicion. The family spent days nervously experimenting with different outfits to downplay James's color, and even tried powdering his face white. Ultimately they settled on a blue coat, short hair, and no makeup.[6] When James presented himself to the family on the morning of the interview, no one was entirely confident that the ruse would work.

The Taylors gambled their reputation because the rewards in case of success were so great. India, like the Caribbean, was a place to make money for those willing to move halfway around the world. It allowed some individuals, with few options at home, to take a chance in the colonies. This was especially true for elite Jamaicans of color attempting eventually to settle down permanently in Britain. They had left the West Indies because of colonial prejudice, lack of schools, and few employment options. They arrived into a British society growing increasingly wary of non-white people at the end of the eighteenth century. A final migratory jaunt to India before returning to Britain could help redefine their status as returning nabobs, rather than as Caribbean grandees. It would also allow for the building of professional networks and assets, divorced from the sugar fortunes of their fathers that were not guaranteed to devolve to them as illegitimate children. In fact, Robert confided to his brother John that it would be impossible to get James "any thing half so good" as a position in the East India Company Army.[7] Other families agreed and undertook the same endeavors, as well as the same risks. This article examines three different Jamaican families of color – the Morses, the Rosses, and the Taylors – who traveled to India. Their experiences reveal that global migration was a key pathway by which mixed-race elites reframed Atlantic identities and financial futures.

Colonial Jamaica was a horrific place for those of African heritage. Over the seventeenth and eighteenth centuries, the island became a hothouse for slavery, with nearly one million Africans brought forcibly to its shores.[8] Enslaved workers endured miserable conditions, a harsh climate, and an effectively year-long cycle of work on sugar plantations that took a heavy mortal toll.[9] By the turn of the nineteenth century, there were 10 slaves for every white person, and the free terrorized the enslaved with brutal violence in the hopes of keeping the colony under control. But this campaign of oppression was not limited to bound laborers. Free people of color – most of whom were the products of white sexual attacks on black and mixed-race women – faced prohibitions from holding office, voting, sitting on juries, matriculating into schools, testifying against whites, and serving in certain professions. Colonial legislation also taxed them more heavily, and limited the amount of money that they could inherit.[10] Although the island's legislature made exceptions to these rules for rich residents of color, even the wealthiest of them experienced regular prejudice in a society so organized around racial segregation. Those who could often left for the greener pastures of Great Britain.

Mixed-race Jamaicans crossed the Atlantic either to find permanent safe harbor, or to use Britain as a first-stop on a global migration. In some cases, they arrived with explicit directions to stay. One Jamaican planter demanded that his two "mestee" sons "never return to Jamaica or any other part of the West Indies."[11] Britain appeared a far more tolerant place, and one in which children of color had greater opportunities for an education and employment. Other parents hoped to have a child return from time spent abroad, under the belief that a refined British upbringing would put them on a higher social footing once they came back. Robert Stirling, for instance, sent his daughter Charlotte to Scotland in part to "qualify her to enjoy the privileges and immunities of a white woman in this island," when she returned. After her father died, though, she stayed in Britain.[12] Although it is unclear why Charlotte made this decision, if she was reticent to rejoin Jamaican society, she had just cause: a number of observers commented on the frequent taunts facing British-educated Jamaicans when they returned to the island.[13] Yet, many individuals of color did travel back because of the advantages conferred by an elite upbringing. Dugald Clarke, a mulatto man who developed a steam-powered sugar mill in Britain, brought his invention to the Caribbean in the hopes of turning high profits. Like more than 650 other Jamaicans of color in the eighteenth century, he petitioned the island's legislature for exemptions to certain laws against mixed-race people. He, along with 70 of those petitioners, noted time spent in Britain as a justification for these special dispensations after returning to their birthplace.[14]

But elites of color were not limited to the two options of Britain and the Caribbean. The wider English empire offered its own potential as well. For Jamaicans accustomed to plantations profiting from the exploitation of large swaths of people, India seemed a familiar place. Britain's Asian outposts were known for dramatic wealth built upon the suffering of a native population. Moreover, East India Company agents and military officers had the reputation of gaining massive sums of money through oriental commerce, as well as outright corruption. A period of largely unfettered fraud and illegal trading started to draw to a close in 1773, when the Company came under closer Parliamentary supervision. Nevertheless, India was still a place to make a great deal of money.[15] Colonial opulence on the subcontinent certainly would have reminded Jamaicans of Caribbean spoils.

The global movement of mixed-race individuals in pursuit of social advancement and economic security raises new questions regarding Atlantic racialization, kinship, and mobility in the early nineteenth century. Linda Colley has shown how military service and other types of imperial participation helped subjects otherwise marginalized in the colonies to claim British identity.[16] Yet, as Isaac Land has argued, Britishness was not attainable for all. Family wealth, in many cases, could not always help subjects with African ancestry surmount institutional barriers.[17] Indeed, scholars have identified a sharp turn against individuals with dark skin in Britain at the end of the eighteenth century.[18] What of mixed-race elites, though, who held kinship with some of the most prominent merchants and planters in the Empire? Most studies of free people of color either place them firmly in the Americas, or see their travels in this period as occurring principally within the circum-Caribbean as revolutionary agents.[19] Some scholarship has emerged to reveal a resettlement in Europe as well.[20] It is worth considering, however, the *worldwide* reach of mixed-race individuals. Colley conducted her own study of a Jamaican woman, potentially of mixed ancestry, who eventually found her way to India. But she presents the story as a unique biography of imperial wandering.[21] Instead, this was a tried-and-true method of advancement for people of color connected to admittedly elite families. Kinship networks were vital in building the British Empire, and mixed-race Jamaicans tapped into their own family associations to navigate global citizenship.[22]

Three members of the Morse family undertook such a journey from the Caribbean to Britain to India in order to capitalize on this potential for advancement. Robert, Sarah, and Ann were born in Jamaica to Elizabeth Augier, a moderately wealthy free woman of color, and John Morse, a rising English planter who died with a significant fortune.[23] Robert studied law at London's Inns of Court, and became a barrister, seemingly without anyone knowing his ethnic background. He achieved some influence arguing cases in front of England's most prominent judges. But anticipating a greater degree of success abroad, Robert boarded the *Seahorse*, bound for Bengal, in May of 1777. Sharing the voyage with him was a Mr. Arnott, the "natural son of the Honourable Frederick Maitland, a post-captain in the Navy and son to the Earl of Lauderdale, by a native woman of Jamaica."[24] As the "natural" – in other words, illegitimate – son of a "native woman of Jamaica" – parlance for a woman of color – Arnott and Morse shared a common path. Most likely they embarked on this journey because they knew other Jamaicans of color who had found success in following it.

Once in India, Robert Morse again took up law though he immediately met challenges. Morse carried a letter of introduction from a Welsh judge whom he knew only through associates. It was intended for the judge's friend, Stephen Cesar Lemaitre, a justice of Bengal's Supreme Court. By the time Morse had landed in India, though, Lemaitre had died. Moreover, when Morse read the letter, he was not encouraged by its potential to win him new contacts. The judge had written, "This will, I believe, be delivered to you by a Mr. Morse, who the devil he is or what sort of a man I cannot tell, never having seen him in my life!" Nevertheless, Morse was soon admitted as an advocate with a generous salary.[25] Yet he grew tired of the profession, as his inclinations were "naturally averse" to the law.[26] He eventually joined the East India Company as paymaster for a troop battalion, and later won a sheriff's appointment.[27] These positions cultivated a strong loyalty to the Company and its officials. When Bengal's governor Warren Hastings was impeached by Parliament for corruption, Morse signed a petition declaring a "general Satisfaction in the whole Tenour" of his administration.[28] As a fellow-recipient of the spoils of Britain's Asian colonies, Robert Morse could not help but support a regime that facilitated the types of bribery and illegality that made a residence in India so potentially lucrative.

Just as Morse may have been motivated by other mixed-race Jamaicans to set off for India, his sisters were inspired by his travels to the subcontinent. Both Sarah and Ann followed their brother to Bengal, although not for any kind of professional appointment. In less of a position than Robert to advance themselves through employment, they instead broadened their networks through marriage. With so many single men making large fortunes, India was a good spot to meet a husband, even if it was not considered an appropriate place for an unmarried woman.[29] They came nonetheless, and not in vain. Ann met a junior servant, and later East India Company official, Nathaniel Middleton after she arrived in Bengal. Middleton had taken up the bachelor's life: he had both an Indian bibi and at least three children by her.[30] But upon meeting Ann he decided to settle down; perhaps her father's large Jamaican estate enticed him. The two wed in Calcutta in the autumn of 1780.[31] One week later, Sarah married William Cator, an East India Company merchant factor and associate of her brother Robert.[32] Both Middleton and Cator had strong ties to the colonial administration. In fact, Middleton had been a regular correspondent of Warren Hastings, who had appointed him as a representative in Lucknow. Although he and Hastings would eventually have a falling out, Middleton stayed loyal. He and Ann named their firstborn son "Hastings," and Middleton claimed forgetfulness when testifying at his former boss's impeachment trial.[33] Sarah and Ann, then, tied themselves closely to an Indian administration that might help advance them once they returned to Britain.

Not long after the sisters' marriages, the Morse siblings all traveled back to England. Ann moved with Nathaniel to Hampshire, while Sarah and William took up residence just north of London. Robert's lodgings were in the capital as well, and he began building an extensive art and book collection.[34] Each of them settled comfortably into English respectability, now significantly divorced from Caribbean roots. The siblings certainly hoped to tamp down any personal association made to Jamaica, or even to India itself.

Immediately prior to leaving Bengal, they sat for a portrait that would present this desired image once in Britain (see Figure 1). The painting eliminated any evidence of time spent in India, and it by no means invoked the Caribbean. Instead, the siblings dressed in refined English fashion, framed by classical architecture, and sitting with European instruments.[35] It asserted visually what they had attempted to claim through travel: they were white Britons with an uncomplicated, domestic identity. Indeed, the family took great pains to instill this notion in their children. Ann and Nathaniel's son Hastings, for instance, later declared to a correspondent that he was unsure if his parents had met in India, or if he had even been born there himself.[36] Global migrations had enriched the family, but these travels had also effectively laundered its members' heritage by complicating the origins of their colonial past.

Figure 1. "The Morse and Cator Family," by John Zoffany, 1784. Courtesy of the Aberdeen Art Gallery and Museums.

The Morses' strategy was attempted by other Jamaicans of color who came to Britain as well. James Taylor, whose family considered whitening his face to pass the East India Company Army interview, most likely did not know the Morses. Their mothers came from two entirely different social groups: one enslaved, the other an elite woman of color. Moreover, their fathers' times in Jamaica did not overlap, so they probably never met. But the island's white society was incredibly small – roughly 20,000 in number at the end of the eighteenth century – and quite closely knit.[37] When fathers discussed plans for their children of color, they often reflected on friends' examples. One Jamaican attorney sent his "Molato Boy" to a school in Yorkshire, having heard that there were others at the institution.[38] Robert Taylor thought of other mixed-race children in Britain when originally making plans for James to leave the Caribbean. He cautioned his brother about sending James to London in fear that his nephew would be reminded too much of a colonial status: "such has been the fate of two thirds of the Young men who I have known of his description." Eventually, Robert found a school – also in Yorkshire – recommended by a friend with his own son in attendance there.[39] After James completed his education, the family looked once more to associates for guidance.

The Taylors did not have to search far for inspiration. They had a longstanding, though estranged, connection with Hercules Ross, who had managed to get two of his Jamaican sons of color into the East India Company Army. Both families grew up in the small seaside town of Montrose, in northeast Scotland. Ross moved to Jamaica in 1761 and established himself as a merchant with the help of Simon Taylor, the cousin of Robert and John. Simon's branch of the family had migrated to the Caribbean a generation earlier, and he would eventually become one of the richest Jamaicans of the eighteenth century.[40] Hercules and Simon became close friends, but the relationship broke down in 1788 when Ross struck up correspondence with William Wilberforce and agreed to provide information to Parliament on the brutality of the slave trade. Perhaps the mixed-race children whom he had in Jamaica, and who had moved with him to Britain, convinced him of the need to attack slavery.[41] Regardless, even though the Taylors and Rosses were no longer on speaking terms, they could not help but notice one another. When James's father John returned to Scotland in 1792, he moved back to the family estate, roughly 10 miles from Hercules Ross's home.

The people of Montrose all likely knew about Ross's attempt to get his sons appointed as officers in the East India Company. Like white society in Jamaica, Montrose was a small, familiar place. Despite its size, though, Montrose was something of a cosmopolitan outpost. It was one of the wealthiest towns in the region, supported by the fortunes of a large number of people – like the Rosses and Taylors – returning from the East and West Indies. In fact, it had the largest proportion of genteel residents in the Scottish county of Angus.[42] Montrose was also near Dundee, a vital port in the coastal trade to London that eventually went on to India. This location inspired many residents to consider a life in Asia. Andrew Mackillop calculates that nearly three dozen men from Angus became officers in the East India Company Army from 1791 to 1807, and that the region had the highest proportion of Company commanders in Scotland. In addition, Dundee's Parliamentary representatives had close ties to the Company, with three of them serving as its director in the eighteenth century.[43] Hercules Ross capitalized on these close associations, as well as his friendship with the rising naval captain Horatio Nelson, when beginning to plan for his sons' employment.

In his first two attempts, Ross was successful in getting his sons appointed to the Company.[44] Daniel Ross entered the Bombay Marines in 1795 at age 14. He would go on to have an illustrious career with the Army, sailing back and forth to India. David was next to interview in 1799, and joined the Bombay Marines as well, aged 17. His story is harder to track, but David did not have the same longevity with the Company as his brother. He left the Army sometime after 1807.[45] Nevertheless, Ross was undoubtedly proud of his sons, and of his own abilities to put them on a solid professional footing. His neighbors were most certainly impressed and aware of the feat as well. With confidence, Ross sent his youngest son in 1800 to interview with the East India Company in London.

Hercules Ross junior, however, would not be as lucky as his older brothers. He interviewed for a spot as third mate on a Company ship, but afterward received a distressing report. "[F]rom the appearance of Mr. Ross," the interviewing committee wrote, it "apprehend[ed] that both his Parents were not Europeans," and declined his application. The committee members went further. They implemented a ban on accepting any future officers who were "Persons born in the West India Islands, whose Complexion evidently shews [sic] that their Parents are not severally Natives of Great Britain or Ireland." This was a sweeping change, but it was not without precedent. Nine years earlier, the Company had instituted a similar ban on officer candidates with East Indian ancestry, after declining the application of John Turing, a Eurasian man living in Britain who had deep familial connections to the Company.[46] The directors did not make their thinking known, although it is telling that the first prohibition began the same year as the Haitian Revolution. Many in Europe attributed that conflict to a prior revolt of French-educated men of color in the colony, and Company officials may have grown nervous about non-white elites in their ranks whom they believed had the same potential to lead an uprising in India.[47] Regardless, the East India Company Army, once a refuge for mixed-race Jamaicans to enter the professional British class, was now officially closed off.

Despite the new ban, the Taylors attempted to secure an appointment for James. They did so knowing full well of Hercules Ross's failure. But the family felt certain that their personal networks were strong enough to ensure success. James's uncle Robert had spent much of his youth in India, and had a number of contacts still in the East India Company.[48] He began fervently soliciting letters of support. James's father John did the same, and reached out to the highest-ranking individuals with whom he was acquainted. "Could I get [James] to India as a Cadet," he implored his friend Sir John Stuart, "I think his Chance of Success would be better than in any other area of life I know."[49] Robert and John's cousin, Sir David Carnegie, also pledged his assistance to help obtain, "a Cadetship for your young Man." As the number of requests grew, the potential damage to the family's reputation mounted in turn. Should James's heritage be found out, not only would the Taylors lose the confidence of their friends, but their associates would be implicated in the deceit as well. Some of those contacts, such as Carnegie, were undoubtedly aware of James's African ancestry because of their own kinship to him, and therefore risked exposure. Moreover, letters from knighted supporters were helpful, but they guaranteed nothing when it came to the issue of race. Even after Carnegie managed to obtain an interview through his friendship with former Prime Minister Henry Addington, the Taylors nevertheless worried about the next steps. Robert notified his brother that a former governor of Bengal had a mixed-race son rejected "whose appearance was by no means worse than James's."[50] It is no wonder that the family obsessed over James's wardrobe, and its supposed effect on his color, prior to the interview.

Ultimately, though, James managed to demonstrate his qualifications effectively to the Company, as well as to convince them that both his parents were European. Relief spread over the whole family. After informing his brother that James had passed through, Robert admitted that he had been unable to sleep after first witnessing his complexion. He even claimed that his nephew's anxiety prior to the interview caused him to grow "a Shade Darker."[51] But James's success calmed everyone's nerves. In fact, the East India Company's declaration that James was white may have opened up his access to other members of the family. Perhaps reluctant to associate too directly with James before his interview, those relatives were now more comfortable letting him into their inner ranks. James met with Sir David Carnegie to thank him for his support, and Carnegie noted that he was "much pleas'd with his appearance."[52] Some unexpected members of the family also introduced themselves. In one of the few surviving letters between him and his father, James noted that he went to see a play with George McCall, John's father-in-law, shortly before McCall took him to Gravesend to ship off to Madras.[53] It may have surprised John that the father of his wife, whom he married soon after returning to Scotland from Jamaica, would have socialized with his son in-law's illegitimate child from the colonies. But step-families were by no means rare in the period, illegitimate children were frequently accepted into Scottish families, and McCall may have recognized James's potential as a future East Indian contact.[54]

Yet, even though James had made it into the Company, his family's reputation was not entirely in the clear. The East India Company had become so concerned with the racial purity of its officer corps that members of its interviewing committee grew distressed that they had not properly vetted the candidate. Indeed, Robert wrote to John immediately after hearing the news of James's success, "some of my friends at the India House told me that no One ever Pass'd under so many Objections." A month later, Robert grumbled that he was still receiving complaints: "[James] was uncommonly lucky in Passing some of the Directors have said since, they are not at all satisfied with their own Conduct in passing him – as they still think he must have some black blood."[55] Although these rumors appear to have died down soon after, they reveal just how precarious things had become for Jamaicans of color. Whereas the Morses had much freer access to India in the 1770s and 1780s, by the turn of the nineteenth century, racial attitudes in Britain were turning even more strongly against those of African descent. The Ross and Taylor families experienced this firsthand, as the doorway to India slowly started to close. Not only did this limit the options for elite Jamaicans of color, but it put added burdens onto relatives who might want to assist them as well.

Even if it was now more challenging to join the East India Company, it was nevertheless still worth the trouble. For James Taylor, service in the Company Army helped him to cultivate a genteel English identity. This process had begun at his Yorkshire schoolhouse, but it would gain full sanction as an Army officer. Indeed, it emerged almost immediately after boarding the *Devonshire* to Madras in 1805. The voyage was not particularly happy. James lost his trunk in Portsmouth, and experienced the normal ravages of sea sickness, boredom, bad food, and nasty weather. Compounding these afflictions was the ever-present threat of French attack. But here James started to meld his own plight with that of the military. As the *Devonshire* neared the Azores, James wrote boastfully to his father about Horatio Nelson's blockade of Napoleon's navy at Cadiz. The victory was even sweeter for James, as his father was an associate of Nelson.[56] This identification with the British military emboldened James in the face of perceived slights. In particular, he grew to resent the ship's captain, James Murray, for failing to acknowledge him. Robert Taylor had successfully won his nephew a spot at the captain's table, a high honor for a young officer. However, Murray ignored the young cadets as they dined: "[H]e never I believe spoke 2 words to any one of us during the voyage," James later complained to his father. This was an especially vicious affront as James had taken such pains to cultivate a refined status through his English education and entrance into the East India Company. "[H]ad he even paid us the common civilities due from one Gentleman to another," he continued in protest, "it would not have been required to have done more."[57] James's choice of wording reveals his own sense of high status as an English gentleman. If he had any memories of an enslaved childhood in Jamaica, they did not influence his emerging public persona. Like the Morses, he felt himself to be British, and he used time spent in India to put an official stamp on such an assertion.

The depth of this personal belief was no more discernible than when James encountered those of non-European ancestry on his way to Madras. As the *Devonshire* cruised along the African coast, it occasionally docked for supplies, allowing its passengers to take sight of the local inhabitants. When James looked upon the people, he drew no connections between his ancestry and theirs. This first occurred when a number of Africans performed the traditional "crossing the line" ceremony for the crew after they passed the equator. Writing to his father, James recoiled at the, "bodies bare and painted in different places with white spots, [who] upon the whole in my opinion […] had a most grotesque appearance." This may have been a performative gesture to provide relatives assurance of his loyalties, but this was not a solitary comment. At a later stop at the Cape of Good Hope James reiterated his disgust, remarking that the black inhabitants who surrounded him wished only to "cheat the unwary stranger."[58] As a young man in Jamaica he had seen thousands of Africans. Indeed, his father built the family fortune as a slave trader in Kingston. But those images had undoubtedly vanished from memory, and James witnessed Africa as many English visitors did. If his removal from the West Indies and schooling in Britain sought to cut any ties he might have had to an African heritage, then the process was complete by the time he set sail for South Asia.[59]

James was most explicit in these personal attitudes once he finally arrived in Madras. Frustration and annoyance saturate his letters back home. He found India to be a completely foreign place: too hot, too unhealthy, and – to his surprise – too expensive. Immediately he complained about his salary, which he now understood would not come close to enriching him at a quick pace. In fact, soldiers' pay had stayed relatively stagnant after Parliament started cracking down on illicit trade.[60] As his resentment mounted, James lashed out against the Tamil people he saw. He described them as "a set of ignorant & careless fools," "cursed rascals," and "expert thieves."[61] These expressions were quite similar to Robert Morse's first sight of India. Upon landing, Morse and his shipmates laughed openly at the "ludicrous figures and postures the black people put themselves into."[62] Like many English visitors to the colonies, James Taylor also made the false assumption that native women worked too hard while their husbands did nothing. He crowed, "the natives are a most effeminate set of wretches one stout Englishman would be more than a match for ½ a dozen of them."[63] James took the colonizer's position. He believed himself different from the Indian people because of his color, his education, his financial status, and his supposed masculinity. The same markers of difference that white Britons used to distinguished themselves from colonial others separated James from the natives with whom he interacted as well.[64] His relatives sensed this transformation. After reading of James's grumbles, Robert Taylor wrote to his brother rather dismissively, "commencing the Gentleman all at once, was too much for him."[65] Robert's comments reveal that, irrespective of James's self-identification, his birth into slavery as the child of a mixed-race woman might never qualify him fully as an elite white, at least in the minds of those who knew his past.

Once in India, James wrote occasionally to his family in Britain, but what happened to him while there is unclear. He pressed his father to help him return home, but to no avail. By 1811, James's letters to his father stopped. There may have been a falling out that did not survive in the correspondence. More likely, his father's diminishing health contributed to the lack of contact. By 1811, James had fought with the Company Army in Île de France (Mauritius) and later Île Bourbon (Réunion). From there, his record trail dries up. Some of the evidence of these travels comes from his mixed-race brother, who wrote to their father about the news in the hopes of joining James in the East India Company.[66] The pull of global travel continued to draw him, and other Jamaicans of color, well into the nineteenth century.

The paths of their Scottish neighbors, the Rosses, are also murky. David Ross is noted as having left the Company and, "turned Turk."[67] It is possible he stayed in Asia for the remainder of his life, living as an East Indian, rather than as a West Indian transplant. His brother Hercules, whose rejection from the Company's officer corps inspired the general ban against individuals of color, eventually made his way to the subcontinent. He served on an East Indiaman ship, but his whereabouts after leaving are unknown.[68] Daniel Ross was the most successful of the brothers. He rose through the Army's ranks to the position of Captain in the Bombay Marines. During his tenure, he undertook a number of important land surveys in Asia, culminating in his election to the Royal Society. It appears that he spent most of his life in India, and that he had several children while there.[69] As one of the last Jamaicans of color to enter the East India Company legally, he made the most of his opportunity. But the timing was not entirely on his, or his peers', sides. Although he may have come close to divorcing himself from a Caribbean past, it would never fully leave him. According to family lore, Daniel returned to his father's home in Montrose in 1801 after completing an initial tour of duty. But Hercules senior had just welcomed the birth of a new son, this one legitimate, by a European bride. He did not greet Daniel welcomingly, perhaps because he did not wish to see his two families come together. Daniel rightfully felt betrayed, and cut off ties to his father.[70] Global travel could still alter one's status significantly, but it did not necessarily transform familial relations.

Such struggles did not beset the Morses, who went to India a generation earlier. British attitudes had not shifted so strongly against elites of color in the 1770s when the Morses began their journeys to Asia. Soon after their return to Britain, however, a cousin did send a letter, which was later published, to the *Morning Herald* that uncovered their "mulatto" status. However, this was to help prosecute an inheritance lawsuit that he was waging against them.[71] The revelation appears not to have significantly diminished their social standing. In fact, a later family history makes no mention of their mixed-race heritage, either because that information had been prohibited from being discussed, or because the Morses' intentions to distance themselves from their Caribbean past had worked.[72] Future generations of the family may not have known about their African ancestry, but the ties to Jamaica still endured. Frank Green – the nephew of Robert, Sarah, and Ann through their sister Catherine – managed the estate that the family still held there in the early nineteenth century. He took over affairs at the moment that anti-slavery activists began calling for the complete eradication of slavery in the British Empire. Echoing pro-slavery supporters of the time, Green's response was, "the condition of the *Blacks* in Jamaica is better than that of the Peasantry in England."[73] His family had long profited from enslaved labor, and so there was not necessarily any reason for him to connect his own heritage in slavery to the abolitionist cause. But he may have also been one of the first members of the family to live without any knowledge of this past, secure in a white identity constructed through tireless global migration.

The movement of well-financed colonists throughout the British Empire is a typical story. Wider imperial adventures offered a chance at social mobility for those who undertook the risks. Yet, this is not a traditional tale told of mixed-race West Indians. The reasons for this are obvious. Most children of interracial relationships in Jamaica were enslaved, and white fathers primarily felt little compulsion to care for them.[74] But of the small number who were freed and offered support, genealogical ties to slavery and African heritage were not an automatic disqualification for a globetrotting life. In fact, migration could prove essential to forming a new identity, distanced from colonial and African roots. Moreover, these travels were not strictly "Atlantic," in that they were limited only to nearby islands, or even back to the metropole. Instead, they took advantage of a widespread and integrated empire that could, with varying levels of toleration, permit them to participate.[75] British policy-makers narrowed these allowances as the nineteenth century dawned, but Jamaicans of color nevertheless continued to work aggressively to redefine their colonial statuses into more rarified British ones.

Notes

1. James's father, John, changed his branch of the family's name from Tailyour to Taylor, although the original version is used in John's records and will appear behind his name here.
2. Robert Taylor to John Tailyour, 5 April 1805, William Clements Library, The University of Michigan, Ann Arbor, MI (hereafter WCL): Tailyour Papers (hereafter TP), Letter Book (1804–1810).
3. Kingston Baptisms. Island Record Office, Central Village, Jamaica (hereafter IOR): Copy Register, Vol. 1, f. 371.
4. Directors Court Minutes, 19 February 1800, British Library, London (hereafter BL): Asia Pacific, and Africa Collections (hereafter APAC), IOR/B/130, ffs. 997–998.
5. Military Department, Cadet Papers, BL: APAC, L/MIL/9/114/211–212.
6. Robert Taylor to John Tailyour, 5 April 1805, TP; Livesay, "Extended Families," 3.
7. Robert Taylor to John Tailyour, 17 February 1806, TP.
8. Rawley and Behrendt, *Transatlantic Slave Trade*, Table 7.3, 145.
9. Brown, *Reaper's Garden*.
10. Heuman, *Between Black and White*, 5–7.
11. A "mestee," in Jamaican parlance, was an individual with one-sixteenth African ancestry, with the remainder of their heritage from Europe; Whittaker vs. Green et al., 18 May 1802, Jamaican Court of Ordinary Records, 1B/11/13/1, ffs. 179–204, Jamaica Archives, Spanish Town, Jamaica (hereafter JA).

12. *Journals of the Assembly of Jamaica* (hereafter *JAJ*), Vol. 5, 8 December 1763, 431; Ibid., Vol. 8, 23 November 1784, 26; *Votes of the Honourable House of Assembly of Jamaica*, 54.
13. *The State of Slavery*, 232; Long, *History of Jamaica*, 328–329; Renny, *A History of Jamaica*, 190n; Walker, *Letters on the West Indies*, 170; Stewart, *A View of the Past and Present*, 328; Cooper, *Facts Illustrative*, 24; *Marly*, 182–184.
14. The petitions can be found in: Acts of the Assembly of Jamaica. The National Archives, UK, Kew (hereafter TNA): Colonial Office (hereafter CO), 139/13–51; Sessional Papers of the Assembly of Jamaica. TNA: CO, 140/23–96; Commissioners of Legal Enquiry in the West Indies Records. TNA: CO, 318/76, ffs. 101–106. See also: Hurwitz and Hurwitz, "A Token of Freedom," 423–431.
15. For a review of these changes in Company policy and Parliamentary oversight, see: Marshall, *East Indian Fortunes*.
16. Colley, *Britons*.
17. Land, "Bread and Arsenic," 89–110; Ibid., *War, Nationalism*, esp. Chap. 4.
18. Wheeler, *The Complexion of Race*; Nussbaum, *The Limits of the Human*; Wahrman, *The Making of the Modern Self*, esp. 83–119; Wilson, *The Island Race*; Molineux, *Faces of Perfect Ebony*, Chap. 4.
19. For a partial list, see: Cohen and Greene, eds., *Neither Slave Nor Free*; Handler, *The Unappropriated People*; Heuman, *Between Black and White*; Garrigus, *Before Haiti*; Newton, *The Children of Africa in the Colonies*; Landers, *Atlantic*, 226–253.
20. Palmer, *Intimate Bonds*; Livesay, *Children of Uncertain Fortune*.
21. Colley, *The Ordeal of Elizabeth Marsh*, xxiii.
22. Rothschild, *The Inner Life of Empires*; Buettner, *Empire Families*; Pearsall, *Atlantic Families*.
23. Jamaica House of Assembly Minutes. TNA: CO, 140/33, f. 66.
24. Hickey, *Memoirs*, Vol. 2, 103–107.
25. Ibid., Vol. 2, 122–130; Vol. 3, 156.
26. Nathaniel Middleton to Elijah Impey, 12 August 1782. BL: Correspondence of Sir Elijah Impey, Add. MS 16263, ffs. 273–274.
27. Hickey, *Memoirs*, Vol. 3, 191.
28. *Minutes of the Evidence*, 2451–2452.
29. There are some literary references to this at the time. In *The Nabob*, Matthew Mite offers to transport two women "to Madrass or Calcutta, and there procure them suitable husbands": Foote, *The Nabob*, 9.
30. Bowyer, "Middleton, Nathaniel," 73–75; Ghosh, *Sex and the Family in Colonial India*, 76. See, also: Will of Nathaniel Middleton, August 1824. TNA: PROB, 11/1470; *Robson and Robson vs. Leake and Smith*, 1834. TNA: PROB, 37/909.
31. Returns of Marriages, 26 October 1780. BL: APAC, N/1/2 f. 145v.
32. Ibid., 4 November 1780; Hickey, *Memoirs*, Vol. 2, 123; Vol. 3, 155.
33. Middleton's letters to Hastings are found in: Warren Hastings Official and Private Correspondence. BL: Add. MS 29142, ffs. 214–215; Add. MS 29143, ffs. 172–173; Add. MS 29146, ffs. 274–275; Add. MS 29155, f. 478. For a discussion of Middleton's bad memory at Hastings's trial, see: Hickey, *Memoirs*, Vol. 3, 155–156; Farington, 18 October 1817, *The Diary of Joseph Farington*, Vol. 14, 5090; Marshall, *The Impeachment of Warren Hastings*, 44–52.
34. Details of Robert's possessions come from announcements of his estate sale: *The Morning Chronicle* (London), 10 June 1816; 29 March 1816; 18 April 1816; 19 June 1816.
35. Other nabobs also distanced themselves from India in their portraits: Leppert, "Music," 68–88; Tobin, *Picturing Imperial Power*, 121–123; Dresser and Hann, "Introduction," xiii.
36. Hastings Nathaniel Middleton to William Leake, 7 November 1819, City of Westminster Archives, Westminster, UK: Hastings Nathaniel Middleton Letterbook, 796/1, f. 213.
37. Heuman, *Between Black and White*, 7; Higman, *Slave Population*, 61–62. For a discussion of their close social networks, see: Petley, *Slaveholders in Jamaica*.
38. JF to [More?] and Bayly, 28 April 1763. Guildhall Library, London: Attorneys Letter Book, MS 14280, f. 28.
39. Robert Taylor to John Tailyour, 4 January 1792. TP; Ibid., 1 February 1792.
40. Sheridan, "Simon Taylor," 285–296; Higman, *Plantation Jamaica*, Chap. 6.

41. William Wilberforce to Hercules Ross, 8 December 1790. National Library of Jamaica: MS 587; Butterfield, *Hercules Ross*, 55–56, 94–96. Many thanks to Mr. J. H. St J. McIlwaine for allowing me to read a copy of his aunt's manuscript.
42. Jackson and Lythe, eds., *The Port of Montrose*, xix–xxv; Harris, "Towns," 195–212; Ibid., "Merchants," 243.
43. Armitage, "The Scottish Diaspora," 280, 297; Mackillop, "Dundee," 160–185.
44. Nelson acted as godfather to Ross's firstborn legitimate son: Horatio Nelson to Hercules Ross, 9 June 1801, in Nelson, *The Dispatches*, 404.
45. Marine Records Miscellany. BL: APAC, L/MAR/C/689, f. 3, 11; Ibid., L/MAR/C/683, f. 16; Butterfield, *Hercules Ross*, 96–128.
46. Directors Court Minutes, 19 April 1791. BL: APAC, IOR/B/113, f. 17; Ibid., 19 February 1800. BL: IOR/B/130, ffs. 997–998. For other discussions of these decisions, see: Butterfield, *Hercules Ross*, 95; Hawes, *Poor Relations*, 55–63; Fisher, *Counterflows to Colonialism*, 201–207; Colley, *The Ordeal of Elizabeth Marsh*, 302.
47. Several months prior to the uprising of Saint Domingue's enslaved population, a group of free men of color, led by Vincent Ogé, organized a small coup that was quickly put down. Although scholars see little connection between the two, a number of European observers at the time pointed to Ogé's rebellion as the spark that lit the fire. See: French National Assembly, *An Inquiry*, 10, 28; Edwards, *An Historical Survey*, 7–10; Garrigus, "Thy coming fame," 20; Daut, *Tropics of Haiti*, 126–129, 560–566.
48. Robert Taylor to John Tailyour, 2 October 1804, TP.
49. John Tailyour to John Stuart, 18 January 1805, Letter Book (1804–1810), TP.
50. Robert Taylor to John Tailyour, 8 May 1805, TP. Sidmouth was James's official recommender in the Company's records: Record of Incoming Cadets. BL: APAC, L/MIL/9/258/96–97.
51. Robert Taylor to John Tailyour, 5 April 1805, TP.
52. Ibid., 6 April 1805.
53. James Taylor to John Tailyour, 9 April 1805, in ibid.
54. Wilson, *A History of Stepfamilies*; Grassby, *Kinship and Capitalism*, 234; Collins, "Reason, Nature and Order": 312–324; Nenadic, *Lairds and Luxury*, 123–149.
55. Robert Taylor to John Tailyour, 5–6 April 1805. TP; Ibid., 8 May 1805.
56. James Taylor to John Tailyour, 3 May 1805, TP.
57. Ibid., 27 June 1805.
58. Ibid.
59. Fanon, *Black Skin*, 11–15, 25.
60. Marshall, *East India Fortunes*. Marshall focuses on Bengal, but the changes in East India Company policy affected all areas of India.
61. James Taylor to John Tailyour, 29 November 1805. TP; Ibid., 7 January 1806.
62. Hickey, *Memoirs*, Vol. 2, 119–120.
63. James Taylor to John Tailyour, 7 January 1806, TP.
64. Scottish identity, in particular, was an important part of British governance in India: McLaren, *British India*.
65. Robert Taylor to John Tailyour, 5 October 1809, TP.
66. John Taylor to John Tailyour, 16 July 1811, in ibid; Ibid., 17 August 1811.
67. Marine Records Miscellany. BL: APAC, L/MAR/C/683, f. 16.
68. Butterfield, *Hercules Ross*, 95–96.
69. Ibid., 102–118; *The Morning Post* (London), 22 February 1821; *Glasgow Herald*, 22 November 1822; *The Times* (London), 6 November 1820; Ibid., 23 April 1822.
70. Butterfield, *Hercules Ross*, 102–103.
71. *Morning Herald* (London), 12 July 1786. The cousin, Edward Morse, did not attach his name to the submission, but its arrival at the *Herald* was timed exactly when the inheritance trial was beginning.
72. Manning, *The Cators*, 6–23.
73. Farington, *The Diary*, 12 October 1815, Vol. 12, 4717.

74. Barry Higman estimates that roughly one-fifth of mixed-race offspring fathered by white men were freed in the nineteenth century: *Slave Population*, 141. Richard Dunn finds the same numbers for the eighteenth: *A Tale of Two Plantations*, 169.
75. For more on the broader connections between the Americas, Britain, and India, see: Games, *The Web of Empire*; Eacott, *Selling Empire*.

Acknowledgements

I would like to thank Rob Taber, Chaz Yingling, and two anonymous reviewers for their careful feedback and suggestions for this article. Their guidance has been incredibly helpful.

Disclosure statement

No potential conflict of interest was reported by the author.

ORCID

Daniel Livesay http://orcid.org/0000-0003-0365-3851

References

Armitage, David. "The Scottish Diaspora." In *Scotland a History*, edited by Jenny Wormald, 272–303. New York, NY: Oxford University Press, 2005.
Bower, T. H. "Middleton, Nathaniel (1750–1807)." In *Oxford Dictionary of National Biography*, edited by H. C. G. Matthew and Brian Harrison, Vol. 38, 73–75. New York, NY: Oxford University Press, 2004.
Brown, Vincent. *The Reaper's Garden: Death and Power in the World of Atlantic Slavery*. Cambridge, MA: Harvard University Press, 2008.
Buettner, Elizabeth. *Empire Families: Britons and Late Imperial India*. New York, NY: Oxford University Press, 2004.
Butterfield, Agnes M. *Hercules Ross of Kingston, Jamaica, and Rossie, Forfar 1745–1816*. Unpublished Manuscript, 1982.
Cohen, David, and Jack Greene, eds. *Neither Slave Nor Free: The Freedmen of African Descent in the Slave Societies of the New World*. Baltimore, MD: Johns Hopkins University Press, 1972.
Colley, Linda. *Britons: Forging the Nation, 1707–1837*. New Haven, CT: Yale University Press, 1994.
Colley, Linda. *The Ordeal of Elizabeth Marsh: A Woman in World History*. New York, NY: Pantheon, 2007.
Collins, Stephen. "'Reason, Nature and Order': The Stepfamily in English Renaissance thought." *Renaissance Studies* 13, no. 3 (1999): 312–324.

Cooper, Thomas. *Facts Illustrative of the Condition of the Negro Slaves in Jamaica*. London, 1824.

Daut, Marlene L. *Tropics of Haiti: Race and the Literary History of the Haitian Revolution in the Atlantic World, 1789–1896*. Liverpool: Liverpool University Press, 2015.

Dresser, Madge, and Andrew Hann. "Introduction." In *Slavery and the British Country House*, edited by Madge Dresser and Andrew Hann, 1–12. Swindon: English Heritage, 2013.

Dunn, Richard. *A Tale of Two Plantations: Slave Life and Labor in Jamaica and Virginia*. Cambridge, MA: Harvard University Press, 2014.

Eacott, Jonathan. *Selling Empire: India in the Making of Britain and America, 1600–1830*. Chapel Hill: University of North Carolina Press, 2016.

Edwards, Bryan. *An Historical Survey of the French Colony in the Island of St. Domingo*. London, 1797.

Fanon, Frantz. *Black Skin, White Masks*. Translated by Charles Lam Markhamm. Sidmouth: Pluto Press, 2008.

Farington, Joseph. *The Diary of Joseph Farington*. Vol. 14. Edited by Kathryn Cave. New Haven, CT: Yale University Press, 1984.

Fisher, Michael H. *Counterflows to Colonialism: Indian Travellers and Settlers in Britain 1600–1857*. Delhi: Permanent Black, 2004.

Foote, Samuel. *The Nabob; A Comedy, in Three Acts*. London: T. Sherlock, 1778.

French National Assembly. *An Inquiry into the Causes of the Insurrection of the Negroes in the Island of St. Domingo*. London, 1792.

Games, Alison. *The Web of Empire: English Cosmopolitans in an Age of Expansion, 1560–1660*. New York, NY: Oxford University Press, 2008.

Garrigus, John. *Before Haiti: Race and Citizenship in French Saint-Domingue*. New York, NY: Palgrave, 2006.

Garrigus, John. "'Thy Coming Fame, Ogé! Is Sure': New Evidence on Ogé's 1790 Revolt and the Beginnings of the Haitian Revolution." In *Assumed Identities: The Meanings of Race in the Atlantic World*, edited by John Garrigus and Christopher Morris, 19–45. College Station, TX: Texas A&M University Press, 2010.

Ghosh, Durba. *Sex and the Family in Colonial India: The Making of Empire*. New York, NY: Cambridge University Press, 2006.

Grassby, Richard. *Kinship and Capitalism: Marriage, Family, and Business in the English-Speaking World, 1580–1740*. New York, NY: Cambridge University Press, 2001.

Handler, Jerome S. *The Unappropriated People: Freedmen in the Slave Society of Barbados*. Baltimore, MD: Johns Hopkins University Press, 1974.

Harris, Bob. "Towns, Improvement and Cultural Change in Georgian Scotland: The Evidence of the Angus Burghs, c. 1760–1820." *Urban History* 33, no. 2 (2006): 195–212.

Harris, Bob. "Merchants, the Middling Sort, and Cultural Life in Georgian Dundee." In *Dundee: Renaissance to Enlightenment*, edited by Charles McKean, Bob Harris, and Christopher A. Whatley, 243–267. Dundee: Dundee University Press, 2009.

Hawes, Christopher. *Poor Relations: The Making of a Eurasian Community in British India, 1773–1833*. Richmond: Curzon Press, 1996.

Heuman, Gad. *Between Black and White: Race, Politics, and the Free Coloreds in Jamaica, 1792–1865*. Westport, CT: Greenwood Press, 1981.

Hickey, William. *Memoirs of William Hickey*. 3 vols. Edited by Alfred Spencer, Vol. 2. New York, NY: Hurst & Blackett, 1948.

Higman, B. W. *Slave Population and Economy in Jamaica, 1807–1834*. Kingston: Press University of the West Indies, 1995.

Higman, B. W. *Plantation Jamaica, 1750–1850: Capital and Control in a Colonial Economy*. Kingston: University of the West Indies Press, 2005.

Hurwitz, Samuel, and Edith Hurwitz. "A Token of Freedom: Private Bill Legislation for Free Negroes in Eighteenth-Century Jamaica." *The William and Mary Quarterly* 24, no. 3 (July 1967): 423–431.

Jackson, Gordon, and S. G. E. Lythe, eds. *The Port of Montrose: A History of its Harbor, Trade, and Shipping*. Wainscott, NY: Georgica Press, 1993.

Land, Isaac. "Bread and Arsenic: Citizenship from the Bottom Up in Georgian London." *Journal of Social History* 39, no. 1 (Fall 2005): 89–110.

Land, Isaac. *War, Nationalism, and the British Sailor, 1750–1850*. New York, NY: Palgrave Macmillan, 2009.

Landers, Jane G. *Atlantic Creoles in the Age of Revolutions*. Cambridge, MA: Harvard University Press, 2010.

Leppert, Richard. "Music, Domestic Life and Cultural Chauvinism: Images of British Subjects at Home in India." In *Music and Society: The Politics of Composition, Performance and Reception*, edited by Richard Leppert and Susan McClary, 68–88. New York, NY: Cambridge University Press, 1987.

Livesay, Daniel. "Extended Families: Mixed-Race Children and the Scottish Experience, 1770–1820." *International Journal of Scottish Literature* 4 (Summer 2008): 1–17.

Livesay, Daniel. *Children of Uncertain Fortune: Mixed-Race Jamaicans in Britain and the Atlantic Family, 1733–1833*. Chapel Hill: University of North Carolina Press, forthcoming.

Long, Edward. *History of Jamaica*. Vol. 2. London: T. Lowndes, 1774.

Mackillop, Andrew. "Dundee, London and the Empire in Asia." In *Dundee: Renaissance to Enlightenment*, edited by Charles McKean, Bob Harris, and Christopher A. Whatley, 160–185. Dundee: Dundee University Press, 2009.

Manning, Pat. *The Cators of Beckenham and Woodbastwick*. Eastbourne: Antony Rowe, 2002.

Marly; or, a Planter's Life in Jamaica. Glasgow: Richard Griffin, 1828.

Marshall, P. J. *The Impeachment of Warren Hastings*. New York, NY: Oxford University Press, 1965.

Marshall, P. J. *East Indian Fortunes: The British in Bengal in the Eighteenth Century*. New York, NY: Clarendon Press, 1976.

McLaren, Martha. *British India & British Scotland, 1780–1830: Career Building, Empire Building, and a Scottish School of Thought on Indian Governance*. Akron, OH: University of Akron Press, 2001.

Minutes of the Evidence Taken at the Trial of Warren Hastings Esquire, Late Governor General of Bengal, at the Bar of the House of Lords, in Westminster Hall, upon an Impeachment Against him for High Crimes and Misdemeanors, by the Knights, Citizens, and Burgesses, in Parliament Assembled, in the Name of Themselves, and of all the Commons of Great Britain. Vol. 6. London, 1788.

Molineux, Catherine. *Faces of Perfect Ebony: Encountering Atlantic Slavery in Imperial Britain*. Cambridge, MA: Harvard University Press, 2012.

Nelson, Horatio. *The Dispatches and Letters of Vice Admiral Lord Viscount Nelson*. Vol. 4. Edited by Sir Nicholas Harris Nicolas. London: Henry Colburn, 1845.

Nenadic, Stana. *Lairds and Luxury: The Highland Gentry in Eighteenth-Century Scotland*. Edinburgh: John Donald, 2007.

Newton, Melanie J. *The Children of Africa in the Colonies: Free People of Color in Barbados in the Age of Emancipation*. Baton Rouge, LA: Louisiana State University Press, 2008.

Nussbaum, Felicity. *The Limits of the Human: Fictions of Anomaly, Race, and Gender in the Long Eighteenth Century*. New York, NY: Cambridge University Press, 2003.

Palmer, Jennifer. *Intimate Bonds: Family and Slavery in the French Atlantic*. Philadelphia, PA: University of Pennsylvania Press, 2016.

Pearsall, Sarah M. S. *Atlantic Families: Lives and Letters in the Later Eighteenth Century*. New York, NY: Oxford University Press, 2008.

Petley, Christer. *Slaveholders in Jamaica: Colonial Society and Culture During the Era of Abolition*. London: Pickering & Chatto, 2009.

Rawley, James A., and Stephen D. Behrendt. *The Transatlantic Slave Trade, A History*. Lincoln: University of Nebraska Press, 2005.

Renny, Robert. *A History of Jamaica*. London: J. Cawthorn, 1807.

Rothschild, Emma. *The Inner Life of Empires: An Eighteenth-Century History*. Princeton, NJ: Princeton University Press, 2011.

Sheridan, Richard. "Simon Taylor, Sugar Tycoon of Jamaica, 1740–1813." *Agricultural History* 45, no. 4 (October 1971): 285–296.

Stewart, James. *A View of the Past and Present State of the Island of Jamaica; with Remarks on the Moral and Physical Condition of the Slaves, and on the Abolition of Slavery in the Colonies*. Edinburgh: Oliver & Boyd, 1823.

The State of Slavery, in the British West Indies, Delineated and Considered. London: Institute of Commonwealth Studies Library, n.d.

Tobin, Beth Fowkes. *Picturing Imperial Power: Colonial Subjects in Eighteenth-Century British Painting.* Durham, NC: Duke University Press, 1999.

Wahrman, Dror. *The Making of the Modern Self: Identity and Culture in Eighteenth-Century England.* New Haven, CT: Yale University Press, 2004.

Walker, James. *Letters on the West Indies.* London: Rest Fenner, 1818.

Wheeler, Roxann. *The Complexion of Race: Categories of Difference in Eighteenth-Century British Culture.* Philadelphia: University of Pennsylvania Press, 2000.

Wilson, Kathleen. *The Island Race: Englishness, Empire and Gender in the Eighteenth Century.* New York, NY: Routledge, 2003.

Wilson, Lisa. *A History of Stepfamilies in Early America.* Chapel Hill: University of North Carolina Press, 2014.

Votes of the Honourable House of Assembly of Jamaica; In a Session Begun October 19th, and Ended December 23, 1784; Being the Ninth Session of the Present Assembly. Spanish Town: Alexander Aikman, 1785.

"A mass of *mestiezen*, *castiezen*, and *mulatten*": Contending with color in the Netherlands Antilles, 1750–1850

Jessica Vance Roitman

ABSTRACT
This article shows that the boundaries between free people of color and enslaved people were blurry on the Netherlands Antilles from the mid-eighteenth through the mid-nineteenth centuries. This blurriness stemmed from a few factors. One factor was the predominantly urban slavery system, in which enslaved people were hired out to work for others. Urban slavery allowed for a relative degree of liberty for enslaved people to move about the islands, and a concomitant freedom to determine the course of their days – with whom they associated, where they worked, and, most importantly, the chance to earn money with which to buy their freedom, thereby increasing the number of freed people of color. This system, in turn, also made it harder to differentiate who was enslaved and who was free, thus scrambling entrenched categories between enslaved and free people. Another related factor was demographic. In part due to the possibility to buy freedom afforded by urban slavery, in part due to the recurring periods of economic malaise in the Netherlands Antilles, which made it attractive for slave owners to manumit their chattel, free people of color made up a large percentage of the total free population of the Dutch islands, sometimes more than 70%. However, unlike in the Spanish, British, and, especially, the French Atlantic, free people of color did not form a sort of intermediary middle class to any great degree, which further lessened the perceived difference between the two groups. Lastly, free people of color fell into a sort of "legal limbo" on the Dutch islands, with no clear distinction between the rights of the enslaved and the free.

Trouble seems to have followed John Francis, a free black porter who resided on the Dutch side of the island of St. Maarten.[1] In 1861, he was arrested for beating up his mistress's husband, and later, in 1870 for public drunkenness.[2] But it was his conflict with Mr. A.A. van Romondt, scion of the most prominent family on the island, and holder of various public positions, including a seat on the Island Council, that caused the biggest stir.[3] On Tuesday 26 and Wednesday 27 August 1856, A.A. van Romondt approached John Francis and a man named Travis, also a free black porter, presumably near the harbor of the island. Van Romondt claimed Travis owed him money. Words were exchanged, and, according to Van Romondt, he "gently" took John Francis' hat as a security for Travis' debt, at which point John Francis tried to hit Van Romondt.[4] John Francis was charged with assault, but Van Romondt was not pleased with the rather mild reaction of the Lt. Governor who had sentenced the porter to several days in jail, and he appealed directly to the Governor of the Netherlands Antilles in Curaçao. In his appeal, he claimed that,

> Every Negro in this town [Philipsburg] seems identified with the case; the exultation and the most aggravating remarks were made, some stating that the day had arrived when any negro could strike a white man and that this Colony would shortly become a second St. Domingo.[5]

That "St. Domingo," as the people of St. Maarten referred to Saint-Domingue [Haiti], could loom large in the rhetoric used by both free blacks and the whites, even more than half a century after the Haitian Revolution, illustrates a few important points about the role of free blacks in the Netherlands Antilles, particularly the Dutch Leeward island of St. Maarten and the Dutch Windward island of Curaçao, which this article will discuss.[6] Clearly, it shows the enduring place of the Haitian Revolution in the imagination of Caribbean people. It was a source of fear and insecurity for whites, while serving as a vivid reminder of power and the possibility of (full) freedom for enslaved people and free blacks alike.

As this article will show, the boundaries between free people of color and enslaved people were blurry on the Netherlands Antilles between in the mid-eighteenth through the mid-nineteenth centuries.[7] This stemmed from a few factors. One factor was the predominantly urban slavery system, in which enslaved people were hired out to work for others. Urban slavery allowed for a relative degree of liberty for enslaved people to move about the islands, and a concomitant freedom to determine the course of their days – with whom they associated, where they worked, and, most importantly, the chance to earn money with which to buy their freedom. This system, in turn, made it harder to differentiate who was enslaved and who was free, thus scrambling entrenched categories between enslaved and free people. Another related factor was demographic. In part due to the possibility to buy freedom afforded by urban slavery, in part due to the recurring periods of economic malaise in the Netherlands Antilles, which made it attractive for slave owners to manumit their chattel, free people of color made up a large percentage of the total free population of the Dutch islands, sometimes more than 70%. However, unlike in the Spanish, British, and, especially, the French Atlantic, free people of color did not form a sort of intermediary middle class to any great degree, which further lessened the perceived difference between the two groups. Lastly, free people of color fell into a sort of "legal limbo" on the Dutch islands, with no clear distinction between the rights of the enslaved and the free.

The Netherlands Antilles: an overview

Except for the years 1828–1845, the Dutch possessions in the Caribbean – Curaçao, Aruba, Bonaire, St. Maarten, Saba, and St. Eustatius, and, in South America, Suriname – never formed a single political unit.[8] This is hardly surprising. Suriname was a relatively profitable plantation colony hanging on to the mainland of the South American continent. In contrast, the so-called *Benedenwindse Eilanden* (Windward) islands of Curaçao, Aruba, and Bonaire, largely lived up to their Spanish moniker of *islas inútiles* (useless islands), which is no doubt one of the reasons the Spanish did not put up much of a fight when the Dutch West India Company (WIC) seized Curaçao in 1634. Likewise, although Columbus first sighted the *Bovenwindse Eilanden* (Leeward Islands) of Saba, St. Eustatius, and St. Maarten in 1493, settlement began only after the British arrived in the seventeenth century. Though the various Leeward Islands changed hands frequently through the centuries, their dry climate meant that their economic importance was small in comparison to Barbados and Saint-Domingue and mainland territories on the Caribbean rim such as Suriname and Guyana. Nevertheless, the Dutch, British, French, Danes, and Swedes maintained their Leeward island colonies for strategic reasons.[9]

In any case, the Dutch Leeward islands were 900 km away from the seat of colonial power, which was vested in Curaçao beginning in 1845, English-speaking, oriented towards the Anglo-American world, and economically marginal by the early nineteenth century, with comparatively small populations of enslaved people. In contrast, Papiamentu, an Iberian-based creole was, and still is, the lingua franca on the Dutch Windward islands, and historically they have been focused on the Spanish-speaking South American mainland, particularly Venezuela and Colombia. What all the Netherlands Antilles have in common is the arid conditions and the concomitantly relatively small enslaved population, certainly in comparison with islands such as Jamaica, Cuba, and Saint-Domingue. This, in turn, meant that on both Curaçao and St. Maarten, urban slavery became predominant. Due to the dynamics of urban slavery, as well as the economic and geographic contexts, free people of color made up 45% of the total free population of Curaçao in 1789, while, in Jamaica, they were 30% of the free population.[10] Slavery was not abolished in the Dutch Atlantic possessions until 1863, more than three decades after abolition in British territories, and more than a decade and a half after the French, Swedes, and Danes ended slavery in their Atlantic possessions.

Urban slavery and the paradox of profit

Curaçao was not a typical Caribbean plantation colony due to its arid climate that made it unsuited for the cultivation of tropical cash crops. What plantations there were on the island hardly deserved to be called as such, certainly as the term is generally understood. These *hacienda*-type estates mainly concentrated on the production of subsistence food crops and on cattle ranching. They were largely a symbol of status and prestige for their owners rather than profit-making enterprises. The island's favorable location close to the colonies on the Spanish main, its role as an important regional slave market during the late seventeenth and early eighteenth centuries, its excellent natural harbor, and its status as a free port, all contributed to its development into a busy trade hub, rather than a plantation colony. In 1789, the only year for which there was a reliable census in the eighteenth century, more than half of the population, both enslaved and free, lived in Willemstad, the only urban center of any real importance on the island, and its environs. It was a small walled city, which barely contained its inhabitants and, by the mid-eighteenth century, had begun to spill beyond its gates and into neighborhoods such as *Otrabanda*.[11]

Although St. Maarten was less mercantile and more focused on agriculture than was Curaçao, the general characteristics were similar. St. Maarten never became a large-scale plantation colony. The plantations that were on the island were decidedly modest in comparison with the size of estates in other plantation colonies. For example, a sugar plantation in Suriname produced an annual average of 158,058 kg around 1836, and 187,566 kg around 1853. In comparison, the average annual sugar production of the 18 largest plantations on St. Maarten taken together was 155,981 kg.[12] M.D. Teenstra, who visited the Dutch Leeward islands in the 1830s, remarked on the pervasive poverty on the island. As Teenstra noted, the common slave lived in "A miserable hut, with walls made of twigs, smeared with mud, and roofs covered with leaves of sugarcane."[13] These dwellings were occupied by family units and were usually grouped in small settlements on the modest plantations. The whites, though certainly better off, also lived in comparatively modest dwellings.

Travelers noted the relative freedom of enslaved people on Curaçao and on St. Maarten. They thought this meant that enslaved people were better off than in the Guianas, but actually they were probably worse off due to periodic shortages of food. Slave owners saved on feeding their enslaved people during times of economic hardship. During the economic crisis in the mid-1700s, for example, Curaçaoan slave owners started giving their enslaved people two or three days a week off from their work for their masters to earn money. This regulation freed the masters from their obligation to feed their enslaved people on those days.[14]

It is not known if there was a similar practice on St. Maarten. It is known, however, that enslaved people on St. Maarten were also rarely confined only to the plantations on which they labored. As agriculture declined on the island in the early part of the nineteenth century, more and more enslaved people were sent to sell produce in the local markets, as well as to hire themselves out as day laborers, often loading and unloading the small crafts that came into the small harbors of the islands, and, in some cases, serving as sailors on the vessels that plied the routes between the islands.[15] A list of occupations of enslaved people from 1854 showed that field work was still the most common job for both men and women, but 27% were domestic servants, there were also masons, carpenters, cobblers, and tailors who were hired out.[16] Women often worked as laundresses, seamstresses, and market vendors, as well as domestic servants.[17] A bondsman or woman would have had to have worked a long time to free him or herself. A male field hand was sold for *f* 400 in 1843 on St. Maarten.[18] Moreover, enslaved people were sent to work in St. Maarten's saltpan. In 1789, there were more than 1000 laborers working in the pan, and it was an important source of income for whites, free people of color, as well as enslaved people.[19]

According to historian and anthropologist Harry Hoetink, the process was similar on Curaçao, with a great deal of freedom of movement for enslaved people. Moreover, the mercantile character of the Curaçaoan economy had important consequences for the frequency of slave manumission. Many of the enslaved people were in fact "luxury servants," acting as gardeners, house servants, or coachmen.[20] A high percentage of enslaved people in Curaçao were seamen (16%), carpenters (9.4%), and fishermen (6.4%), while 17.6% of women were laundresses, 14% seamstresses, and over 10% vendors.[21] The money that they earned could be used to free themselves. A field worker had to pay 300 *pesos* or approximately *f* 750 to free him or herself.[22] This was no small mount. The average price for a slave in Curaçao between 1740 and 1795 was *f* 233 or 93 *pesos*.[23] Despite these barriers, of the total number of manumissions in the period between 1737 and 1800, 10–15% were made by free colored men and, even more so, women.[24]

Of course, slave owners were the main source of manumissions on Curaçao, just as they were on St. Maarten.[25] Sometimes this manumission was less an act of charity on the part of their masters than a convenient way for the latter to free themselves of the legal responsibility for feeding and caring for their enslaved people in periods of economic depression. Plantation owners on Curaçao were known to manumit old, unproductive enslaved people in times of prolonged drought and general poverty.[26] In the middle of the eighteenth century, recurrent periods of commercial depression had caused a relatively large number of manumissions on Curaçao.[27] In fact, in the 1750s attempts were made to reduce the number of manumissions with a stipulation that an amount of money (50–100 *pesos*) was to be paid for each slave who was officially freed.[28]

This was similar to what happened on St. Maarten. When the British abolished slavery in their possessions in 1834, the ownership of enslaved people became increasingly unprofitable on St. Maarten. This was because the British had put a stranglehold on selling enslaved people onwards, as well as because of the ease with which enslaved people on this island could escape to British territory and, therefore, be free due to so-called free soil principles.[29] Emancipations grew apace. There were 685 letters of manumission issued between 1806 and 1845, and more than 202 between 1846 and 1853.[30] In fact, many slave owners turned a blind eye to their enslaved people escaping to nearby British possessions, so that they would not have to feed extra mouths, nor pay the high costs of legal emancipation.[31] The fact that there were not more manumissions likely had to do with the, as it turned out, erroneous expectations for the quick abolition of slavery in the Dutch possessions, which many slave owners were actually agitating for.[32]

Though slavery was not officially abolished in the Dutch possessions until 1863, enslaved people in St. Maarten were treated de facto, if not *de jure*, as free beginning in 1848. After a series of urgent meetings in the immediate aftermath of French emancipation, the planters of the island wrote to the governor in Curaçao that from 1 August of the same year they would treat their enslaved laborers as hired workers. They had decided on this because they feared losing not only their property but also their lives.[33] In the words of one desperate missive, "The spirit of insubordination rules and they are guilty of rebellion."[34] The white residents wrote an urgent letter to the colonial government about the

> highly excited feelings of all the Slaves in this colony, loudly and vehemently demanding to be placed on a footing of freedom, with their neighbors, proof of which, that the gangs of several estates of Cul de Sac in the Dutch part of this Island, are now in the public roads and have struck work.[35]

That the enslaved people of St. Maarten had, essentially, freed themselves meant that on that island, at least, there was even less of a real difference between free people of color and those who were officially enslaved than there had been before. Moreover, the fact that these enslaved people could exercise enough power to affect their own emancipation no doubt heightened the whites' feelings of insecurity.

Even without such an upheaval, due to manumissions, the total number of free people of color increased rapidly during the late eighteenth and early nineteenth centuries on Curaçao until, as the following figures demonstrate, they came to be twice as numerous as whites; and at some point between 1817 and 1833, they even surpassed the total number of enslaved people. That there were "twenty Blacks to a single White" on Curaçao as was contended time and again, was clearly an exaggeration.[36] But the argument does show that free people of color and enslaved people were conflated in the rhetoric used by whites, and, moreover, that both free and enslaved people were perceived by the white population as threatening. A little over half of the total population at that time lived in Willemstad and its immediate surroundings; 42% of the enslaved people, 95% of the Whites, and nearly 90% of the free people of color were town dwellers, making the perceived threat from the non-white group, particularly the predominant free people of color, especially acute in the tightly packed city of Willemstad.[37]

As historian Linda Rupert points out, Curaçao, in general, and Willemstad, specifically, was a contradictory place, at once bound by the conventions of a colonial American slave society, while also supported by an economy that was based on intercolonial trade – a trade requiring the free movement of commodities, vessels, and workers, many of whom were enslaved.[38] Residents of Willemstad from every socioeconomic sector depended on trade for their very survival, and the city and its port drove the entire island economy. Rather than a landed gentry or planter class, the island's most powerful citizens were urban merchants. Similarly, slavery centered on maritime commerce, and many enslaved me were freed temporarily in order to sail with their owners' ships, a legal situation which further blurred the boundaries between enslaved and free people of color (Table 1).[39]

When A.A. van Romondt sent his letter to the Governor of the Netherlands Antilles in 1856 complaining about the light punishment meted out to John Francis, his arguments echoed those made on Curaçao. He wrote that he lived on a part of the island on which there were "only eight white men to a negro population of two-fifths of the Island."[40] Amid the fading sugar economy on St. Maarten, economic malaise, and a perception of dwindling prestige, Van Romondt's statement exemplifies what was for whites a disquieting change in the island's population composition. By the early-to-mid-nineteenth century, whites had seen within their lifetimes their own numbers shrink alarmingly, and a formerly relatively insignificant population group loom large. As Table 2 shows, the free colored group had more than doubled in a little over 50 years, while the number of whites had shrunk by two-thirds. Small wonder, then, that whites on St. Maarten and on Curaçao were, and would continue to be, fearful of both the free people as well as the enslaved people.

An extremely destructive hurricane ravaged St. Maarten in 1819. Reports made from directly after the hurricane detailed the devastation. Over two hundred people and countless animals were killed, 384 houses were destroyed, while 76 houses were damaged.[41]

Table 1. Population of Curaçao, 1789–1840.

	Whites	Free colored	Enslaved people	Total population	% of total population composed of free people of color	% of total free population composed of free people of color
1789	4410	3714	12,864	20,988	17	45
1816	2780	4549	6741	14,070	32	62
1820	2555	5195	6983	14,733	35	67
1825	2884	5203	5781	13,868	37	59
1830	2682	5921	5908	14,511	40	64
1833	2602	6531	5894	15,027	43	71
1835	2402	6176	4949	13,527	45	71
1840	2734	6432	5750	14,916	43%	70%

Source: Hoetink, "Suriname and Curaçao," 71 (for 1816, 1833); Klooster, "Subordinate but proud," 331 (for 1789); Renkema, Curaçaose plantagebedrijf, 336–7 (1816, 1840); Hanneke Lommerse, "Population Figures," in ed. Gert Oostindie, Dutch Colonialism, Migration and Cultural Heritage (Leiden: KITLV, 2008), 315–42, 332.

Table 2. Population of St. Maarten, 1790–1842.

	Whites	Free colored	Enslaved people	Total population	% of total population composed of free people of color	% of total free population composed of free people of color
1790	1151	194	4226	5571	3	14
1816	715	293	2551	3559	8	29
1842	491	405	1730	2626	15	45

Source: C.Ch. Goslinga, *The Dutch in the Caribbean and in Surinam, 1791/5–1942* (Assen: Van Gorcum, 1985), 154; NL-HaNA, 1.05.08.01, f. 351, Gouverneur-Generaal der Nederlandse West-Indische Bezittingen.
Note: There is far more data available for Curaçao than for St. Maarten.

When Reverend Bosch visited the island in 1828–1829, a decade after the storm had struck, his descriptions would seem to show that the island had not really recovered. Not only had the population declined, as Table 2 shows. It would seem that the urban centers, such as they were, had also struggled to rebuild. Bosch remarked that Philipsburg, the only city of any real size on the island, was "Nothing more than a gathering of wooden houses which for the main part looked like sheds, and which appeared to me to be badly kept and painted."[42] M.D. Teenstra, who visited the islands at around the same time as did Bosch, reported that islanders told him that, after the hurricane, only 26 houses in Philipsburg were still habitable. There were a few other tiny villages on the Dutch side of the island, such as Simpson Bay, though they were little more than conglomerations of shacks in which fishermen lived. After the hurricane, Simpson Bay became isolated because the connection with the rest of the island was flooded. In 1829, there were "twelve houses that hardly deserved the name, 24 negro huts in this miserable place, around which piles of trash lay."[43]

Clearly, then Philipsburg had little in common with Willemstad, with its dense population, walls surrounding the city, and vibrant street and port culture. Moreover, the difference between maritime and trade focused Curaçao with its panoply of languages, particularly the creole language of Papiamentu, predominantly Catholic majority amongst the people of color, enslaved and free, and its distinctly Latin culture was different than that of the rather sleepier St. Maarten, where English was spoken, and most of the enslaved and free people of color were Methodists. Therefore, we must be careful in exaggerating the similarities. Nevertheless, the comparison between these two islands is useful. Of course, they were both ruled by the Dutch, which led to more or less the same legal structures and governmental institutions. Both islands, as has been shown in Tables 1 and 2, had very large percentages of free people of color. Moreover, on both islands enslaved people had a relative freedom of movement, and many enslaved people were hired out, or hired themselves out, within the urban slavery system which predominated on Curaçao and St. Maarten. This meant that the boundaries between the enslaved and free were ever more blurred, which led to the same sorts of concerns on the parts of whites on both islands about this ever-growing population of people of color.

"The riotous state, and demoralizing influence, exercised by the negroes generally is to be feared"[44]

Enslaved people hiring themselves out and a degree of spatial mobility within and even across the Netherlands Antilles was quite similar to urban slavery in colonial Latin

America. It certainly did not mean that slavery had vanished, but it does imply that the contours of slavery were different. This, in turn, illustrates that, to paraphrase Rebecca Scott, slavery and freedom had different gradations of gray.[45] In fact, the relative freedom with which the enslaved people on the Dutch islands moved around alarmed some colonial officials, and led them to issue proclamation after proclamation demanding that the enslaved people carry passes, to be renewed daily, from their owners to show they were authorized to travel away from their homes.[46] The multitude of proclamations issued demonstrates just how ineffective they were on these relatively small islands.

On Curaçao, largely as a result of the earliest of the periodic economic recessions that plagued the economy of the island, by the 1740s there were so many free people of color that a large volume of complaints began to appear about their behavior. Many of them had organized into two gangs.[47] The conflicts between the groups resulted in a 1741 ordinance that was directed exclusively against the free people; it prohibited them from participating in any meeting of more than six persons, including weddings and burials, even though as free people, such ordinances should not have been applicable to them. A 1745 decree prohibited both enslaved people and freedmen from walking on the streets after 9 pm without a lantern, an ordinance which shows that the groups were lumped together legally, though enslaved people also needed night permits from their masters. Enslaved people and freedmen were not allowed to carry sticks or other weapons, nor could they make music or buy liquor after that hour, again demonstrating that the boundaries between enslaved and free were virtually non-existent and, instead, color was the determinant factor on Curaçao.[48]

These ordinances were very similar to the ones passed on St. Maarten. No blacks or mulattoes (generally the term used for free people of color) were allowed out after 8 pm.[49] It was prohibited to "sell strong drink to soldiers, blacks, or mulattoes."[50] There were continual attempts, all futile, to limit enslaved people and free people of color traveling back and forth between the French and Dutch sides of the island.[51] Intriguingly, an ordinance from 1806 stated that all free people of color must wear a red ribbon on their chests to "prove their freedom," which would seem to illustrate the concern with maintaining social distinctions, as well as the general porousness of the boundaries between enslaved and free people on the island.[52] There was also concern for their physical safety. Neither enslaved people nor freed people of color were allowed to approach "gentlemen" with rakes, hoes, or anything else that might be used as a weapon, which demonstrates that both groups were viewed as potentially threatening.[53]

This fear of the free people of color manifested itself in repeated complaints about their undisciplined behavior and social intractability.[54] In 1789, a report written by Dutch commissioners W.A. Grovestins, W.C. Boey, and R. van Suchtelen observed that

> a mass of *mestiezen, castiezen,* and *mulatten* can be found, as well as many free Negroes and free maids, all of whom have lost completely the highly necessary ties of discipline; also, the undersigned can testify that they have never visited any colony where the Negroes are as impertinent as here in Curaçao.[55]

The wording of this claim makes clear that all people of color were grouped indiscriminately together. Similarly, on St. Maarten, in 1803 there were complaints made about the "obstinate character" of the free people of color. Their "undisciplined and proud" behavior to whites was decried, and it was ordered that all people of color, whether enslaved or free, must remove their hats when they saw a white person.[56] Whites could not be approached with any implement that might be used as a weapon including sticks and brooms, again showing both the perception of threat and the lack of delineation between enslaved and free people of color.[57]

A 1791 report to the States General complained about the "unruliness" of the slave population on Curaçao, but added that because of the limited natural resources on this "barren rock," there was always a scarcity of food and hence the enslaved people were materially worse off than elsewhere in the Caribbean.[58] The report worried about the enslaved people's "insolence." Likewise, European contemporaries visiting the colony expressed concern about the independence of the free colored segment.[59] The 1791 report urged the authorities to instill more discipline in this group, clearly in reference to the troubling situation in French Saint-Domingue.

And, indeed, there was a slave revolt on Curaçao. It broke out on 17 August 1795 when around 50 enslaved people on the De Knip plantation apparently protested against some alteration in their daily routine, refused to work, and marched off to neighboring plantations.[60] At its height, the revolt comprised 2000 enslaved people out of a total slave population of some 12,000 (see Table 1), and became an island-wide revolution inspired by the ideals and example of the Haitian revolt. The leader of the Curaçaoan revolt, Tula, also went by the name of Rigaud, a reference to the mulatto general, Benoit Joseph Rigaud, who was a military leader of the uprising in Saint-Domingue.[61] Some scholars believe that Tula had ties with the Saint-Domingue rebels, but this is difficult to ascertain with any degree of certainty.[62] What is clear is that there was a very clear understanding of the geopolitical context in which the Curaçao rebellion had taken place, including the French and Haitian revolutions and the French invasion of the Netherlands in January 1795. Father Schink, a Roman Catholic priest whom local authorities sent to negotiate with the rebels reported that Tula said, "The French blacks have their freedom. Holland has been taken by the French, thus we should also be free here." Schink also reported that the rebels sang French freedom songs.[63]

By late August, however, the rebellion had been crushed, and dozens of enslaved people were executed on the spot. The official reports about the 1795 on rebellion on Curaçao gave considerable attention to the numerous free people of color who maintained close contacts with the rebels and kept them informed of the moves and plans of their adversaries.[64] Yet free blacks were also involved in suppressing the uprising. A corps of free blacks, albeit under white command, forced the rebels to disperse. In fact, almost half of the two hundred troops that attacked and captured the rebels were blacks or mulattoes.[65] This fact alone illustrates the contradictory position of free people of color in the society. The reports also emphasized that free people from the French islands had taught revolutionary ideas to the enslaved people and had made them aware of the dramatic events in Saint-Domingue.[66] Phillip Troutman describes how enslaved peoples throughout the Atlantic world acquired, disseminated, and applied geographic and geopolitical knowledge in a process he calls "geopolitical literacy," and this was certainly the case for free people of color in the Netherlands Antilles.[67] In fact, the Curaçaoan government was worried about enslaved people from Saint-Domingue being sold on the island, an eyewitnesses to the revolt on the island testified that he heard the rebels singing French revolutionary songs, and one of the rebel leaders was nicknamed Toussaint.[68]

Not much had changed in the new century. An 1802 report by the British interim governor (the island was under British rule between 1800–1803, and 1807–1816), Carlyon Hughes, reported a lack of discipline in the militias, both white and colored.[69] This was a complaint echoed by the militia commander on St. Maarten, who despaired of the lack of professionalism of the troops, and also wondered how wise it was to have so many blacks, presumably free people of color, serving "when the enslaved people are so restive," showing that he believed all people of color would be allies.[70] Visitor to Curaçao M.D. Teenstra wrote in 1830 that,

> The colored men mostly are lazy and dirty drunkards, and exceptionally bold, so that the sensible thing to do is to avoid them […] The colored are treated with much greater contempt in Curaçao than in Surinam; with regard to the Negroes, however, the situation is the reverse.[71]

These ordinances, travel accounts, and reports sent back to the Netherlands illustrate both the lack of distinction made between enslaved people and free people of color in the legislation and ordinances promulgated on the islands, which will be discussed below, but also the pervasive fear of free people of color. This fear stemmed, of course, from their high percentage of the total free population. It also resulted from their presumed lack of respect to whites, as was illustrated above. People of color were not doffing their hats to whites, were using foul language, and were not acknowledging the social position whites felt was theirs to enjoy.[72]

These examples clearly show that whites were afraid for their physical safety, and that that fear did not seem to materially differentiate between enslaved and free people. Rather, it seemed to be based solely on color. It was ominously predicted that the enslaved and free people of color would rise up in rebellion if they were not forced to pay proper respect towards whites for, as one Curaçaoan official stated,

> This sort of people is always out to dominate the Whites … and in the end it will come to a situation where no white person will dare to go out in the streets for fear of being molested or attacked.[73]

On St. Maarten, a similar fear was expressed quite forcibly. The signatories of the petition in support of A.A. van Romondt's call for John Francis' punishment warned that, "This Wanton, and Unprovoked assault, petitioners affirm, is only the prelude to Similar Acts of Aggression, which will inevitably follow, and no peaceful inhabitants, will henceforth be safe from the Attacks of the Negro population."[74]

It also would seem to show that whites needed to assert their difference from the free coloreds in order to maintain what may have been perceived to be a rather tenuous social distance. As the visiting Dutch Reverend G.B. Bosch remarked, the whites felt that the coloreds on Curaçao were "already too pretentious" as it was.[75] For example, in the eighteenth and nineteenth centuries some free colored people owned enslaved people, which set them up as social equals to whites.[76] In fact, despite the restrictions imposed on free people of color, and the overall poverty of most of them, some individuals did quite well. For example, Gaspar Antonio Quirigazo was one of several free black captains who made a good living off of contraband.[77] Thus, it is not surprising that there were legal measures implemented specifically aimed at curbing the economic opportunities of the free people of color, likely in order to maintain a social distance. Free people of color were barred from keeping shops.[78] There was an ordinance passed on St. Maarten to keep free people of color from engaging in retail trade.

Sections of the white elite on Curaçao and, less so, on St. Maarten were worried about the frequent occurrence of intermarriage between whites and people of color. There were complaints that the free people of color managed to "tempt" whites into marriage, and that they were also becoming so self-assured that they even imagined themselves "to be the equals of Whites."[79] Around the middle of the eighteenth century, several white Curaçaoans petitioned the States General to issue a ban on the solemnization of marriages between whites and people of color. It was stated in the petition that under the then prevailing marriage regulations it was more difficult to prevent mixed marriages and it was feared that "pure white families, which until now are free of such unions, are exposed daily to the danger of being contaminated with this stain."[80] Moreover, whites on both Curaçao and St. Maarten openly stated in petitions to government authorities that, "Associating too closely with them [free coloreds] was to be avoided in order to prevent them from becoming too self-assured."[81]

This concern was likely exacerbated because the economic position of many whites was not particularly good. For example, in 1816, the newly appointed Governor, Albert Kikkert, would report that the enslaved people of Curaçao were treated very well and that urban enslaved people were better off than the poor whites and people of color living in Willemstad.[82] He went on to exclaim at the number of impoverished whites, an observation other visitors to the city had also made.[83] The whites on St. Maarten were not necessarily much better off. As was already mentioned, the plantations were not large, and there were many small farms. The impressive plantation houses built in classic style such as on Jamaica and Guadeloupe were not to be found on St. Maarten. Even one of the largest estates, Belvédère, was quite basic by the standards of other Caribbean islands.[84] When Reverend Bosch visited the island after his stay in Curaçao, he remarked that Philipsburg, the only city of any real size on the island, was "Nothing more than a gathering of wooden houses which for the main part looked like sheds, and which appeared to me to be badly kept and painted."[85] After 1848, the value of plantations on St. Maarten was estimated to have been about a quarter of what it had been only a few years before.[86]

Thus, the whites of Curaçao and St. Maarten seem to have felt an economic and social threat to their dominant position. This perceived peril was at the root of an urge to keep both the enslaved and the free people of color under strict control. The alleged dangers to social stability posed by a numerically superior non-white population constituted the recurrent argument used to defend oppressive and restrictive measures towards the free and enslaved people of color which, in turn, perpetuated this ever-growing body of locally issued legislation.[87] That this legislation could be made locally illustrates the confusion around the actual status of free people of color, and illustrates the legal limbo in which they lived their lives.

"Free enslaved people" and the confusion of color

The legislation or ordinances issued on Curaçao and St. Maarten were designed to keep the entire non-white population under strict control. Very few of the ordinances made any distinction between free and enslaved people of color. Take, for instance, the proclamation made in 1773 on St. Maarten against "serving drink to blacks." The ordinance states that white innkeepers were not to serve drink to "blacks, enslaved people as well as free people."[88] On Curaçao, the same grouping of all people of color, whether enslaved or free, was also the norm. Local legislative authority on both islands was used to issue proclamations on, as was described above, everything from people of color gathering together, playing loud music, being out on the streets after dark unless carrying a lantern, or carrying sticks or anything else that might be construed to be a weapon. In fact, the only real differentiation that was made on either island was that enslaved people had to carry a note from their owners if they were out and about, a regulation that was pointless for free people. That said, free people of color were often asked to show papers proving that they were, in fact, free.

That "blacks, enslaved people as well as free people" was the phrasing almost always used in any locally issued legislation in the Netherlands Antilles shows clearly that there was a conflation of racial categorization. When they were not 'blacks, enslaved people as well as free people' they were called "free enslaved people" whether they were born free or not – a contradictory term that speaks volumes. And herein lay the crux of the matter. As historian Han Jordaan points out, though in the metropolitan Netherlands there was no legal differentiation between free and enslaved people based on color, this was a distinction that was made in the Netherlands Antilles.[89] "Blacks, enslaved people as well as free people" were grouped together based on race in the colonies, not on their legal status as free or enslaved, despite the shaky judicial foundations for such categorizations. Thus, there was a clear divergence in the application of law between the metropolitan Netherlands and the colonies when free people of color were involved – a divergence that illustrates how deeply entrenched racially based attitudes were, as well as the great latitude whites in the colonies had for the application of justice.

The treatment of free people of color in the Netherlands Antilles brings to light an interesting tension. Dutch law was based on Roman law. As Alan Watson in his analysis of slave law in the Americas shows, in ancient Rome, slavery was not based on race, which is reflected in the law: slaveholding was strictly considered a matter between master, and slave and manumission by the owner was relatively unrestricted. Citizenship was also generally easily granted to a freed slave. Although in the Dutch (and French, Spanish, and Portuguese) American colonies slavery was based on race, each colony had received a system of law based on Roman law when it was founded, and, insofar as slave law remained unchanged or developed from its European tradition, the law remained nonracist in its rules. Law for the colonies was primarily made in the mother country, and hence nonracist in character.[90] Thus, for example, when a young public prosecutor, Hubertus Coerman, arrived on Curaçao from the Netherlands in 1766, he was shocked by the practice of distinguishing between whites and non-whites, regardless of whether or not they were free.[91]

Yet this was a deeply entrenched practice on the Dutch islands, and Coerman created quite a stir with his attempts to bring the practice of law on the islands in line with the letter of the law in the Netherlands. He was accused of "favoring mulattoes to the detriment of whites."[92] When Coerman brought up standardizing laws regarding people of color in one of the Island Council meetings, it immediately led to clashes with the Captain of the Militia, who openly declared that he would never permit one of his citizens, tellingly equating citizenship with being white, to receive any corporal punishment for any wrongdoing against "some negro or Mulatto," a statement condoned by the Governor.[93] In this sense, the actual application of laws in the Dutch colonies were closer to that of the

English American colonies based on common law, and in which law was racially based from the start.

These lopsided legal relations between whites and people of color had even come to a point that when a white person killed a person of color, irrespective of whether the latter was free or enslaved, punishment would usually only consist of a fine. Whites were allowed to punish by wielding a single blow of a cane on black or colored persons for behavior that they considered impertinent. Some of these regulations were repeated on several occasions, which no doubt explains A.A. van Romondt's outrage when John Francis struck him back on that fateful day at the end of August 1856 on St. Maarten. Not only had he been within his rights to strike the black porter, regardless of the fact John Francis was a free man, but local custom dictated that the Lt. Governor and police should have acted swiftly and forcefully to punish him, preferably corporally and in a very public manner. As Van Romondt's supportive petitioners so eloquently put it, "[We] do not pretend to be Analysts of these Conflicting Opinions, as regards Caste or Color. But [we] foresee the most disastrous, and pernicious effects likely to occur from this transaction [...]"[94]

The legal asymmetry on the Netherlands Antilles went so far as to prohibit the calling of a witness of color, regardless of whether he or she were free or not, because their testimony lacked any legal recognition. A white witness was allowed, however. If a white person was found guilty of a crime, publicity was limited. If a person of color was determined to be guilty, the punishment was made as public as possible. And perhaps most damaging to people of color, as was seen in the case of John Francis, if a person of color wounded or insulted "a white person of irreproachable conduct," no judicial inquiry was opened, but the white man was simply taken at his word, and the alleged colored aggressor was exiled or received corporal punishment.[95]

The fact that the Lt. Governor on St. Maarten did not punish John Francis – at least not as severely as, apparently, local custom demanded – shows that there were also limits to how much local authorities could translate racially based attitudes into regulations restricting the freedom of free people of color. Firstly, there were limits to local legislative powers; only by-laws with a public function could be issued. For instance, it was not possible for colonial administrators to fundamentally change regulations regarding manumission, inheritance, or marriage law to the disadvantage of free people of color. Secondly, the very existence of a large number of free people of color meant that local officials did not have free reign. This limitation on local officials was not due just to the demographic prominence of free people of color; it also had to do with the economic and social importance of some of these people, particularly on Curaçao. Moreover, there were often long-standing blood ties between white and non-white families. Lastly, the military importance of free people of color in the local militias as a whole forced the (Lt.) Governor and Councilors to be careful not to alienate the free people of color.[96]

Conclusion

The petitioners who lobbied for a harsher punishment for the free man of color, John Francis', offense of striking a notable white resident of the island of St. Maarten claimed that they were "Activated by a love of Justice, but are not desirous of having the barriers of Society Annihilated, and surely the introduction of the Wild, and extravagant tenets of the French Revolution established among them – A System of Equality."[97] Yet John Francis hit A.A. van Romondt more than 50 years after the French and Haitian Revolutions. Despite the passage of half a century, the fear and insecurity these revolutions caused whites reverberated through the Caribbean and through time, while serving as a rallying point for enslaved and free people of color alike. This was especially poignant in the Netherlands Antilles, where slavery was only abolished in 1863, far later than in the British, French, Swedish, and Danish colonies.

Perhaps whites on the Netherlands Antilles knew of the vital role free people of color had played in the Haitian Revolution, and this might explain their particular fear of the free people of color on the islands of Curaçao and St. Maarten. We have no evidence to prove that point, but it is clear that between the mid-eighteenth and the mid-nineteenth centuries boundaries between free and enslaved people of color were blurred. The two groups were often conflated in the minds of whites, as well as in the legislation and ordinances promulgated on the islands. These blurred boundaries were the result of a combination of factors. The system of urban slavery in which enslaved people were hired out to work for others allowed for a relative degree of liberty for enslaved people to move about the islands, and a concomitant freedom to determine the course of their days – with whom they associated, where they worked, and, most importantly, the chance to earn money with which to buy their freedom. This system, in turn, made it harder to differentiate who was enslaved and who was free, thus scrambling easy entrenched categories between enslaved and free people. Another related factor was demographic. Sometimes more than 70% of the total free population of the Dutch islands was composed of free people of color – a presence that struck fear in the hearts of white residents. This high percentage was due to a few reasons. One was the possibility to buy freedom afforded by urban slavery. Another was how attractive it was for owners of slaves to manumit their chattel due to the recurring periods of economic malaise in the Netherlands Antilles. Lastly, free people of color fell into a sort of "legal limbo" on the Dutch islands, with no clear distinction between the rights of the enslaved and the free, leading to confusion and mistrust on both sides.

Notes

1. The island is shared between the Dutch and the French, with the Dutch side known as St. Maarten and the French side as St. Martin.
2. National Archives of Curaçao (hereafter AN NAC) 3757. Brieven aan de Gezaghebber van St. Maarten.
3. For more on the Van Romondt family, see Roitman and Veenendaal, "We Take Care of Our Own," 69–88. doi:10.18352/erlacs.10119
4. AN NAC 3756. Brieven aan de Gezaghebber van St. Maarten.
5. AN NAC 3756. Brieven aan de Gezaghebber van St. Maarten. The Netherlands Antilles were governed from Curaçao after 1845. The other Dutch Antillean islands of Saba, St. Eustatius, St. Maarten, Aruba, and Bonaire were so-called subordinate islands and each had a Lt. Governor who reported directly to the Governor in Curaçao.
6. Confusingly, the islands are known as the "Windwards" (*Bovenwindse Eilanden*) in Dutch, while the Windward islands of Bonaire, Aruba, and Curaçao are known as the *Benedenwindse Eilanden*. For the sake of consistency and to avoid confusion, I use the standard Leeward/Windward distinction as it is understood in the English-speaking world.
7. This article will focus on St. Maarten and Curaçao. These were the islands with the greatest number of enslaved and free people of color in the Netherlands Antilles. This article will not discuss Suriname, because the prevalence of large-scale (plantation) slavery there and

its location on the mainland of South America meant that the dynamics of how enslaved and free people of color functioned in the society were different than on the Antilles. For a comparison of free and enslaved people of color between Curaçao and Suriname, see Hoetink, "Surinam and Curaçao," 59–83. For information specifically on Suriname, see Hoefte and Vrij, "Free Black and Colored Women," 145–168; and Hoefte, "Free blacks and coloureds," 102–129.

8. During these years, the Governor General of the West Indian possessions was located in Suriname's capital city of Paramaribo. After 1845, the Antilles were governed from Curaçao, and Suriname became a separate entity.
9. At the end of the 1840s, salt was the most important export commodity of the Dutch Leeward islands, with St. Maarten producing 311,114 barrels per year. Calculations based on Renkema, *Het Curaçaose Plantagebedrijf in de negentiende eeuw*; and Paula, *'Vrije' Slaven*.
10. For Curaçao, see Klooster, "Subordinate but Proud," 331. For Jamaica, see Burnard, *Planters, Merchants, and Enslaved people*, 173.
11. Klooster, "Curaçao as a Transit Center to the Spanish," 25–51.
12. Calculations for St. Maarten based on Paula, *'Vrije' Slaven*, 37–38. Calculations for Suriname from van Stipriaan, "Suriname and the Abolition of Slavery," 117–141, esp.117, note 3.
13. Teenstra, *De Nederlandsche West-Indische Eilanden*, vol. 2, 295.
14. National Archive of The Netherlands (hereafter NL-HaNA): Tweede West-Indische Compagnie (hereafter NWIC), 1.05.01.02, inventory number 607, ffs. 61617, 14 August 1770 and 22 July 1771, 1.05.01.02, inventory number 608, ffs. 300–301. This led to an increase in crime, because a few days a week was not enough to earn what they needed legally. Sheep and goats were the most frequently stolen items. In 1789 on Curaçao, there were 31,401 sheep and 9201 goats. See Hartog, *Curaçao*, vol. 1, 372.
15. NL-HaNA: Ministerie van Koloniën, 1814–1849, 2.10.01, inv. nr. 3865, 6 June 1835.
16. Paula, *'Vrije' Slaven*, 111.
17. NL-HaNA: St. Eustatius, St. Maarten en Saba tot 1828, 1.05.13.01, inv. nr. 485.
18. *Tweede Rapport der Staatscommissie benoemd bij koniklijk besluit van 29 november 1853*, 313. The price of such an enslaved field hand declined by two-thirds in 1847 to a mere f 150. See Roitman, "Land of Hope and Dreams," 375–398, 385; and "The Price You Pay," 196–223.
19. Paula, *'Vrije' Slaven*, 54. This number includes both enslaved and free people from both the Dutch and the French side of the island.
20. Hoetink, "Suriname and Curaçao," 67.
21. NL-HaNA: NWIC, 1.05.01.02, inv. nr. 1166, f. 124, cited in Klooster, "Subordinate but Proud," 285.
22. Klooster, "Subordinate but Proud," 286.
23. Visman, "Van slaaf tot plantagehouder," 39–51, 40–41; Postma, *The Dutch in the Atlantic Slave Trade*, 268.
24. Oostindie, "Curaçao," 253. Oostindie summarizes the data in Jordaan, *Slavernij & Vrijheid op Curaçao*, 274–276.
25. Jordaan, *Slavernij & Vrijheid op Curaçao*, 274–276 for Curaçao, and Paula, *'Vrije' Slaven*, 112 for St. Maarten.
26. Hoetink, "Suriname and Curaçao," 67.
27. Hoetink, "Suriname and Curaçao," 79–80.
28. Hoetink "Suriname and Curaçao," 68; Schiltkamp and de Smidt, eds., *West Indisch plakkaatboek*, vol. 1, nos. 67, 97, 143, 150, 223, 256, 288, 290; vol. 2, nos. 391 (7), 395 (4), 430; and Watson, *Slave Law in the Americas*, 109.
29. See Roitman, "Land of Hope and Dreams," 386–387; and "The Price You Pay."
30. NL-HaNA: St. Maarten na 1828, 1.05.13.03, inv.nr. 33, Register van vrije lieden binnen het Nederlandsch gedeelte des Eilands Sint Maarten, 1806–1845; Paula, *'Vrije' Slaven*, 143–148.
31. Roitman, "Land of Hope and Dreams," 387–388.
32. Ibid., 384.
33. NL-HaNA: Ministerie van Koloniën, 1814–1849, 2.10.01, inv. nr. 3878, 20 June 1848.
34. Ibid., 12 June 1848.
35. NL-HaNA: Collectie C.Ph.C.E. Steinmetz, 1.13.21, inv. nr. 1a, 1 June 1848.

36. Klooster, "Subordinate but proud," 286, 289.
37. Population figures from Klooster "Subordinate but Proud," 286, 289.
38. Rupert. *Creolization and Contraband*, 104.
39. Ibid., 119. Rupert discusses temporarily freed sailors throughout her book. Women made up 60% of the port's population, though only 16% of the registered heads of household. See NL-HaNA: NWIC, 1.05.01.02, inv. nr. 1149. With so many men temporarily away at sea for extended periods of time, women were likely the de facto heads of many more households. See Rupert, 125. Women were also significant property owners in town. Twenty-five percent of Willemstad's houses were owned by women, 85% of whom were widows. NL-HaNA: NWIC, 1.05.01.02, inv. nr. 206, 35–42.
40. AN NAC: 3756, Brieven aan de Gezaghebber van St. Maarten, 25 August 1856.
41. Archives of Dutch St. Maarten (ASM): Commander's Journal, 22 September 1819.
42. Bosch, *Reizen in West-Indie: Eerste deel*, 73.
43. Teenstra, *De Nederlandsche West-Indische eilanden*, 246.
44. AN NAC: 3756, Brieven aan de Gezaghebber van St. Maarten, 25 August 1856.
45. See Scott, *Degrees of Freedom*; and Reis, *Slave Rebellion in Brazil*, 175–186.
46. AN NAC: 3746, 4 June 1845; AN NAC: 4753, 13 September 1847; AN NAC: 3897, 3 April 1848; AN NAC: 4543, 12 October 1852, to list but a few of the many examples.
47. These gangs were given the unexplainable names *Borosi* and *Japans,* and had started fighting on every conceivable occasion. It is tempting to suppose that this division correlated with that between free mulattoes and free Negroes, a distinction that authorities often made, which usually correlated to a difference in status. "Free mulattoes," by virtue of their lighter skin color were awarded higher social status. Moreover, those who had been born free, versus those who had been manumitted, were accorded a higher rank. Though a clear social distinction did exist between these two groups (a distinction which the government emphasized by dealing separately with them in administrative and military matters), there is no proof for the supposition. Hoetink, "Surinam and Curaçao," 67.
48. Hoetink, "Suriname and Curaçao," 67.
49. NL-HaNA: WIC, 1.05.01.02, inv. nr. 1309, 6 February and 24 March 1781.
50. NL-HaNA: St. Eustatius, St. Maarten en Saba tot 1828, 1.05.13.01, inv. nr. 295, ffs. 357–358, 25 May 1795. This ordinance was repeated multiple times, including 2 December 1797, f. 443.
51. NL-HaNA: St. Eustatius, St. Maarten en Saba tot 1828, 1.05.13.01, inv. nr. 292, f. 81, 29 November 1768.
52. NL-HaNA: St. Eustatius, St. Maarten en Saba tot 1828, 1.05.13.01, inv. nr. 343, f. 42, 25 January 1806. This ordinance had been issued before, including on 25 November 1786 and 12 January 1787.
53. NL-HaNA: St. Eustatius, St. Maarten en Saba tot 1828, 1.05.13.01, inv. nr. 292, f. 31, 15 August 1770. This was an oft-repeated ordinance, including in 1780, 1785, 1787, and had already been issued in 1741.
54. Hoetink, "Suriname and Curaçao," 71.
55. Goslinga, *Emancipatie en emancipator*, 37.
56. NL-HaNA: St. Eustatius, St. Maarten en Saba tot 1828, 1.05.13.01, inv. nr. 343, f. 23a.
57. Ibid.
58. Grovestins and Boey, "Rapport betreffende het eiland Curaçao (1791)," 123.
59. Klooster, "Subordinate but Proud."
60. Oostindie, "Slave resistance, colour lines, and the impact of the French and Haitian revolutions in Curaçao," 8.
61. Rupert, 208.
62. Rego, *Sklabitut I rebellion 1795*.
63. Goslinga, *Dutch in the Caribbean and in the Guianas*, 10 and Rupert, 208–209.
64. Hoetink, "Suriname and Curaçao," 69.
65. Rupert, 207.
66. Wim Klooster argues that the French revolutionary message had a more direct impact on free people of color in the Caribbean than on enslaved people. According to Klooster, they hoped

to achieve full legal equality as promised by the Declaration of the Rights of Man, while enslaved people were more often inspired by the notion of a royal decree that emancipated them. Klooster, "The Rising Expectations of Free," 57–74.

67. Troutman, "*Grapevine in the Slave Market*," 203–233. More research must be done on the effects of the Haitian Revolution on the Dutch Leeward islands of St. Maarten, Saba, and St. Eustatius. It is clear, however, that the enslaved and free people on these islands were well aware of what was going on in the rest of the region, as well as further afield. See Roitman, "The Price You Pay," and "Land of Hope and Dreams."
68. Oostindie, "Slave Resistance, Color Lines," 10. Wim Klooster examines the networks of Curaçaoan people of color and enslaved people throughout the Caribbean, including St. Thomas, Louisiana, and the mainland of Venezuela. See also his, "The Rising Expectations of Free," 66–69.
69. Hughes, "Economic and Strategic Importance," 146.
70. AN NAC: 4952, Registratie op de Gouv. Correspondenties St. Martin & St. Eustatius 1845–1854, 18 October 1848.
71. Teenstra, *De Nederlandsche West-Indische Eilanden*, 165–166.
72. AN NAC: 3866, no. 32 17/39, 14 August 1848
73. NL-HaNA: NWIC, 1.05.01.02, inv. no. 605, f. 565.
74. AN NAC: 3756, Brieven aan de Gezaghebber van St. Maarten.
75. Bosch, *Reizen in West-Indie: Eerste deel*, 34.
76. Hoetink, "Suriname and Curaçao," 74.
77. Rupert, 147.
78. NL-HaNA: NWIC, 1.05.01.02, inv. no. 1176, f. 453; See also Klooster, "Subordinate but Proud," 289.
79. Kunst, "Van zaak tot person," 56.
80. Schiltkamp and de Smidt, eds., *West Indisch plakkaatboek*, 66; Kunst, "Van zaak tot persoon," 205–206.
81. Jordaan, "Free Blacks and Coloreds, and the Administration of Justice in Eighteenth-Century Curaçao," 67; NL-HaNA: St. Maarten na 1828, 1.05.13.03, inv. nr. 49.
82. Kikkert, "Economische toestand op Curaçao, Bonaire en Aruba (1817)," 164.
83. Grovestins and Boey, "Rapport", 124–125; Hughes, "Economic and Strategic Importance," 161.
84. Bergsma and Dijkshoorn, "Traditional Architecture on the Windward Islands," 92–93.
85. Bosch, *Reizen in West-Indie: Eerste deel*, 73.
86. AN NAC: 3756, 16 May 1852. Union Farm, a 180-acre sugar plantation with 58 enslaved people sold for ƒ 8000 in 1851. Twenty-two years earlier, it had sold for ƒ 30,000. In 1848, enslaved people on the French side of the island were emancipated, and as a consequence, enslaved people on the Dutch side were treated as de facto if not *de jure* free. See Roitman, "Land of Hope and Dreams," 185.
87. Jordaan, "Free Blacks and Coloreds," 84.
88. NL-HaNA: St. Eustatius, St. Maarten en Saba tot 1828, 1.05.13.01, inv. nr. 292 (3), f. 152a, 3 August 1773. This ordinance was clearly ineffective as it was repeated in 1785, 1.05.13.01, inv. nr. 294, ffs. 1–4 and in 1795, 1.05.13.01, inv. nr. 205, 1795. It had already been proclaimed earlier in 1745.
89. Jordaan, "Free Blacks and Coloreds."
90. Watson, *Slave Law in the Americas*, 128, 130–133.
91. Coerman is discussed at length in Jordaan, "Free Blacks and Coloreds," but was first reviewed in Klooster, "Subordinate but Proud," 290–291.
92. NL-HaNA: NWIC, 1.05.01.02, inv. nr. 318, 30 December 1766.
93. NL-HaNA: NWIC, 1.05.01.02, inv. nr. 604, 3 July 1765, 1420–1422, cited in Jordaan, "Free Blacks and Coloreds," 66.
94. AN NAC: 3756, Brieven aan de Gezaghebber van St. Maarten.
95. NL-HaNA: NWIC, 1.05.01.02, inv. nr. 318, 30 December 1766; Schiltkamp and De Smidt, vol. 1, 259; cf. Klooster, "Subordinate but Proud," 289.
96. Jordaan "Free Blacks and Colored," 84.
97. AN NAC: 3756, Brieven aan de Gezaghebber van St. Maarten.

Acknowledgements

The author would like to thank the two anonymous reviewers for their insightful and helpful comments. She would also like to thank Charlton Yingling for including her in this project, and both Charlton and Robert Taber for putting together this special edition. This work was supported by the Dutch Organization for Scientific Research (NWO), grant number 858.14.011.

Funding

This work was supported by Nederlandse Organisatie voor Wetenschappelijk Onderzoek "The Dutch Windward Islands: Confronting the Contradictions of Belonging, 1815–2015" [grant number 858.14.011].

ORCID

Jessica Vance Roitman http://orcid.org/0000-0003-2908-2364

Bibliography

Bergsma, Grietzen, and Siem Dijkshoorn. "Traditional Architecture on the Windward Islands." In *Building Up the Future from the Past*, edited by Henry Coomans, et al., 89–98. Zutphen: Walburg Pers, 1990.

Bosch, G. B. *Reizen in West-Indie: Eerste deel*. Utrecht: Van der Monde, 1829.

Burnard, Trevor. *Planters, Merchants, and Enslaved People: Plantation Societies in British America*. Chicago, IL: University of Chicago Press, 2015.

Goslinga, Ch. *The Dutch in the Caribbean and in the Guianas, 1680–1791*. Assen/Maastricht: van Gorcum, 1985.

Goslinga, Ch. *Emancipatie en emancipator: De geschiedenis van de Slavernij of de Benedenwindse Eilanden en van het werk der Bevrijding*. Assen: Van Gorcum, 1956.

Grovestins, W. A. S. and W. C. Boey. "Rapport betreffende het eiland Curaçao (1791)." In *Breekbare banden: Feiten en visies over Aruba, Bonaire, Curaçao na de Vrede van Munster, 1648–1998*, edited by Maritza Coomans-Eustatia, et al., 109–126. Bloemendaal: Stichting Libri Antilliania, 1998.

Hartog, Johan. *Curaçao*. 2 Vols. Aruba: De Wit, 1961.

Hoefte, Rosemarijn, and Jean Jacques Vrij. "Free Black and Colored Women in Early-nineteenth-century Paramaribo, Suriname." In *Beyond Bondage: Free Women of Color in the Americas*, edited by David Barry Gaspar, and Darlene Clark Hine, 145–168. Urbana: University of Illinois Press, 2004.

Hoefte, Rosemarijn. "Free Blacks and Coloureds in Plantation Suriname." *Slavery & Abolition* 17, no. 1 (1996): 102–129.

Hoetink, Harry. "Surinam and Curaçao." In *Neither Slave Nor Free: The Freedmen of African Descent in the Slave Societies of the New World*, edited by David W. Cohen, and Jack P. Greene, 59–83. Baltimore, MD: Johns Hopkins University Press, 1972.

Hughes, W. Carlyon. "Economic and Strategic Importance of Curaçao (1802)." In *Breekbare banden: Feiten en visies over Aruba, Bonaire, Curaçao na de Vrede van Munster, 1648–1998*, edited by Maritza Coomans-Eustatia, et al., 143–150. Bloemendaal: Stichting Libri Antilliania, 1998.

Jordaan, Han. "Free Blacks and Coloreds, and the Administration of Justice in Eighteenth-Century Curaçao." *New West Indian Guide* 84, nos. 1–2 (2010): 63–86.

Jordaan, Han. *Slavernij &Vrijheid op Curaçao: De Dynamiek van een Achttiende-Eeuws Atlantisch Handelsknooppunt*. Zutphen: Walburg Pers, 2013.
Kikkert, A. "Economische toestand op Curaçao, Bonaire en Aruba (1817)." In *Breekbare banden: Feiten en visies over Aruba, Bonaire, Curaçao na de Vrede van Munster, 1648–1998*, edited by Maritza Coomans-Eustatia, et al., 163–168. Bloemendaal: Stichting Libri Antilliania, 1998.
Klooster, Wim. "Curaçao as a Transit Center to the Spanish Main and the French West Indies." In *Dutch Atlantic Connections, 1680–1800: Linking Empires, Bridging Borders*, edited by Gert Oostindie, and Jessica Vance Roitman, 25–51. Leiden: Brill, 2014.
Klooster, Wim. "The Rising Expectations of Free and Enslaved Blacks in the Greater Caribbean." In *Curaçao in the Age of Revolutions, 1795–1800*, edited by Wim Klooster, and Gert Oostindie, 57–74. Leiden: Brill, 2011.
Klooster, Wim. "Subordinate but Proud: Curaçao's Free Blacks and Mulattoes in the Eighteenth Century." *New West Indian Guide* 68, nos. 3–4 (1994): 283–300.
Kunst, A. J. M. "Van zaak tot persoon: De handel in slaven en de slavernij op de Nederlandse Antillen." In *Verzekeringen van vriendschap: Rechtsgeleerde opstellen aangeboden aan prof. Mr. T.J. Dorhout Mees*, edited by R. Savatier, et al., 49–60. Deventer: Kluwer, 1974.
Oostindie, Gert. "Curaçao: Insular Nationalism vis-à-vis Dutch (Post) Colonialism." In *Exploring the Dutch Empire: Agents, Networks and Institutions, 1600–2000*, edited by Cátia Antunes, and Jos Gommans, 245–266. London: Bloomsbury, 2015.
Oostindie, Gert. "Slave Resistance, Colour Lines, and the Impact of the French and Haitian Revolutions in Curaçao." In *Curaçao in the Age of Revolutions, 1795–1800*, edited by Wim Klooster, and Gert Oostindie, 1–22. Leiden: Brill, 2011.
Paula, A. F. *'Vrije' Slaven: een social-historische studie over de dualistische slavenemancipatie op Nederlands Sint Maarten, 1816–1863*. Zutphen: Walburg Pers, 1993.
Postma, Johannes. *The Dutch in the Atlantic Slave Trade*. Cambridge: Cambridge University Press, 1990.
Rego, Charles Do. *Sklabitut I rebellion 1795*. Curaçao: Asosiashon Promoshon Konsenshi Istoriko, 1995.
Reis, João José. *Slave Rebellion in Brazil: The Muslim Uprising of 1835 in Bahia*. Baltimore, MD: Johns Hopkins Press, 1993.
Renkema, W. E. "Het Curaçaose Plantagebedrijf in de negentiende eeuw." PhD diss., Vrije Universiteit, Amsterdam, 1981.
Roitman, Jessica Vance. "Land of Hope and Dreams: Slavery and Abolition in the Dutch Leeward Islands, 1825–1865." *Slavery & Abolition* 37, no. 2 (2016): 375–398.
Roitman, Jessica Vance. "The Price You Pay: Choosing Family, Friends, and Familiarity Over Freedom in the Leeward Islands, 1835–1863." *Journal of Global Slavery* 1, nos. 2–3 (2016): 196–223.
Roitman, Jessica Vance, and Wouter Veenendaal. "We Take Care of Our Own: The Origins of Oligarchic Politics in St. Maarten." *European Review of Latin American and Caribbean Studies* 102 (2016): 69–88. doi:10.18352/erlacs.10119.
Rupert, Linda. *Creolization and Contraband. Curaçao in the Early Modern Atlantic World*. Athens, GA: University of Georgia Press, 2012.
Schiltkamp, J. A., and J. Th. de Smidt, eds. *West Indisch plakkaatboek: Publikaties en andere wetten alsmede de oudste resoluties betrekking hebbende op Curacao, Aruba, Bonaire*. 2 Vols. Amsterdam: S. Emmering, 1978.
Scott, Rebecca. *Degrees of Freedom: Louisiana and Cuba After Slavery*. Cambridge, MA: Harvard University Press, 2005.
Stipriaan, Alex van. "Suriname and the Abolition of Slavery." In *Fifty Years Later: Antislavery, Capitalism and Modernity in the Dutch Orbit*, edited by Gert Oostindie, 117–141. Leiden: KITLV, 1995.
Teenstra, M. D. *De Nederlandsche West-Indische Eilanden*. 2 Vols. Amsterdam: Sulpke, 1837.
Troutman, Phillip. "Grapevine in the Slave Market: African American Geopolitical Literacy and the 1841 *Creole* Revolt." In *The Chattel Principle: Internal Slave Trades in the Americas*, edited by Walter Johnson, 203–233. New Haven, CT: Yale University Press, 2004.
Tweede Rapport der Staatscommissie benoemd bij koniklijk besluit van 29 November 1853.
Visman, M. A. "Van slaaf tot plantagehouder: een aspect van het 18e eeuws plantagewezen op Curaçao." *New West Indian Guide* 55, no. 1 (1981): 39–51.
Watson, Allan. *Slave Law in the Americas*. Athens, GA: University of Georgia Press, 1989.

Index

Note: Italic and **boldface** page numbers refer to figures & tables, pagenumbers followed by "n" denote endnotes

Addington, Henry 102, 126
Africanity and universalism 75–9
Age of Atlantic Revolutions 1, 2, 4, 6, 15, 25
Aldiquir, Pierre 109
Allan, John 63
Aly, Paul 84, 85
Appau, Augustin 109
Appeal to the Colored Citizens of the World (Walker) 2
Ardouin, Beaubrun 80, 83–6, 88n49
Ardouin, Céligny 82–5
Armée d'Orient 97
Atlantic Creoles 3
Atlantic economy 96
Augier, Elizabeth 122
August 1791 revolt 82, 83
Axis Rule in Occupied Europe (Lemkin) 93

Balborda, Abraham 65, 66
Balborda, Samuel 56, 62, 65
Barbé-Marbois, François 100
Begouen, Jacques François 100
Belley, Jean-Baptiste 4, 108
Benedenwindse Eilanden 138–9, 150n6
Benet, Rose 109
Benis, Paul 109
Benton, Lauren 57
Bergstedt, Anders 63, 64
Berlin, Ira 51n28
Bermuda 57
Bernadotte, Charles Jean 59
Bicou, Charles 109
Bigard, Philippe 56, 65, 66
Bissette Affair 66
Blanquezel, José Concepción 39
Blanquezel, Manuel 39
Blanquezel, Mateo 39
Bois Caïman ceremony: Ardouin's portraitof 85; Dumesle's account of 79; omission of 82

Bolívar, Simón 2, 65
Bombay Marines 126, 129
Bonaparte, Joseph 103
Bonaparte, Napoleon 93
Bongie, Chris 76, 77
Bosch, G. B. 146, 147
Boulay, Antoine 104
Boyer, Jean-Pierre 77, 79, 80
Brown Fellowship Society 45
Bruix, Étienne Eustache 98, 99

calidad 16
Cambacérès, Jean Jacques 104
Carbonell, Pedro 13, 20, 21
"Caribbean Genocide" (Girard) 95
Carnegie, David 126, 127
Cartagena 35; artisans of African descent in 36, 39; artisan work and militia service 40; Charleston *vs.* 42; free people of color 37, 39, 47; "*fuero militar*" 41, 47; legal challenges 50n19; 1777 census 37–8, 49n3; pardo and negro artisans 38, **38,** 40, 42, 50n6; racial classification of artisans 37–8, **38**; Romero, Pedro 34, 38–40, 47, 50n16
Cator, William 123
Certeau, Michel de 7
Chanlatte, Juste 75–7; critique of race 76; *Le Cri de la nature* 75, 76; slavery attacks, discussion of 76–7
Charleston 35, 51n23, 52n42; artisans of color 46, 48; free people of color 42, 44–8; Jones, Jehu 34, 44–6; 1848 census 43, 51n27, 52n39; 1831 directory of 43; racial classification of artisans **43**; racial-occupational patterns 42; social prestige and stability in 36; South Carolina's legislature 44; *vs.* Cartagena 42
Chatelot, Alexander 109
Chavanne, Jean-Baptiste 77
Chevalier de l'Empire français 110
Chretien, Pierre Nicholas 106
Christophe, Henry 63–4, 75–7
civil equality 97
Clarke, Dugald 122

INDEX

coartación process 6
Coclanis, Peter 96
Coerman, Hubertus 148
Cohen, David 1
Colley, Linda 122
Colonial Department 61–2
Constitution of the Year (1795) 97–8
"créole et grand planteur de St.Domingue" 99
Cressé, A. J. Bouvet de 76
"Crisscrossing Empires" (Scott) 57
Crosby-Arnold, Margaret 8
"Cry of History, The: Juste Chanlatte and the Unsettling(Presence) of Race in Early Haitian Literature" (Bongie) 76
Curaçao 57–8; Caribbean plantation colony 139; Dutch possessions in 138; economic recessions 144; enslaved people 140; manumissions on 141; non-white population 147; population of **142**; rebellion on 145; slave population 145; slave revolt 145
Curry, Leonard 51n23, 51n28

Danish Caribbean 57
Dash, J. Michael 78
Daut, Marlene 78
de Pombo, José Ignacio 40
depopulation, biological techniques of 94
dépôts 92
Dessalines, Jean-Jacques 74, 83; assassination 75
Diferencias entre lo Temporal y lo Eterno (Nieremberg) 22
Ducoudray-Holstein expedition 65–8
Dumas, Thomas Alexandre 100
Dumesle, Hérard 79–80; *Voyage dans le nord d'Hayti* 79
Dutch Leeward islands 138–40
Dutch possessions 138, 141
Dutch Windward islands 139
Dwyer, Philip 92, 94, 95, 99, 110

East India Company Army 120, 125–7, 129
Echeverri, Marcela 15, 26n13
economic imperialism, mission of 107
economic technique, genocide 94
État des deportés 107
Europe, anti-black sentiment in 4
"Expédition Secrète prepare à Brest" 101

Ferrer, Ada 98
France: administration 94; colonial commodity production 96; colorblind liberty in 98; diplomatic relations with Britain 100; economic reality 96; experiment 97; French Revolutionary wars 92, 97; Laveaux, Étienne 97; Napoleonic wars 92, 94; National Convention 97; overeign domains of 97; re-export trade, economic centrality of 96; Roederer, Pierre Louis 99; Sieyés, Emmanuel Joseph 99; sugar business 96
Francis, John 137, 138, 142, 149
Frank, Zephyr 36
free ports, in Caribbean 57–8
"French mania" 98
French republicanism 23
French Revolution 14, 23, 150
French Revolutionary wars 92, 97
Friendly Moralist Society 45
Friendly Union Society 45

Gaffield, Julia 57, 59
Garraway, Doris 78
genocide: biological techniques 94; conception of 94; critical studies 94; economic technique 94; hiding and denying 109–11; Jewish populations 93; Lemkin, Raphaël 93–4; Napoleonic 103–9; policies of 93; political technique 94; religious technique 94; social technique 94; state-sponsored, objects of 99–101
German genocide 93
German hegemony 94
Girard, Philippe 95, 101
Globalization and History (O'Rouke & Williamson) 95
gracias al sacar process 6
Greene, Jack 1
Green, Frank 130
Grégoire, Abbé 76
Grenville, William 101
Grimm, Jacob 110
Gustavia, St. Barthélemy 60, 67, 68

Haitian literary production 74–5, 86; Africanity and universalism 75–9; Ardouin, Beaubrun 80, 83–6, 88n49; Ardouin, Céligny 82–5; Chanlatte, Juste 75–7; Dumesle, Hérard 79–80; Madiou, Thomas 80–3; Vastey, Pompée Valentin 75, 77–9
Haitian Revolution 138, 150
Haitian Romanticism 80
Haitian War of Independence 103
Harding, Richard 96
Hastings, Warren 123, 124
Higman, Barry 133n74
Hoetink, Harry 140
"homme de couleur" 100
Hughes, Carlyon 146
hyperbolic statements 95

Jarvis, Michael J. 57
Johnson, Lyman 36
Joly, Rene 106
Jones, Jehu 34, 44–6
Jordaan, Han 148
Journal d'Économie 99

INDEX

Kerverseau, François 103, 107
Kiernan, Ben 94
Kikkert, Albert 147
Klooster, Wim 152n66

Labielais, Louis 109
Landers, Jane 3
Land, Isaac 122
Lardenoy, Antoine Philippe de 65
"*la République Français une et indivisible*" 101
Laveaux, Étienne 97
Le Belvoir 106
Leborgne, Pierre de 103
Leclerc, Charles 95, 103, 105
Le Cri de la nature 75, 76
Lefranc, Jean Baptiste Antoine 106
Lemaitre, Stephen Cesar 123
Lemarchand, René 95
Lemkin, Raphaël 93–4
Levene, Mark 96
Livesay, Daniel 8
Loi de promulgation du traité d'Amiens 105
Loi relative à la traite des noirs et au régime des colonies 105
Louverture, Toussaint 83–5, 98, 100, 101, 103, 105, 108

Mackillop, Andrew 125
Madiou, Thomas 80–3
Magallon, François-Louis de 106
Maitland, Thomas 98, 100
manumissions, on Curaçao 141
Margerison, Kenneth 99
Marks, John Garrison 7
Martí, Don Mariano 19, 24
McCall, George 127
Menichetti, Johan 99
Mentor, Étienne Victor 99
Middelanis, Carl Hermann 79
Middleton, Nathaniel 123, 124, 131n26
Mills, Jean-Baptiste 108
mixed-race Jamaicans 5, 120; children of interracial relationships 130; colonial Jamaica 121; global movement of 122; migration to Britain 121–2; Morses family 122–4, *124*, 127; Rosses family 125–6, 129, 130; Taylors family 120–1, 125–9
Montrose 125
More, Hannah 64
Moreno, José Ignacio 20
Morgan, Philip D. 36, 51n23
Morse, John 122, 123, 128
Morse, Robert 123
"*mourir civilement*" 104
Mulich, Jeppe 57
multilateral cooperation 101–3
Murray, James 128

Napoleonic Europe, people of color 99–101; Bonaparte, Napoleon 93; civil rights to free 97; destruction 101, 103; disintegration and destruction 101–3; French Revolutionary and 92; genocide 95, 96, 103–10; German people during 93; heterogeneous population 93; imperialism 95
National Convention 20, 97, 108
Nau, Ignace 80
Negrophiles 93
Neither Slave nor Free: The Freedmen of African Descent in the Slave Societies of the New World (Cohen & Greene) 1
Nelson, Horatio 125, 128, 132n44
Netherlands Antilles 6; *Benedenwindse Eilanden* 138–9, 150n6; citizenship 148; Curaçao 139–40, 150n5; Dutch Leeward islands 138–40; Dutch Windward islands 139; economic malaise in 138; enslaved people 138, 140; free blacks in 138; freedom of movement 140; free enslaved people 147–9; free people of color 148–50; French and Haitian revolutions 138, 145; "geopolitical literacy" 145; intermarriage 147; marriage law 149; overview 138–9; plantation colony 139–40; Saint-Domingue rebels 145; Simpson Bay 143; slavery 141; St. Maarten 139, 151n7; urban slavery 138, 139; West India Company 139
neutral Scandinavian ports 58–60
'New European Order' 94
Newton, Melanie 61
Nicholls, David 86n2
Norderling, Johan 56, 61, 65, 66
Norvins, Jacques de 110

Odoards, Louis-Florimond Fantin des 110
Ogé, Vincent 5, 77, 79
Olivares, Juan Bautista 13–15, 29n61, 29n64; Bishop of Caracas 19; Catholic faith 15; ecclesiastical authorities 14, 20; education 17, 19, 23; family 18, 19; General-Captain 21–2, 25; hardships 23; petition 20, 24; political identity 25; prison in Caracas 14, 21; royalism 15; School of Music of Chacao 19; seditious public readings 20; "true vassal of the King" 21–5
Olivares, Juan Manuel 18
"One Drop Rule" 5
1831 directory of Charleston 43
1791 slave revolt 76, 77, 79
O'Rouke, Kevin 95
Osío, José de 18

Pålsson, Ale 7
Panilio, William 60
pardo literacy and political identity, in Venezuela 13; Age of Revolutions 15, 25;

INDEX

calidad 16; Carbonell, Pedro 13, 20, 21; colonial communities 16; demographic growth 17; "dispensation of color" 24; economic improvement 17; in eighteenth-century 14, 26n7; literacy skills 14; mulattos 16, 17; pardo literacy in 16–19; population of 16; quality of public schools 18; social hierarchies 16–19; social mobility 24, 26n9; social reality 18; socio-racial groups 16, 20; traditional historiography 26n6
Peele, Robert 75
Peltier, Jean-Gabriel 75
"people of non-related blood" 94
"perpetual detention" 104
Pétion, Alexandre 75
physical annihilation, notion of 94
political technique, genocide 94
Portalis, Jean 104
post-Napoleonic Europe 5
Power, Samantha 93
"process of liquidation" 93
purity of blood *(Limpieza de sangre)* 16, 27n19, 92, 110

Quasi-War (1798-1800) 101
Quirigazo, Gaspar Antonio 146

racial labels 78–9
Raimond, Julien 100
Ramsey, Kate 82
re-export trade, economic centrality of 96
Régiment Royal Africain 108
Reid-Vazquez, Michele 36
religious technique, genocide 94
Report of Saint Bartholomew, The 63, 66
Restall, Matthew 36
"revolutionary contagion" 14
"revolutionary system of France" 98
Rewbell, Jean-François 97
Rigaud, André 83, 103
Rochambeau, Donatìen-Marie-Joseph 95
Roederer, Pierre Louis 99–100
Roman law 148
Romero, Pedro 34, 38–40, 47, 50n16
Rosensvärd, Johan 59
Ross, Daniel 126, 129
Ross, David 129
Ross, Hercules 125–6
Rupert, Linda 57, 142, 152n39

Sainte Clique 62
Saint-Georges, Chevalier de 4
Saint-Méry, Moreau de 110
Sartorius, David 15, 26n13
Scandinavian colonialism, in Caribbean 58
Scandinavian neutral ports 58–60
Schink, Father 145
Scott, Julius 57

Scott, Rebecca 144
Secrétaire d'État 92
Sieyés, Emmanuel Joseph 99
Silencing the Past: Power and the Production of History (Trouillot) 75
slave ownership 52n42
"Slavery: A Poem" (More) 64
Slave Schedule 52n42
social technique, genocide 94
Société des Observateurs de l'Homme 103
Sojo, Pedro Palacios 18, 19
Solano, Sergio Paulo 36, 40
Somois, Charle 106
Soulouque, Faustin 81, 83
South Carolina's legislature 44
Spanish reformism 15, 18
state-sponsored genocide 99–101
St. Barthélemy 56, 58; Ducoudray-Holstein expedition 65–8; free people of color 60; Gustavia 60, 67, 68; neutral Scandinavian ports 58–60; Norderling, Johan 56, 61, 65, 66; petitioning for equality 60–3; *Report of Saint Bartholomew, The* 63, 66; revolutionary operations in 62; Swedish acquisition of 59
Stephen, James 103
St. Eustatius 60
Stirling, Robert 121
St. Kitts 60, 62–3
St. Maarten: agriculture 139; British abolished slavery in 141; enslaved people 141; hurricane 142; intermarriage 147; non-white population 147; population of **143**
St. Martin 60, 65
strategy, Certeau's use of 7
St. Thomas 57–8; free people of color 58
Stuart, John 126
Swedish acquisition of St. Barthélemy 59
Swedish colonialism 7
Sweet, James 3

tactics, Certeau's use of 7
Taylor, James 120–1, 125, 126–9
Taylor, Robert 125, 128, 129
Taylor, Simon 125
Teenstra, M. D. 143, 146
Topik, Steven 96
Treaty of Amiens (1802) 92
Trouillot, Michel-Rolph 75
Troutman, Phillip 145, 153n67
Turing, John 126
Turnbull, John 102
Twinam, Ann 16, 24, 26n6, 36
2010 Haitian Earthquake 75
Tybell, Carl 62

urban Atlantic World, free artisans of African descent in 35–6, 49
urban slavery 138–43, **142, 143**

INDEX

Valentin, Aimé 109
Valentin, François 109
van Romondt, A. A. 137–8, 142, 146, 149, 150n3
Vastey, Pompée Valentin 75, 77–9; Essai sur les causes de la Révolution et des guerres civiles d'Hayti 78; racial labels 78–9
Vaucrosson, Anthony 62
Velázquez, José Francisco 19
Velázquez, Sebastiana 19
Vinson, Ben 36
Vodou, Haitian 80
voting rights 61, 66
Voyage dans le nord d'Hayti (Dumesle) 79

wait-and-see approach 98
Walker, Charles 50n12
Walker, David 2
"war of extermination" 103
Watson, Alan 148
"Western democratic triumphalism" 3
Whitman, T. Stephen 36
Wilberforce, William 125, 132n41
Williamson, Jeffrey 95
Wilson, John L. 45
Wilson, Victor 58
Woodson, Carter G. 52n42

Zavitz, Erin 8